notes on MORAL THEOLOGY 1981 through 1984

Richard A. McCormick, S.J.
*Kennedy Institute of Ethics
(Georgetown University)
and Woodstock Theological Center*

UNIVERSITY
PRESS OF
AMERICA

Copyright © 1984 by

University Press of America,™ Inc.

4720 Boston Way
Lanham, MD 20706

3 Henrietta Street
London WC2E 8LU England

Library of Congress Cataloging in Publication Data

McCormick, Richard A., 1922-
  Notes on moral theology, 1981 through 1984, 1985,
c1984.

  Composed of articles originally appearing in
Theological studies.
  Includes bibliographical references and index.
  1. Christian ethics—Catholic authors—Addresses,
essays, lectures. 2. Social ethics—Addresses, essays,
lectures. I. Theological studies (Baltimore) II. Title.
BJ1249.M25   1985   241'.042   84-19672
ISBN 0-8191-4351-0 (alk. paper)
ISBN 0-8191-4352-9 (pbk. : alk. paper)

For Terry and Traug
Who Define the Meaning of Friendship

TABLE OF CONTENTS

PREFACE

Several years ago I was persuaded to publish *Notes on Moral Theology 1965-1980*. The response to that volume, all 892 pages of it, was not only encouraging, it was quite literally overwhelming. It was this response that heightened my arrogance level sufficiently to brave this addition to the original tome.

Notes on Moral Theology 1981-1984 will not serve the multiple purposes of the earlier volume (e.g., Christmas tree prop, door stop, cure for intractable insomnia). But I am confident that the subjects critically reviewed will remain alive in the Church and of interest to the general public for years to come. For instance, the problems of divorce, preservation of life, sterilization, woman's role in the Church, social morality, abortion, and nuclear weapons are far from "solved." The same may be said for the methodological concerns touching on moral norms, the place of narrative in moral theology, the moral magisterium, and doctrinal development. There are those, of course, who believe that such areas of moral concern have been officially settled once and for all by past formulations. I do not share such a view. Different times, different circumstances, different questions and different language mean different formulations and emphases, a point explicitly admitted by the Congregation for the Doctrine of the Faith (*Mysterium Ecclesiae*, 1973). If the publication of this volume serves no other purpose than that of a standing reminder of this truth, it will have been worth the effort. For it is unfortunately the case that institutionalized ecclesial life can easily lead some in the Church to sherk their critical responsibilities, and even to suppress efforts to face them.

I should note in passing that the dates 1981-1984 refer to the publication dates in *Theological Studies*, just as did 1965-1980 in the first volume.

Finally, it is a dutiful pleasure once again to thank the Detroit Province of the Society of Jesus, and its remarkable provincial, Howard J. Gray, S.J., for a generous grant, making possible a reduced price for this volume.

Richard A. McCormick, S.J.

CURRENT THEOLOGY

NOTES ON MORAL THEOLOGY: 1980

RICHARD A. McCORMICK, S.J.

Kennedy Institute of Ethics and Woodstock Theological Center, D.C.

This edition of the "Moral Notes" will deal with the literature touching on four subjects: (1) methodology in moral decision-making; (2) liturgy, character, and moral theology; (3) the preservation of life; (4) the Synod of 1980.

METHOD IN MORAL DECISION-MAKING

For some years now, Catholic moral theologians have been attempting to explore the methodological implications of some quite concrete moral formulations traditional in the Catholic community. These explorations touch many areas and raise many questions; but above all, they have centered on the understanding of moral norms. Because the matter is difficult and highly sensitive, the literature has continued to abound. A brief sampling must suffice here.

Johannes Gründel, professor of moral theology at the University of Munich, clearly adopts a teleological understanding in his most recent book.[1] Behind this understanding is a conflict model of decision-making.[2] Within this model, things traditionally prohibited by deontologically understood norms (contraception, sterilization, artificial insemination by husband, etc.) become discussable, indeed at times justifiable. Gründel's work is reported and some questions put to it by Heinz J. Müller.[3] Müller's questions do not attack the theory as such but attempt to make it more precise.

The same is true of the overview article of Karl Hörmann.[4] It concentrates on and summarizes the perspectives of Joseph Fuchs, Bruno Schüller, Peter Knauer, Helmut Weber, Bernard Häring, and Rudolf Ginters. Hörmann does not challenge the substantial direction of these studies but insists on the importance of situating the conflict model within an adequate concept of the vocation of persons.

J. R. Flecha Andres presents an overview study on norms in which he argues that traditional presentations of intrinsically evil actions do not

---

[1] Johannes Gründel, *Die Zukunft der christlichen Ehe* (Munich: Don Bosco, 1978).

[2] Cf. ibid. 90, 94.

[3] Heinz J. Müller, "Theologische Durchblicke: *Die Zukunft der christlichen Ehe*," *Theologie der Gegenwart* 22 (1979) 233–38.

[4] Karl Hörmann, "Are There Absolutely Binding Moral Norms?" *Melita theologica* 30 (1978–79) 44–53. The article is terribly translated and is at times almost unintelligible; I do not recommend it.

1

consider the situation, the ends, the conflict of values.[5] The principle of double effect he regards as a "pseudo solution." He then briefly presents seven theses about moral norms. One such thesis is that moral norms must take into account "the 'objective' reality of the living person in his specific time and real situation," affected by external sociological factors as well as by congenital or educational influences. Another thesis: moral norms must distinguish evil (premoral) from perversity (moral evil). The overview concludes by noting that norms have the provisional character of our journey into the future. They are an orienting force in a history which is both fulfilment and promise.

It is clear that an increasing number of theologians insist on understanding moral norms within the conflict model of human reality.[6] Conflicted values mean that occasionally our choices (actions or omissions) are inextricably associated with evil. Thus, we cannot always successfully defend professional secrets without deliberately deceiving others; we cannot at times protect ourselves against aggressors without violent response; we cannot secure a stable professional and political atmosphere without hurtfully revealing the faults of others. Many theologians have come to believe that such evils (and others) may be done and intended if, all things considered, they are proportionately grounded.

This has led to the accusation by some that these theologians are violating the Pauline axiom (Rom 3:8) that a good end does not justify an evil means. Thus Richard Roach, in referring to a recent volume edited by Paul Ramsey and myself,[7] states: "I wonder if whoever chose the title for this volume pondered the text of Romans 3:8."[8] Roach's essay is a vigorous[9] defense of the absoluteness of the prohibition of the direct

---

[5] J. R. Flecha Andres, "Reflexión sobre las normas morales," *Salmanticensis* 27 (1980) 193–210.

[6] Cf. Franz Böckle, *Fundamentalmoral* (Munich: Kösel, 1977) 306.

[7] *Doing Evil to Achieve Good* (Chicago: Loyola University, 1978).

[8] Richard R. Roach, "Medicine and Killing: The Catholic View," *Journal of Medicine and Philosophy* 4 (1979) 383–97.

[9] Of those with whom he disagrees ("deviating theologians," "deviant moral theology") he writes: "They have coined a wealth of jargon. They speak of commensurate reason, proportionality, the method of proportionality; they speak of the preference principle or the principle of compromise; they distinguish between ontic and moral evil, or between premoral and moral evil etc." Their analyses are referred to as "argumentative ploys." Finally: "In short, these persons are all characterized by espousing a position on a substantial matter which contradicts the teaching of the Church *to which they claim to belong*" (389, emphasis added). Merely to cite such language is to deplore it. One must fault the editors for tolerating such a collapse of courtesy. For a gentle warning against this type of thing, cf. B. Schüller, "Die Bedeutung der Erfahrung für die Rechtfertigung sittlicher Verhaltensregeln," *Christlich glauben und handeln* (Düsseldorf: Patmos, 1977) 283. Hans Schilling notes that the more personal and accusatory theological language becomes, the less capable is the accuser of even understanding the position under discussion ("Theologische Wissenschaft und kirchliches Lehramt: Erwägungen zur Therapie einer kranken Beziehung,"

killing of the innocent. He contrasts this with a view that would approach the prohibition in an effort "to calculate the beneficial consequences of violation and find them to outweigh the 'evil.' "[10] Roach argues that this misses the point of the moral life, "which is whether our actions fit us for communion with God or not." Certain acts (e.g., fornication) break communion with God here and now "because of the purposes He has implanted by design into the sexual natures we are right now." There is no need of "appeal to consequences or future states." This is true of direct killing of the innocent. "It makes us unfit for communion with Him." Why? Because it usurps God's sovereignty "and any act which usurps that sovereignty is a bad act and one which is absolutely prohibited."

Several things about this essay call for comment. First, I agree with Roach that all practical moral reasoning is teleological in form (sc., it begins with the end in view). I also agree that the right end is communion with God. I further agree that actions which unsuit us for communion with God are morally wrong. But how does one get from these very

---

Stimmen der Zeit 198 [1980] 291–302). In this respect one should read the wise analysis and suggestions of Archbishop John F. Whealon, "Unity and Pluralism as a Pastoral Concern of Bishops," *Catholic Mind* 78, no. 1344 (June 1980) 34–42.

[10] In any number of places Roach misrepresents the authors he attacks. For instance, to those who contemplate possible exceptions to rules he considers absolute he attributes the following: "We are obliged to follow them only when they promote what we calculate will make for human happiness." I know of no Catholic theologian who holds such a eudaimonistic position or who consistently must in terms of his/her principles. In another place Roach is cited as follows: "Consequentialism involves a person in subjective assessments of his actions. For instance, if a man is committing adultery he can excuse himself by rationalizing that he is not breaking up a family; that his mistress is lonely and needs him to comfort her; that the adultery puts him in a good mood, thereby facilitating a happy relationship with his wife" (*National Catholic Register*, Nov. 23, 1980, 10). If this is put forth as representing the position of many contemporary moral theologians, it is not only erroneous; it is unjust.—In their exchanges, theologians have a right to have their positions presented accurately. Those who oppose what they dub "proportionalism" frequently fail in this regard. For instance, the position has been described as follows: "The argument, basically, is that a hoped-for good-to-come-about can justify the deliberate, direct intention to do evil now" (*Hospital Progress* 61, no. 9 [Sept. 1980] 39). Here we have evil *now*—good *to come*. Thus it is sometimes said that adultery now justifies a future good. This misrepresents what Fuchs–Schüller–Böckle–Janssens–Scholz–Weber–Curran and many others are saying. What they are saying is that the good achieved *here and now* (though it may perdure into the future) is sometimes inseparable from premoral evil. Thus, an act of self-defense achieves *here and now* the good of preservation of life. A falsehood achieves *here and now* the protection of the professional secret. Taking property (food) of another saves the life of the taker *here and now*. The contraceptive act prevents *here and now* a further conception. In Knauer's terms, these theologians are speaking of the *finis operis* of the action. Indeed, one might counterargue that it is the principle of double effect which condones evil *now* for good *to come*; for the condition that the bad effect must be equally immediate is not understood temporally but causally.

general assertions to the conclusion that direct killing of the innocent always unsuits us for communion with God? Roach's answer: this is God's moral purpose "expounded in Scripture as taught by the Church." This purpose "is that God wills to retain direct sovereignty over each and every instance of innocent human life." To say anything else is to propose a contradictory purpose and one that makes our action "unfitting for communion with God." Roach applies this same reasoning to all sexual acts not "in conformity to the Church's teachings." They are bad in themselves without appeal to "consequences or future states."

Here I believe Roach misreads his own tradition and falls into a form of ecclesiastical positivism. He argues that God's purposes are clear independently of consequences and future states, even in situations of conflict. However, James Gustafson rightly notes that "the teleological framework of Catholic theology and ethics has always set the concern for consequences in a central place in moral theology."[11] Even the deonto-logically understood rules that did develop had a teleological basis. Thus, as Gustafson notes, adultery not only violates a covenant, but the rule against it has validity because adultery is harmful to the parties involved.

One can see this form of teleology at work in the process of restrictive interpretation given over the centuries to the commandment "Thou shalt not kill." If we adhere to the prohibition literally, we find that our hands are tied against unjust aggressors who disdain the rule. The result is that more lives are lost than if we had not adopted the rule. Therefore we qualify the rule, interpreting it as forbidding the taking of *innocent* human life. Then there are cases (birth-room conflicts) that are not covered by the exceptions comprised under "innocent." So we refine the rule further, distinguishing between direct and indirect killing, the latter being at times permissible. The rule is, in a sense, as acceptable as it is capable of being restricted to accommodate our sense of right and wrong, and our firm commitment to save more lives than we lose in situations of conflict.[12] To ignore this teleological substructure to the development of the rule against direct killing of the innocent and to read God's purposes

---

[11] James Gustafson, *Protestant and Roman Catholic Ethics* (Chicago: University of Chicago, 1978) 49.

[12] Cf. the interesting study of Joseph Fuchs on epikeia. Medieval theologians held that the *ratio justitiae* could not change but that the *materia* could. Thus for these theologians there arose the question of what truly constituted unjust killing. Fuchs notes: "Here is pertinent what contemporary opinion states about the teleological nature of right moral judgments—precisely to render the natural law as efficacious as possible." Fuchs concludes his study with this statement: "Where concrete human reality is sacrificed to abstractly formulated human norms—or where certain norms which appear only general are taken to be universal—there the natural law strictly speaking is sacrificed to these norms. That is, the person is sacrificed" ("'Epikeia' circa legem moralem naturalem?" *Periodica* 69 [1980] 251-70).

directly from official formulations is a form of ecclesiastical positivism (the teaching is right, and a manifestation of God's purposes, *because* the Church says so). When such positivism substitutes for moral reasoning, it becomes merely exhortatory or parenetic and begs most of the questions at issue.[13]

My second problem with Roach's essay is his dismissal of the notions of premoral, nonmoral, ontic evil as "jargon" coined by theologians and as "argumentative ploys." Once again, greater familiarity with his own tradition would have prevented this error. For centuries Catholic theologians have referred to certain effects of our conduct as *mala physica*, in contrast to *mala moralia*. For example, what are we to call the killing that occurs in legitimate self-defense? A moral good? Hardly. A moral evil? No, for the defense is *ex hypothesi* morally just and right. *Malum (mere) physicum* was the traditional way of describing such evils.

Contemporary theologians rightly think the word *physicum* is almost invariably misleading, as suggesting and being restricted to bodily harms and harms due to commission. The concept is far broader. It includes not only harm to reputation, etc., but even the imperfections and incompletenesses due to our limitations. Thus Janssens writes: "We call ontic evil any lack of a perfection at which we aim, any lack of fulfilment which frustrates our natural urges and makes us suffer."[14] The terminology "coined" by contemporary theologians, far from being a "jargon," is in substance utterly traditional.

Roach's use of disparaging terms such as "deviant moral theology" (deviant from official formulations) indicates that his primary preoccupation is conformity to official formulations. This makes it apropos to refer here to an interesting article by Karl Rahner on theologians and the magisterium.[15] He begins by noting that in spite of the huge outpouring

[13] Karl Rahner notes that in moral argument the conclusion is often *hineingesmuggelt* in the premises. That represents a begged question. In this case the conclusion so *hineingesmuggelt* is that the creative will of God is simply and in all circumstances identified with the moral will of God, or, in other words, that facticity is identified with God's moral will ("Über schlechte Argumentation in der Moraltheologie," in *In libertatem vocati estis* [Rome: M. Pisani, 1977] 245–57, at 245). For further comments on bad arguments, cf. Richard A. McCormick, S. J., "Moral Argument in Christian Ethics," in Stanley Hauerwas, ed., *Remembering and Reforming: Toward a Constructive Christian Moral Theology* (Univ. of Notre Dame, forthcoming).

[14] Louis Janssens, "Ontic Evil and Moral Evil," *Louvain Studies* 4 (1972) 134. There is some indication that Roach's apologetic fervor has led him even to misunderstand the terminology many theologians are using. Thus he states (393) that were he attacked by a bear in the woods, he would directly kill it; for, other things being equal, "killing bears is a nonmoral good or bad." He continues: "But if I were attacked by a man in the woods, the matter becomes moral." That is not the understanding of the terminology used by contemporary theologians. If my legitimate self-defense resulted in the killing of a person, that killing would be classified as a nonmoral or ontic evil by the theologians in question.

[15] Karl Rahner, "Theologie und Lehramt," *Stimmen der Zeit* 198 (1980) 363–75.

of literature on the magisterium and theologians, the relationship remains very obscure ("immer noch sehr dunkel"). The magisterium presumes that its declarations are persuasive and that the task of theologians is to defend them. Clearly Rahner sees the picture as much more complex. He puts himself in the position first of a member of the Roman magisterium, then of a theologian, to say things that might be mutually helpful, even though he admits that there will always be tension and friction.

As for the magisterium, Rahner begins by insisting that the magisterium admit that it has erred, and even recently ("haben es schon oft bis in unsere Tage getan"). He points out that *Lumen gentium* left many questions unanswered. For instance, he suggests that the time of an "obsequious silence" in the face of authoritative teaching must be much briefer. After all, the present Pope is using language forbidden not long ago (Yawhist authorship). He faults the secrecy of the procedures of the Sacred Congregation for the Doctrine of the Faith. The final procedure with ten cardinals is outmoded. Beyond their seminary schooling, they knew nothing of theology ("salva omni reverentia ... nichts von Theologie verstehen").[16] On the other hand, the magisterium has a right to insist on a presumption for its noninfallible but authoritative declarations. These are themes Rahner has often rehearsed.

What is most interesting is the second half of the article, where Rahner assumes the role of theologian speaking to the magisterium. After acknowledging the appropriate deference due to the magisterium, he turns to the binding force of authoritative statements. He argues that no. 25 of *Lumen gentium* (with its demand of "religious submission of mind and will") is an inadequate portrayal of the appropriate theological response. He states: "If, for example, the statements of *Lumen gentium* (no. 25) on this matter were valid without qualification, then the world-wide dissent of Catholic moral theologians against *Humanae vitae* would be a massive and global assault on the authority of the magisterium. But the fact that the magisterium tolerates this assault shows that the norm of *Lumen gentium* (and many other similar assertions of the past one hundred years) does not express in sufficiently nuanced form a legitimate praxis

[16] Leo Scheffczyk cites this phrase of Rahner and admits that it suggests that the contributions of theologians are necessary even at the highest level. But he argues that the problem is not exhausted by such a suggestion. There is great pluralism in theology itself and eventually the magisterium must make a decision. Furthermore, Scheffczyk believes Rahner has misconceived the character of an authentic faith-judgment of the magisterium. It roots not in theological erudition but in the charism of the magisterium. I believe Scheffczyk has misunderstood the point of Rahner's objection. It is not that theology determines the magisterium. It seems to me to be the much more modest and practical point that, as things are, too often little or no account is taken of theological research in the official statements of the magisterium (cf. Leo Scheffczyk, "Das Verhältnis von apostolischen Lehramt und wissenschaftlicher Theologie," *Internationale katholische Zeitschrift* 9 [1980] 412–24, at 422–23).

of the relationship between the magisterium and theologians."[17] He continues: "What are contemporary moral theologians to make of Roman declarations on sexual morality that they regard as too unnuanced? Are they to remain silent, or is it their task to dissent, to give a more nuanced interpretation?" Rahner is unhesitating in his response: "I believe that the theologian, after mature reflection, has the right, and many times the duty, to speak out against ("widersprechen") a teaching of the magisterium and to support his dissent."[18] Only so does the Church make doctrinal progress. It is possible for the magisterium to proceed "unobjectively and unjustly" in its administrative constraints on theologians, to use evil means to its ends. Of other theologians Rahner allows: "I must say, however, that the number of cases of unjustified restraint that I have experienced in my life is rather large." He concludes by noting that explicit Roman admission of these perspectives would not lessen the authority of the magisterium but enhance it.

Here we have the Church's foremost theologian, a conservative in the authentic sense of that term, saying things that root deeply in the history and growth of the Catholic community. Is it not regrettable that the Church has not found, and seems incapable of finding, a way of dealing constructively with the type of dissent alluded to by Rahner? Instead of being used as an indispensable and positive contribution to the "development of the Church's understanding of her inheritance" (Bishop B. C. Butler's phrase), to the teaching-learning *process* of the Church, it is viewed with suspicion and fear. It is this fact—and the factors behind it—more than anything else that has prevented the Church from exercising the type of prophetic role expected of it in several domains of contemporary life. I would exhort my esteemed colleague Roach (and others who share his perspectives, perspectives I consider one-sidedly juridical, even preconciliar) to ponder Rahner's conciliatory but forthright essay.

If one desires to get a truly balanced and fair outline of some of the issues at stake in this discussion, I recommend Lisa Cahill's excellent essay in the same journal.[19] Cahill has befriended both Ramsey and this author with accurate analysis and tightly reasoned criticism.

The axiom that a good end does not justify an evil means has been treated frequently in the literature, most recently in a careful study by Bruno Schüller.[20] Schüller first notes that the term "evil" can mean two

---

[17] Rahner, "Theologie und Lehramt" 373.

[18] Ibid. 374.

[19] Lisa Sowle Cahill, "Within Shouting Distance: Paul Ramsey and Richard McCormick on Method," *Journal of Medicine and Philosophy* 4 (1979) 398–417.

[20] Bruno Schüller, S.J., "La moralité des moyens," *Recherches de science religieuse* 68 (1980) 205–24.

things: (1) moral evil (*malum morale, peccatum*); (2) nonmoral evil (*malum naturae sive physicum*), e.g., sickness, poverty, error. If it is taken in the first sense, then the axiom positively stated ("a good end justifies a morally evil means") is a formal contradiction; for to say that an action is morally evil is to say that it cannot be justified morally. As Schüller notes, "How is it possible that a good end can morally justify something which by definition excludes all moral justification?" St. Paul had been falsely accused by some Jews of teaching that we ought to sin (moral evil) in order that God's mercy might be more gloriously manifested. The falsity of such teaching is clear when we consider the indivisible nature of moral good. One cannot, e.g., simultaneously stand *for* justice and *against* fidelity.[21] "As a result, the person who takes moral good in any of its manifestations as his/her end, by this very fact eliminates moral evil from the domain of that which presents itself as the object of free will and choice." If one decides to do a morally evil action, one can do so only by ceasing to seek moral good as one's goal.

If, however, "evil means" refers to nonmoral evil, then clearly the end can justify causing such means. For instance, a physician may cause pain to a patient when this is inseparable from truly cognitive measures. This is evident whether one reasons teleologically or deontologically. Schüller, therefore, wonders why theologians with deontological tendencies have the impression that teleologists hold that a good end justifies a *morally* evil means. The only answer is that many means viewed by deontologists as morally evil are not viewed as morally evil by teleologists.[22]

Schüller uses contraception as his example. Catholic theologians of a teleological bent indeed hold that this (nonmoral evil) can be justified by the end. When others (e.g., Roach) conclude from this that they hold that a good end justifies a morally evil means, "they reveal only their incapacity to view the matter even hypothetically from the point of view of a teleologist." For instance, all Catholic theologians defend the moral rightness of blood transfusions. Jehovah's Witnesses see them as morally evil. "Does that mean that Catholic theology must allow itself to be accused by Jehovah's Witnesses of holding that a good end ... justifies a morally evil means? Of course not."

Schüller rightly concludes that whatever one's normative method may be, it should not be used to discredit others by sinister moral insinuations.

Joseph Fuchs, S.J., examines moral norms in the context of the "sin of the world" (Jn 1:29).[23] He indicates three ways in which this "sin of the

---

[21] Cf. the excellent study of John P. Langan, S.J., "Augustine on the Unity and Interconnection of the Virtues," *Harvard Theological Review* 72 (1979) 81–95.

[22] I use these terms reluctantly and merely as space savers. They are patient of so many different renderings as to be misleading.

[23] Joseph Fuchs, S.J., "The 'Sin of the World' and Normative Morality," *Gregorianum* 61 (1981) 51–76.

world" is relevant to the formulation of objective moral norms. First, he notes the different stages in salvation history, especially the present stage and the stage of eschatological glory. In the present stage we are burdened with concupiscence. Therefore there are norms and institutions possible and necessary only because of the actual situation of persons. An example would be private property. In the view of many medieval theologians, division of goods is rooted in our egoism and concupiscence. Catholic theologians are increasingly aware of the "sinful character" of some systems and institutions.

Second, there are what Fuchs calls "objectifications of concupiscence." These are sin-conditioned situations which may require an "adapted" form of human response. Some examples which have been given are: a class hugely dishonest in examinations may modify the demands of honesty on an individual; certain business situations where what is contracted for and what is done need not exactly correspond; certain homosexual relationships resembling marriage; falsehood in unjustly imposed situations.

Fuchs is very careful here. First, he does not specify that any of these situations must be seen as an objectification of sin, e.g., that true homosexuality is a sin-conditioned attraction. He merely asserts that other theologians have approached some of these situations as sin-conditioned and responded with a theology of compromise (e.g., Charles Curran). Second, he distinguishes carefully between a sin-conditioned situation and an objective conflict of values due to our finitude or historical circumstances. The two situations are parallel but different, and the compromise called for in each is different. The compromise that results from the objectified results of sin contains some of these objectified results. This is not the case with compromise that roots in a conflict of values.

Fuchs believes that it is really not possible in practice to make a neat distinction between the two types of compromise. Nor is it necessary; for the "evils or disvalues which are brought about as part of a 'difficult' situation—in spite of their being possibly conditioned by 'sin'—are not moral evils, but are relevant to moral judgment as *premoral* evils or disvalues."[24]

The third way the "sin of the world" can influence norms is through residual concupiscence in the individual. The weakness of an individual can be such that fulfilment of a moral demand is impossible. Fuchs is somewhat sceptical about the way certain theologians present this matter, above all because they see the resultant disorders in our conduct as moral evils. This implies the existence of two moral orders, one that is feasible

---

[24] Ibid. 60.

and one that is ideal. Fuchs rejects this. He prefers to call disorders in our conduct due to weakness "premoral" evils, because they can at times be justified.

With regard to what he calls "difficult" situations, Fuchs summarizes as follows:

Such values therefore do not *absolutely* have to be realized in individual situations. As values which are part of the well-being of the human world, they are not moral values (which always have to be implemented) but premoral values, which have to be implemented as far as possible according to the context. Only values which determine the *person* as such—and not merely the *well-being* of the person—are of themselves moral values. Therefore the compromise solution does not allow the simultaneous realization of the morally right and the morally wrong, but only of the morally right, which, however, contains both nonmoral right (good/value) and nonmoral wrong (evil/disvalue).[25]

Catholic theology has always admitted the existence of conflict situations and it has faced them with a set of exception-making categories (e.g., rule of double effect, material-formal cooperation, etc.). But only relatively recently has it begun to see the source of some conflicts in our sinful situation. In the past, at least some of these conflicts were approached exclusively through the distinction objective-subjective. Thus, in the face of human weakness, some conduct was seen as objectively wrong but subjectively guiltless. Fuchs's essay, without denying the usefulness of this distinction, is an attempt to move beyond it, at least in some cases. He is aware of the dangers in this approach. He notes that "there is a constant danger of using genuinely 'sin-conditioned' situations as a facile excuse for indulging in compromise."

One comment. Fuchs recognizes the difference in a compromise that is occasioned by our sinful situation and one with rootage in the objective incompatibility of premoral goods. He believes the two cannot be easily distinguished in practice. I think that is correct. But I believe it is important to continue to try to do so. Why? Because Fuchs's use of the terms "premoral" ("nonmoral") to analyze conflicts due to our sin-conditioned situation represents an advance, an extension. I believe it is a legitimate one. But the terms are already so badly misunderstood, so frequently distorted, so firmly resisted in some quarters that the analytic gains achieved by them could be easily threatened unless we continue to strive to distinguish as clearly as possible the two types of compromise and to tighten our analysis of each.

In an excellent piece of moral analysis, Lisa Cahill has done just that.[26]

[25] Ibid. 73–74.
[26] Lisa Sowle Cahill, "Moral Methodology: A Case Study," *Chicago Studies* 19 (1980) 171–87.

She uses homosexuality as a case study for highlighting the multiple sources (Scripture on homosexuality, related texts, general biblical themes, descriptive accounts of human experience [e.g., empirical sciences], normative accounts) that must be integrated to achieve a truly Christian outlook. Cahill sees the need of maintaining a balance among the dialectical reference points. Their complexity is respected only by a very nuanced judgment. In her judgment, these sources "point unavoidably toward a heterosexual norm for human sexuality. This norm does not necessarily exclude exceptional applications, in cases where human and Christian values even more important than those protected by the norm are at stake, and when their realization cannot be accomplished without overriding the specific sexual norm."[27]

For Cahill, a genuinely Christian perspective (which sees heterosexuality as normative) will perceive in the homosexual condition the suffering, tragedy, and irreconcilable conflict "which are part of historical existence after the fact of sin, as part of the 'brokenness' in which all creation shares." As for material (genital) acts, they are to be judged by their relationship to moral values (honesty, love, service, self-denial, etc.). "If because of conflictual situations, the material acts [heterosexual] usually conducive to and expressive of moral values do *not* actualize them or in fact inhibit them, then these acts are not to be commended in the situation." Of homosexual actions in such "broken" situations, Cahill says that they are "non-normative but objectively justifiable in the exceptional situation."

She concludes by noting that another way of stating her conclusion is that homosexual acts are evil (as generally to be avoided because not conducive to moral value) but that "they are 'premoral' evils in that their sheer presence does not *necessarily* make the total act or relation of which they are a part 'morally' evil or sinful."[28] There can be sufficient reason for causing such premoral evil. In this Cahill is at one with Fuchs.

Brendan Soane has raised difficulties with these conclusions in his commentary on a report of an Anglican Working Party (of the Board of Social Responsibility) published in 1979.[29] He uses Charles Curran as his example. Curran had argued that, although heterosexual acts are the ideal, still homosexual acts of the invert can be morally justified. Curran based his conclusion on two arguments. First, *agere sequitur esse*. But the invert has a different psychic structure (*esse*), a different sexual humanity. Second, we must distinguish between two states of natural law, before the Fall and after. This secondary (after the Fall) natural law is shaped by the presence of sin in the world. Thus the principles of natural law must be applied differently in different situations of human

[27] Ibid. 183. [28] Ibid. 186.
[29] Brendan Soane, "Homosexual Relationships," *Clergy Review* 65 (1980) 288–94.

history. Since the homosexual condition is a result of sin in the world, the homosexual acts of inverts in loving, permanent relationships are justified "by the principle of proportionate good in a situation affected by sin" (*sic* Soane reporting Curran).

Soane questions both arguments. As for the first, the argument would apply also to alcoholics, compulsive gamblers, kleptomaniacs, etc. Therefore the being we are called to follow (*agere sequitur esse*) "is the human being we are called to become, not the imperfect being we already are." Second, the examples Curran had given of compromise in our postlapsarian world (self-defense, capital punishment, material co-operation, toleration of evils in society, etc.) differ from homosexuality. They are activities necessary if life is to go on at all. Sexual activity is not necessary in the same way. Instead Soane proposes that the problem is better met "by the type of pastoral solution which maintains that homosexual relationships in which there is a physical expression of erotic love are disordered, but may on occasions be the best that is possible in the circumstances as a temporary expedient."

Perhaps Fuchs–Cahill–Curran might respond by saying that the activities and conditions cited by Soane (alcoholism, compulsive gambling, kleptomania) are harmful to the persons involved and to others. In this they differ from expressed homosexuality.

But here we must put a question to Soane. He has said "disordered . . . but the best that is possible in the circumstances." How does that differ from Fuchs–Cahill–Curran? Not at all, as far as I can see, providing Soane understands "disorder" as something other than *moral* disorder.[30] If he does, this pastoral position seems to be exactly that of Fuchs–Cahill–Curran, who insist that the heterosexual, permanent married state is normative for full sexual expression and that therefore deviations from it involve premoral evil. If Soane's "best that is possible in the circumstances" means "not morally wrong," his position is exactly that of the three authors mentioned, as I understand them.

Much of the discussion on norms in the Catholic community was occasioned by Peter Knauer's earlier study.[31] Now, fifteen years later, he returns to the discussion in a very long study.[32] Knauer states at the outset that his perspective is really a middle ground between two positions (deontological, teleological), a synthesis that resolves the polarity.

---

[30] Fuchs discusses this (n. 23 above) on pp. 63–67 and notes that the term "désordre" in the French bishops' pastoral on *Humanae vitae* "should have been understood in a nonmoral sense." In a similar vein, cf. Edward Vacek, "A Christian Homosexuality?" *Commonweal* 107 (1980) 681–84.

[31] Peter Knauer, S.J., "La détermination du bien et du mal moral par le principe du double effet," *Nouvelle revue théologique* 87 (1965) 356–76.

[32] Peter Knauer, S.J., "Fundamentalethik: Teleologische als deontologische Normenbegründung," *Theologie und Philosophie* 55 (1980) 321–60.

We are concerned with determining the moral right and wrong. Traditionally, the principle of the double effect claimed to be able to do this for instances of conflict. Knauer rejects the traditional four-conditioned formulation as a *petitio principii* (it supposes the answer to the question it proposes to answer); for one of its conditions is that the action in itself must not be morally evil.

Knauer next turns to the Thomistic formulation of this principle (2-2, q. 64, a. 7, c) in the analysis of defense against an unjust aggressor. He interprets Thomas as holding that the evil effect (death of the aggressor) is unintended (*praeter intentionem*) when it is necessary to the self-defense. Where it is unnecessary, then such an evil effect is not *praeter intentionem*. In summary: the killing of an aggressor is morally evil when it is intended. It is intended when it is unnecessary to the self-defense. Or, as Thomas says, "Potest tamen aliquis actus ex bona intentione proveniens illicitus reddi, *si non sit proportionatus fini.*"

From this Knauer concludes that the moral rightness or wrongness of any action is gathered from a single criterion: whether the act is proportioned to its end. In the example of self-defense, the end of the act is self-defense. It is the *ratio boni* of the action. "As long as the action is proportioned to this *ratio boni*, then the *ratio boni* occupies the entire field of the 'intended' and effects the moral rightness of the conduct."

What does it mean to say that the action must be "proportionate" to the end? Knauer rejects an understanding of the term which would suppose a weighing of goods, the ethical duty being to choose the "higher." This not only leads to rigorism; it also supposes a criterion for measuring the unmeasurable. The choice, he urges, is not between different goods or values, but *in what way* to seek the good one chooses. If the action involving harm will "generally and in the long run" ("auf die Dauer und im ganzen," a phrase repeated by Knauer over and over again) undermine the very good being sought here and now, it is morally wrong. If not, it is morally right.

Knauer says that this distinguishes his understanding of proportion from those demanding a weighing of different goods against each other.[33] "In respect to the *one and same* value, we ask whether one does justice to it in the long run and generally. ... " Thus, in the instance of self-defense, the death of the aggressor, to be morally right, must be grounded in the overall good of life "in the long run and generally." The good sought in the action must not be eventually undermined. One who seeks

---

[33] Knauer admits that other values can indeed be considered, not precisely because they are "higher" values than the value sought, but "because they are the condition of its realization" (336). In a similar vein, I have spoken of the "association of goods." There are any number of ways of interpreting a "weighing of different goods" without measuring the incommensurable.

wealth through a bank robbery undermines wealth itself. In other words, the action must not be counterproductive. It is this counterproductivity "in general and in the long run" that makes an action morally wrong.

So far I see nothing different in Knauer's study from his 1965 analysis. That analysis had led him to assert that, of the four conditions traditionally stated for the double effect, only the fourth (ratio proportionata) remains.[34] The rest of his study is a systematic application of this notion to several traditional concepts.

The first area is that of the notion of affirmative and negative precepts. Affirmative precepts ("Thou shalt protect life") bind semper sed non pro semper, as the scholastic saying goes. Negative precepts ("Thou shalt not murder") bind semper et pro semper. One can be excused from the former, not the latter. Traditionally, affirmative precepts have been seen as weaker and less fundamental. Knauer denies this. Negative precepts are merely the application of affirmative ones; that is, they state the cases where the conditions of release from affirmative precepts are not fulfilled.

The next area of application is the distinction between direct and indirect. Knauer insists that the evils caused and permitted in our actions (killing, falsehood, taking another's property) must be viewed as premoral evils. Sometimes they can be justified, sc., where there is a ratio proportionata. When this is lacking, the evils caused or permitted are "eo ipso 'directly' willed" in the ethical sense. Therefore we must distinguish clearly between direct in the psychological sense and the ethical sense. Knauer applies this to capital punishment. Such punishment can be justified only if necessary for the protection of life itself. Where it is so necessary, it is indirect in the ethical sense.[35]

Knauer next turns to the traditional notions of object, end, and circumstances as fonts of morality. Traditionally, the object of an act (finis operis) was said to be that end to which the act by its very nature is ordained. The end (finis operantis) was a freely chosen purpose of the agent beyond its object. Knauer rejects this undue separation and sees the purpose of the act as really constitutive of its object (finis operis). We cannot give an ethical qualification or meaning to an ontic or pre-ethical notion such as "taking another's property." More is required. Thus the taking of another's property without commensurate reason has as object "the harming of a fellow man through his property" and is theft. If, however, taking another's property is the only way of preserving one's

---

[34] Cf. also Jean-Marie Aubert, "Morale et casuistique," Recherches de science religieuse 68 (1980) 167–204. Aubert rightly sees this in other studies also: "C'est d'ailleurs dans cette direction que s'orientent bien des recherches actuelles, y voyant l'unique condition essentielle de la règle du double effet" (201).

[35] Cf. the excellent "Statement on Capital Punishment" of the American bishops in Origins 10 (1980) 373–77.

life, "then the *finis operis* is totally different, namely, saving one's life."[36]

Another application Knauer makes is to the axiom that "a good end does not justify an evil means." The axiom supposes, as Schüller had noted, that the means is *morally* evil. "However, when the means to achieve an end consists in the causing or permitting of a harm ... then the means can be morally evil only in the case where the *ratio boni* of the entire action constitutes no commensurate good and therefore the *finis operis* of the whole action is morally evil."[37] One cannot look just at the physical structure of an act and pronounce it *morally* evil. One of Knauer's examples: masturbation for sperm-testing in a sterile marriage.

Similarly, Knauer insists that an action is *contra naturam* only when the harm caused is counterproductive in the sense explained.

Knauer concludes by noting several characteristics of his proposed grounding of moral norms. First, it is pragmatic and looks to the future. For instance, as for the future, we may use medicines with noxious side effects if these are the only means for cure available. When another cure without such effects is available, use of the first becomes morally wrong. Every ontic value makes a claim on us that we promote it and not endanger it without commensurate reason. Hence there is a future-looking thrust away from the harms inseparably a part of our actions.

As for pragmatism, Knauer believes his approach makes an essential place for the empirical sciences. Moral norms can be developed only through trial and error. For instance, it is possible that placing abortion on the penal code would not really reduce abortions at all. Other measures might be more effective. Only experience can tell us that. We learn what is "in general and in the long run" counterproductive through experience.

Second, Knauer grants that his theory has in common with utilitarianism the notion that in every morally right action a utility or goal is sought. It differs, however, because it insists that this goal must not be sought in overall counterproductive (contradictory) ways. This is very close to the way Louis Janssens has formulated the matter.

Third, his theory is a middle path between opposing theories known as deontological and teleological. While it takes consequences into account, still the qualifier "in the long run and in general" distinguishes his approach from standard consequentialism. Thus certain actions are wrong in themselves (counterproductive ones).

I have given here only the main outlines of Knauer's study. Some years ago Germain Grisez stated of Knauer that he "is carrying through a revolution in principle while pretending only a clarification of traditional

---

[36] Here Knauer relies on Thomas' distinction between *species naturae* and *species moris* (1–2, q. 1, a. 3, ad 3).

[37] Knauer 348.

ideas."[38] I believe that is true—and Knauer explicitly admits it in this study. The only question, then, is the following: Is the revolution justified? Is it solidly grounded? Grisez says no. His key objection is that Knauer "cannot exclude a fanatical dedication to any particular genuine value." Thus a mad scientist would, Grisez argues, find support in Knauer's theory. "He could defend any sort of human experimentation, no matter how horrible its effects on the subjects, provided the experimental plan promoted the attainment of truth—on the whole and in the long run."

Is Knauer vulnerable to this objection? I think not. He could answer (as Grisez acknowledges) that the fanatical investigator would really damage the cause of truth "in general and in the long run" in the very means used. And if that were the case, Knauer would say the action is morally evil, and indeed "in itself." If this is the case, the basic question between these two scholars seems to me to be epistemological: How do we know that this is the case? Do we simply intuit it? Or is that conclusion (about counterproductivity) learned from experience by a kind of trial and error? Some statements of Knauer's lead me to believe he would answer in the latter way.

My own tentative view is that the judgment of counterproductivity is probably made in different ways depending on the issues at stake. In some cases we know from experience that certain actions are counterproductive. For instance, we know that private property is essential to the overall well-being of persons, hence that robbery is counterproductive. We know that those who live by the sword die by the sword, hence that violence is most often counterproductive. We know that permanent marriage offers unsurpassable opportunities for human fulfilment, hence that actions that undermine its stability and permanence (adultery) are counterproductive.[39] I think we are getting very close to this in our judgment of war. We are all losers, as experience has so frequently taught us. Experience itself provides a sound basis for such judgments.

There is a second category of actions where we sense very strongly (sense of profanation, outrage, intuition) that the actions are counterproductive. Indeed, so strong is our sense of revulsion that we are grateful that we have not as yet had the experience. In this category I would put the example adduced by Grisez.

Third, there are actions or procedures where we know very little and must proceed to normative statements gradually by trial and error. This would be true of our moral statements about DNA recombinant research, and on many technological matters where dangers and/or abuses are

[38] Germain Grisez, *Abortion: The Myths, the Realities, the Arguments* (New York: Corpus, 1966) 331.

[39] Some of these judgments are confirmed from other sources, e.g., Sacred Scripture.

possible but where no experiential history is available to instruct us.

Grisez's objection to Knauer leads me to ask: Could it be that some of the disagreements being experienced in the area of moral norms are traceable to unexamined suppositions and disagreements about how clear and certain we can or ought to be on all moral matters? Perhaps the mechanizing and quantifying of moral judgments that occurred during several centuries of high casuistry has led us to expect a type of certainty in some moral judgments that is beyond realistic expectation. I leave that to my colleagues and to further discussion.

LITURGY, CHARACTER, AND MORALITY

Moral theology concerns itself with both character formation and decision-making. Perhaps attention has fallen somewhat one-sidedly on the latter to the neglect of the former.[40] Here a brief roundup will have to suffice to point up recent efforts to redress this imbalance.

Jeremy Miller, O.P., uses the book of Bruce Birch and Larry Rasmussen[41] to underline the importance of the Church (as community) for Christian ethics.[42] The Church influences character in three ways: as shaper of moral identity, bearer of moral tradition, community of moral deliberation. For instance, where moral identity is concerned, it is clear that the Church's actions (liturgy, preaching) function as socializing factors. More attention to character formation would tie liturgy more closely with moral theology.

Miller suggests—rightly, I believe—that Vatican II's notion of the Church as People of God would provide a Christian anthropology that would put appropriate emphasis on "the inner discerning power the Christian can claim in living out the demands of discipleship." This would mean also that a more prominent place is required for principles of dissent. Furthermore, an emphasis on the theology of grace would mean a tighter union of morality and spirituality.

The directional emphasis suggested by Miller seems certainly justified. We might say that we have been putting a heavy emphasis on the pair right-wrong, to the neglect of those considerations (virtue, formation, character) involved in the pair good-bad. When appropriate adjustment is made, we will be much more concerned with factors influencing character, especially liturgy and the sources of Christian spirituality. A concrete but not insignificant gesture-of-resolve in this direction might

---

[40] For an interesting article calling attention to the one-sidedness of either of these contrasts, cf. Thomas R. Ulshafer, S.S., "Jacques Maritain as a "Mixed Deontological Ethicist of Agency,'" *Modern Schoolman* 57 (1980) 199–211.

[41] *Bible and Ethics in Christian Life* (Minneapolis: Augsburg, 1976).

[42] Jeremy Miller, O.P., "Ethics within an Ecclesial Context," *Angelicum* 57 (1980) 32–44.

be adoption of the usage "moral-spiritual life."

Enda McDonagh notes the emerging sense of the need to integrate the liturgical life of the Church, personal prayer, and "Christian living in the world (formally treated in moral theology)."[43] His study explores, therefore, the relationship between liturgy and morality.

He notes and develops several links. The first is that of "mystical" experience (the experience of God). In liturgy—which is community remembering—we recall in celebration the life, death, and resurrection of Jesus Christ in such a way that we appropriate more deeply our own present identity. In doing so, we enjoy the present experience of God. "In Christian liturgy history is the way to mystery, the human activity of celebration the way to mystical experience." Thus in liturgy we have celebration, remembering, identity, and mystical experience.[44]

These same four elements occur in the moral life. In moral activity we celebrate others, achieve fuller self-identification and self-transcendence. Finally, "moral response to a human other has the potential of encounter with the divine other." Both liturgy and moral action involve us, through temporalities, in opening to the experience of God as Father of Jesus Christ (McDonagh's so-called "mystical" element).

Second, McDonagh states that by remembering and retelling the story and events of Jesus Christ, the liturgy enters into the essential moral education of Christians. The biblical narratives and their liturgical commentary are intended to reveal the basic meaning and direction of Christian living as discipleship. In his development of this point, McDonagh scores a widespread rationalism in moral theology, as if the "mystical" encounter promoted by liturgy and discernible in moral activity has "no bearing on the analysis and resolution of concrete problems." Rather, the recall of God's relationship with humankind and its realization in Jesus "*illuminates in endless ways* the moral dilemmas one faces from fidelity to a marriage partner to sharing the goods of the earth."[45] Here I wish McDonagh would have been more specific. Concretely, what form does such illumination take? Does it simply reconfirm what is in principle knowable by human insight? Or does it provide a broader, more satisfying context for analyzing concrete problems? Or does it result in substantially different judgments? These are not insignificant questions; they are constantly put to me by my colleagues in moral philosophy. An

[43] Enda McDonagh, "Liturgy: Expression or Source for Christian Ethics?" in Stanley Hauerwas, ed., *Remembering and Reforming: Toward a Constructive Christian Moral Theology* (Univ. of Notre Dame, forthcoming).

[44] For a study on how this happens in terms of models of consciousness, cf. Donald E. Miller, "Worship and Moral Reflection: A Phenomenological Analysis," *Anglican Theological Review* 62 (1980) 307-20.

[45] Emphasis added.

answer is not satisfactory until it deals analytically with a concrete moral problem, and in terms other than the merely parenetic. I shall return to this below.

McDonagh ends his stimulating essay by attending to a third linkage between liturgy and morality, that of liturgy as source of structure and direction for the communities in which we lead our moral lives. Here he very helpfully outlines how liturgy acts as a corrective for dualistic attitudes toward the body and pleasure, toward the earth and our care of it, toward individualistic or collectivistic tendencies, toward triumphalistic assessments of our moral achievements. McDonagh began his study by expressing the hope that he could "carry a little further" the task of relating liturgy and morality. He has done far more than that.

An entire issue of the *Journal of Religious Ethics* is devoted to liturgy and ethics. Just a few items will be lifted out here. Paul Ramsey and D. E. Saliers addressed the relationship of liturgy and ethics at the January 1979 meeting of the Society of Christian Ethics.[46] Ramsey insists that the engendering event gives shape to the engendered liturgical response ("a formed reference to divine events"). But this is true as well for Christian morality and Christian faith. Thus Ramsey refers to the *lex orandi, lex credendi, lex bene operandi* as having the same ordering principle. Between these three responses (*orare, credere, operari*) there is both parity (no one deserves a priority over the other) and reciprocity. In Christian ethics, e.g., the notion of agape must be continually nourished by liturgy and the entire biblical narrative; otherwise it loses its meaning and collapses into a pale philosophical concept.

Ramsey then applies in illuminating fashion the relation of liturgy and morality to two practical instances: second marriages and abortion. In the Eastern Orthodox tradition, theology and ethics are contained, subsumed, and conveyed by the liturgy. The liturgy for a second marriage (after a failed first) is straightforwardly penitential in character and is a way of making a theological statement about marriage.

Next Ramsey turns to abortion. He shows, amply and correctly, the shape of biblical thought on abortion. "And it is the shape of Christian liturgies so far as the Bible has not been excluded from them." Anyone who believes that the Bible says nothing definitive to the abortion question Ramsey believes has not listened to biblical evidence or has responded: "Speak, Lord, and thy servant will think it over." Ramsey urges: "Far more than any argument, it was surely the power of the Nativity Stories and their place in ritual and celebration and song that tempered the conscience of the West to its audacious effort to wipe out

---

[46] Paul Ramsey, "Liturgy and Ethics," *Journal of Religious Ethics* 7 (1979) 139–71; D. E. Saliers, "Liturgy and Ethics: Some New Beginnings," ibid. 173–89.

the practice of abortion and infanticide."[47] So Ramsey is arguing that liturgy affects morality not merely by transforming the moral agent and his/her perspectives and character in a general way (which it does), but also by presenting substantial concrete moral content. This is vintage Ramsey—which means that it is an entertaining, enlightening, and provocative piece.

In rather marked contrast to Ramsey, Donald E. Saliers argues that the relations between liturgy and ethics are most adequately formulated by specifying how certain affections and virtues are formed and expressed in liturgy. By this he does not mean an instrumentalist understanding of worship, where liturgy is viewed as a means to moral exhortation or motivation. Rather, good liturgy, as a rehearsal of narratives, is the imaginal framework of encounter with God in Christ and a continual re-embedding of persons into the perspectives of God's actions toward us and the world. As such, it molds our vision and moral character.

Yale's Margaret Farley, in a thoughtful response to these studies, grants that Ramsey and Saliers have made important points.[48] But they do not "raise the most critical issues confronting us today in the worshiping life of the Church." Many Christians experience liturgy as deadening, impoverishing, and burdensome. Farley identifies three causes of this. First, liturgical structures too often incorporate the divisions of class, race, and sex that violate our deepest Christian convictions about the Church as *koinonia*. Second, there is a disparity between word and reality in worship. *Diakonia* (service) after the example of Jesus is shaped by the model of servant; yet the reality too often is a pattern of power and domination. Furthermore, there are drastically different views of what *diakonia* must mean in our contemporary world. Until these differences and tensions are resolved, they will continue to impact deleteriously on the worshiping community.

Finally, there is the contemporary experience of the death of symbols. Since these are utterly essential to liturgy, it is no wonder that liturgy fails to be for so many a meaningful rehearsal of divine realities.

William Everett notes that Ramsey and Saliers have focused on different aspects of the Word central to faithful life (Saliers on a greater personal openness to God's Word and character formation, Ramsey on the right orders set forth in Scripture).[49] But neither copes successfully with the realities of social pluralism. Social pluralism refers to the fact that any worshiping person is a member of associations, institutions,

---

[47] Ramsey, "Liturgy and Ethics" 162.

[48] Margaret A. Farley, "Beyond the Formal Principle: A Reply to Ramsey and Saliers," *Journal of Religious Ethics* 7 (1979) 191–202.

[49] William Everett, "Liturgy and Ethics: A Response to Saliers and Ramsey," ibid. 203–14.

communities whose interests may compete with, complement, or ignore one another.

In Saliers' approach, Everett sees an accommodation to social pluralism that is, if I understand him correctly, excessively individualistic, even a kind of escapism. Ramsey is much readier, through his emphasis on right structures, to challenge easy social pluralism, but Everett finds the approach a form of emerging sectarianism (the distinction between holy community and profane society). He feels that the impetus toward right social order and right character has to be reworked in our time to lead to critical engagement of social and cultural pluralism.

Everett proposes the notion of "public" as the vehicle of this reworking. "The public is a pattern of ways for acting about important matters." Liturgy disposes us to become "public beings." "Not only do we rehearse the stories of past action, we project new scenarios to test the judgments of the public realm." The article is stimulating, but even after several readings, the notion of publicity remains obscure to me.

The volume of the *Journal of Religious Ethics* ends with a brief but thoughtful essay by Philip Rossi, S.J.[50] Rossi's thesis is that the character of our moral agency as Christians has its most fundamental formative ground in Christian public worship. This is so because it is in liturgy that we are exposed to the narratives that shape our lives. Rossi contrasts the contours of this shaping (God as the Lord of life) with those dominant in our culture (the agent as solitary, morally autonomous individual).

It seems that Rossi's presentation is what we might call the "ideal." That is, the character of our moral agency ought to be fundamentally formed by exposure to biblical narratives in liturgy. But whether that is actually achieved by contemporary liturgy is another question, as Farley has pointed out so clearly.

Since it is liturgy, especially through remembering and rehearsal of narrative accounts, that shapes our moral consciousness and character, it is important that the relation of the biblical narratives to moral life be accurately understood. Two recent studies have focused on this question.

Stanley Hauerwas examines the moral authority of Scripture.[51] He sees it ultimately as one about the kind of community the Church must be in order to make the narratives of Scripture central to its life. The Church's life depends on faithful remembering of God's care for creation through the vocation of Israel and Jesus. Scripture is the vehicle of that remembering. Its dominant mode is narrative. Thus the Bible is not a logical unit or finished whole; indeed, some of its prescriptions strike us as

[50] Philip J. Rossi, S.J., "Narrative, Worship and Ethics: Empowering Images for the Shape of Christian Moral Life," ibid. 239–248.

[51] Stanley Hauerwas, "The Moral Authority of Scripture: The Politics and Ethics of Remembering," forthcoming as in n. 43 above.

irrelevant, even perverse. Only within the narrative context can we place
the explicitly moral sections of Scripture (exhortations, commandments).

Hauerwas argues that those who see Scripture as by and large irrelevant to ethics have mistakenly seen ethics as primarily a matter of
decisions. It is not. It also concerns the character of individuals and of a
community, "what kind of community we must be to be faithful to
Yahweh and his purposes for us." Once we see this, we see that the
narratives of Scripture are as important as the commandments.

James Childress believes that interpretations such as that of Hauerwas
overemphasize some features of the moral life (vision and perspectives,
images and metaphors, stories, loyalty and character) to the detriment of
the role of Scripture in moral justification.[52] These interpretations highlight influence rather than reflection. Actually, Childress argues that
aesthetic interpretations (images, metaphors, stories) aid us to recognize
obligations, but justification of them comes through appeal to principles
and rules. Childress concludes his brief essay by insisting that there is a
variety of uses of Scripture as revealed morality. "To reduce Scripture's
moral requirements to any single category is to distort both morality and
Scripture." Clearly, Childress feels that the restriction of Scripture to
formative narrative is such a reduction.[53]

The literature on liturgy and ethics is relatively young and sparse, but
it is extremely interesting. Here I want to raise one problem that was
hinted at by Childress. It is clear that moral theology has a great deal to
do with character and community formation, and that the biblical stories
through liturgy play an essential role here. It is also clear that moral
theology has a great deal to do with moral deliberation and justification.
But what is the relationship of these two? How do the biblical narratives
as formative relate to justification in moral discourse? It is clear, of
course, that good people will generally make right decisions, as Aristotle
noted. But that is not sufficient as an answer, for moral theology seeks a
more systematic and reflexive understanding.

There are any number of possible answers to this question, no one of
which is adequate or exclusive of others. The problem I am raising here
is indicated in two distinctive emerging tendencies in recent literature.
On the one hand, those who emphasize vision and character (and the
biblical narratives that impact on them) do not often engage in moral
justification with regard to concrete moral problems. When they do, the
moral "justification" (so it seems to some observers) is either not a true
justification or not an original one (sc., it is knowable by other than

[52] James Childress, "Scripture and Christian Ethics," *Interpretation* 34 (1980) 371–80.
[53] The rest of the issue of *JRE* contains interesting articles on concrete aspects of biblical
ethics by Gene Outka, John Howard Yoder, David Little, and Charles M. Swezey.

biblical sources). Thus Childress has referred to this form of writing as an overemphasis.

On the other hand, those who are concerned with concrete moral problems and a disciplined analysis of their solution say little about vision and character and the biblical-liturgical materials that nourish and shape them. In other words, they act like moral philosophers. There is ample witness to this in the literature on bioethics, as James Gustafson has repeatedly pointed out.[54] Unless these two trends are brought together, what goes for moral theology will increasingly become either sectarian exhortation or unbiblical rationalism.

An interesting article by Stanley Hauerwas on abortion will illustrate the concern I am outlining.[55] Hauerwas argues that Christian opposition to abortion has failed because we have accepted a "liberal" culture's presupposition that our convictions must be expressed in terms acceptable to a pluralist society. In doing so, we have not exhibited our deepest convictions, convictions which alone make the rejection of abortion intelligible. Specifically, Hauerwas argues that we have tried to present abortion independently of the kind of people we would like to become. Thus the arguments pro and con abortion are fragments torn from the context that gave them intelligibility.

Hauerwas sees the roots of this dilemma in the presupposition on which our liberal society is founded: how to prevent people from interfering with one another. The government is restricted to this and is expected to be neutral on the very subjects that matter most. Thus liberalism seeks an account of morality divorced from the kind of persons we are or want to be. That falsifies the way moral injunctions function. Taken together, moral injunctions describe a way of life.

As Christians, we have failed because we have tried to argue abstractly. We should rather have presented abortion as an affront to our basic convictions about what makes life meaningful, to our way of life. To do this, we must tell stories that show the correlation between the prohibition of abortion and the story of God and His people. "It is only when we have done this that we will have the basis for suggesting why the fetus should be regarded as but another of God's children."

More positively, Hauerwas urges that the Christian prohibition of abortion rests on our conviction that life is not ours to take. Life is God's creature, under the lordship of Jesus. Furthermore, for Christians, as people determined to live within history, children are seen as duty and

---

[54] Most recently in "A Theocentric Interpretation of Life," *Christian Century* 97 (1980) 754–60.

[55] Stanley Hauerwas, "Abortion: Why the Arguments Fail," *Hospital Progress* 61, no. 1 (1980) 38–49.

gift. It is in displaying themes such as these that we will best serve our society on the abortion question.

Two things in this extremely interesting study could easily be overlooked and need explicit reference. First, Hauerwas notes that "the broad theological claims I am developing cannot determine concrete cases." This means that such themes cannot function as criteria for rightfulness or wrongfulness in individual instances. Second, of the desire for new life that is part of the Christian form of life, Hauerwas says: "Such a desire is obviously not peculiar to Christians." Of the love of those we did not choose, he says that "the existence of such a love is not unique or limited to Christians." Moreover, he concludes that "Christians should certainly wish to encourage those 'natural' sentiments that would provide a basis for having and protecting children."

What have we here? We have (1) an attitude not specific or peculiar to Christians (2) which does not decide rightfulness or wrongfulness in individual cases.

I want to raise several points. First, here is an attitude which does not determine in individual cases the morally right or wrong. What, then, does it do? Must we not say that it nourishes sentiments or dispositions preparatory to individual decisions? That is broadly known as parenesis, at least in so far as it relates to individual decisions. Or, in Childress' language, it is a perspective which helps to *recognize* an obligation, but not to *justify* it or its violation.

Second, if it is not specific to Christians, then are not the Christian warrants for it confirmatory rather than originating? I have suggested elsewhere (on abortion) that "these evaluations can be and have been shared by others than Christians of course. But Christians have particular warrants for resisting any cultural callousing of them."[56] The point I am raising here is epistemological. It is not whether *de facto* and historically Christians have rejected abortion because of their story and the community they wanted to be. One can make a strong case for that, as Ramsey has. The question is rather whether this rejection of abortion is in principle unavailable to human insight and reasoning (sc., without the story or revelation).[57] If it is, then the only way to know that abortion (and many other things) is to be rejected is to be part of the story. That is inherently isolationist. Whatever it is, it is certainly not Catholic tradition or the story of the Catholic community. Its story is precisely that many of these moral demands are epistemologically separable from its story, though confirmed by it. "Particular warrants" of the Christian

[56] Richard A. McCormick, S.J., "Abortion: A Changing Morality and Policy?" *Catholic Mind* 77, no. 1336 (Oct. 1979) 42–59, at 51.

[57] This point has been made recently by P. Gaudette, "Jésus et la décision des chrétiens," *Science et esprit* 32 (1980) 153–59, at 158.

for rejecting abortion do not raise the issue of how one originally knows God's will within a storied community.

Third, if Christian convictions on abortion (and similar concrete moral questions) are indeed in principle available to human insight (sharable by others than Christians), is it not more productive in a pluralistic society to urge one's convictions in the public forum in terms of what is sharable in that forum?[58] That is what many popes and Catholic bishops throughout the world have done. Or negatively, are Christians not argued right out of the current controversy by presenting their convictions in terms of particular and often unsharable warrants? If we argue our conviction in terms of a unique community story, others need only assert that their story is not ours. The conversation stops at that point. Hauerwas is aware of this difficulty (indeed, he raises it), but, in my judgment, he does not adequately answer it.

Hauerwas has pursued these general themes in another stimulating study.[59] In speaking of the Christian commitment to peace, he states that it is not based on "the inherent value of life but on the conviction that the refusal to resort to war cannot be consistent with the Kingdom we have only begun to experience through the work of Christ and his continuing power in the church." He says much the same thing about slavery, sc., that we reject it not because it violates inherent human dignity but because "we have found that we cannot worship together at the table of the Lord if one claims an ownership over others that only God has the right to claim."

Two reflections. The first concerns the nature of moral argument. Appeals to "the type of people or community we want to be" (who acknowledge Jesus as Lord and Lord of life) are certainly true. They are also certainly not moral arguments in the sense of justifications for the moral rightness or wrongness of any individual action. To think that they are is to confuse Christian parenesis with justification.

Concretely, Hauerwas asserts that Christians reject slavery not because it violates human dignity but because "we have found that we cannot worship together at the table of the Lord if one claims an ownership over others. . . . " One might respond: if that is the *only* reason why Christians

---

[58] In contrast to Hauerwas, Walter Kern, S.J., states that Catholic social teaching can make an important contribution to the discussion of fundamental values. However, this is only possible if "it argues on a broadly human basis, that is, not a specifically Christian one" ("Zur Grundwertediskussion," *Stimmen der Zeit* 198 [1980] 579–84, at 580). This does not mean abandoning specifically Christian convictions (e.g., on the indissolubility of marriage). It is simply a recommendation about how one discusses these in the public arena. Christian convictions ought to be presented in the public forum; but this does not mean that they have to be, or should be, presented as Christian.

[59] Stanley Hauerwas, "The Church in a Divided World: The Interpretive Power of the Christian Story," *Journal of Religious Ethics* 8 (1980) 55–82.

reject slavery, perhaps it clarifies why they did not do so for nineteen centuries. Discomfort at the Eucharistic meal helps to *recognize* wrong-doing, to use Childress' language. It is not the only or primary validation (justification) of it as wrong.

In another context Hauerwas notes: "When asked why we do or do not engage in a particular form of activity, we often find that it makes perfectly good sense to say 'Christians just do or do not do that kind of thing.' And we think that we have given a moral reason. But it is moral because it appeals to 'what we are,' to what kind of people we think we should be."[60] I am suggesting here that "moral reason," as Hauerwas uses the term, does not pertain to the genre of moral argument understood as justification.[61]

My second reflection follows immediately from the first. Hauerwas states that, e.g., Christians reject slavery not because it violates inherent human dignity but because we cannot worship together with those who engage in it. Here he contrasts and separates what ought not be separated. Christian warrants are continuous with and interpenetrate human warrants, at least in the Catholic tradition. In this sense Christian warrants are confirmatory. The Christian story does not replace the notion of "inherent human dignity"; it supports and deepens it.

What it seems (and I emphasize "seems") Hauerwas is actually doing is denying the relevance, perhaps even the existence, for the Christian, of what has been badly called for centuries the natural moral law. I suspect he does this because he conceives of it as a set of principles (and their warrants) developed through discursive reasoning. (He would be aided

---

[60] Hauerwas, "Abortion" 42.

[61] Hauerwas writes: "Our theological convictions and corresponding community *are* a social ethic, for they provide the necessary context for us to understand the world in which we live. The church serves the world first by providing categories of interpretation that offer the means for us to understand ourselves truthfully ... " ("The Church in a Divided World" 75). We all would agree to that. "Contexts" and "categories of interpretation" are not in themselves, however, adequate justifications of rightfulness and wrongfulness of individual actions, necessary as they truly are. In this sense they are not a social ethic if by that term we mean to exhaust all that is requisite to moral justification. To think that such "moral reasons" are moral justifications is to ask them to bear a burden they cannot bear. It is not a moral justification to say "Christians do not do these things." It is simply an assertion that reminds one to go back to his/her tradition and find out why. When pressed, I believe Hauerwas would admit this; for he refers to "theological convictions that *shape* our reasoning." They do not replace it. This point is made well by Martin Honecker, "Vernunft, Gewissen, Glaube," *Zeitschrift für Theologie und Kirche* 77 (1980) 325–44. Honecker refers to theological contributions as those which "broaden our horizons and open our insights" (344). In a statement (Oct. 22) explaining his now famous "lust" statement, John Paul II referred to Christ's words as "the basis for a new Christian ethos which is marked by a transformation of people's attitudes." An "ethos" and "transformation of attitudes" are necessary but not sufficient conditions for moral discourse.

and abetted in this distortion by certain Catholic formulations such as that of the then [1940] Holy Office that "direct sterilization is against the law of nature.")

But this is not what the natural moral law in its earliest and most genuine sense means. It refers to *naturaliter nota*, those things known immediately and connaturally.[62] The existence of such knowledge is admitted, so many exegetes argue, in Romans, where the fault of nonbelievers is said to be precisely suppressing such knowledge. Elsewhere Schüller has argued that unless we know (moral consciousness) what faithfulness means, we will have no idea of what faithfulness to Christ could possibly mean and thereby commit the entire moral life to blind obedience, indeed to incoherence.[63] If Hauerwas exalts Christian warrants so much that he denies the existence of such knowledge (cf. his not because of "the inherent dignity of our humanity," "inherent value of life"), I believe it must be said that he has diminished the very Christian story to which he appeals; for part of that story is that basic moral knowledge and correlative justifications are not exclusive to this community. To overlook this is to annex the Christian story to a single reading of it.

There is a great deal in Hauerwas' recent writing that is powerful and compelling. For instance, he is right on target in attacking the assumptions of the modern liberal state which lead it to neutrality where our deepest values are concerned. However, overemphasis (in Childress' words) on those Christian perspectives that attack these assumptions can force on them a burden in moral discourse that they cannot always bear, and in doing so can lead to a sectarianism that could easily be counterproductive.[64]

LIFE AND ITS PRESERVATION

Any number of widely publicized events (living-will legislation, brain-death statutes, the Public Television broadcast of "Choosing Suicide," the Quinlan–Saikewicz–Spring–Fox–Becker cases, the Broadway play *Whose Life Is It Anyway?*, the activities in Britain of EXIT [a voluntary euthanasia society]) have forced public attention on euthanasia. It was probably in light of the problems and doubts created by the aforemen-

[62] Cf. the recently republished essay of Jacques Maritain, "De la connaissance par connaturalité," *Nova et vetera* 55 (1980) 181–87, esp. 185–86. Also interesting in this regard is V. Ferrari, O.P., "Il primo principio morale," *Angelicum* 57 (1980) 45–53.

[63] Bruno Schüller, S.J., "Wieweit kann die Moraltheologie das Naturrecht entbehren?" *Lebendiges Zeugnis*, March 1965, 41–65.

[64] Some of the points raised here have been urged from a different perspective by J. Wesley Robbins, "Narrative, Morality and Religion," *Journal of Religious Ethics* 8 (1980) 161–76.

tioned events that the Sacred Congregation for the Doctrine of the Faith issued in late June its *Declaration on Euthanasia.*[65]

The introduction itself to the document is interesting. After noting that medical advances have created new anxieties and doubts, the SCDF proposes to offer "elements for reflections" that people can then "present to the civil authorities with regard to this very serious matter." Three groups are envisaged as recipients: (1) those who place their faith and hope in Christ; (2) those who profess other religions, but with a basic faith in God; (3) people of good will who, in spite of their philosophical differences, are sensitive to the rights of the human person. Thus the religious appeals are supportive of the human appeals, the SCDF using phrases such as "human and Christian prudence suggest. . . . "

After dealing with the value of life ("necessary source and condition of every human activity") and euthanasia (to be rejected), the SCDF turns to the means that must be used to preserve life. It makes two points. First, who makes the decision? "It pertains to the conscience either of the sick person, or of those qualified to speak in the sick person's name, or of the doctors to decide. . . . " Second, the SCDF turns to the principles in light of which the decision ought to be made. It adverts to the standard terminology ("ordinary," "extraordinary" means) and suggests that, while the principle behind these terms still holds, the terms themselves are "perhaps less clear today." It notes that some advocate the use of "proportionate" and "disproportionate" means. Whatever the term used, the SCDF notes that the judgment is a balancing of two considerations: (1) the type of means used (degree of risk, difficulty, cost, etc.); (2) the result to be expected for the patient. Thus certain treatments can be "disproportionate to the result." The document concludes by applying these principles somewhat more concretely. For instance, it makes it clear that it is morally permissible, with the patient's consent, "to interrupt these means where the results fall short of expectation."

This document received widespread praise, and it deserved it. It said nothing new, but it spoke in new circumstances and what it said it said very well. Thus *Commonweal* states that it "recognizes complexity and respects individual circumstances."[66] The *New York Daily News* editorialized: "We think he [the Pope] has laid down guidelines that will be enormously helpful to both Catholics and non-Catholics in right-to-die controversies."[67] The (London) *Tablet* stated of the declaration that it is "timely, compassionate and rooted in common sense."[68] Such statements

[65] *Declaration on Euthanasia* (Vatican City: Vatican Polyglot Press, 1980); also in *Catholic Mind* 78 (Oct. 1980) 58–64 and *Origins* 10 (1980) 154–57.

[66] *Commonweal* 107 (1980) 420.

[67] *New York Daily News*, July 9, 1980.

[68] *Tablet* 234 (1980) 624.

could be multiplied.[69]

I believe that several things should be highlighted in this declaration. First, the statement makes quite clear in a general way who are the decision-makers as to how the ill shall live while dying. It refers to "the conscience either of the sick person, or of those qualified to speak in the sick person's name, or of the doctors." This is extremely important at a time when the courts are increasingly assuming the prerogative of decision-making in this matter. I said above "in a general way." The SCDF does not address the problem of disagreement among the doctors and "those qualified to speak in the sick person's name," or among doctors themselves. There is surely a place for court appeal here.

Second, the SCDF is sensitive to the "imprecision of the term" (ordinary, extraordinary). I shall return to this below. But in stating the principle that undergirds any language used, the document remains flexible and nuanced. This is important. Many persons, not excluding physicians, expect a principle which will "solve cases" and "give them answers." There is no such thing. Human formulations can direct prudence; they cannot replace it. What some people seem to be looking for is a guideline that will make the decision for them. This is understandable; for these are extremely delicate decisions and weigh heavily on us. We squirm under the terrible burden of risk they involve and would feel more comfortable if a formulated rule could remove from us the burden and anguish of that risk. But it cannot be so. A formulated rule about the proportionate or disproportionate character of a particular treatment, and the elements that go into its making, can only prepare us intellectually and psychologically for a decision; it cannot make the decision for us. To think otherwise is to move in the direction of mechanizing and stereotyping these decisions in a way potentially harmful to the patient and to our best instincts about what is humanly and Christianly appropriate.[70]

The great relativity of the terms "ordinary" and "extraordinary" is underscored in a brief study by James J. McCartney, O.S.A.[71] He reviews the history of this usage from Soto (1582) and Bañez (1595) to Pius XII's Allocution to Physicians and Anesthesiologists (1957), then summarizes the theological reaction to the papal allocution. Pius XII clearly gave families an important, indeed decisive role where the patient is unconscious—a point of no little importance in our time. McCartney concludes

---

[69] "The Right to Life Question," *Overview*, Oct. 1980, 1–8.

[70] This same point is made by Ph. Delhaye, "Aspects de cette déclaration," *Esprit et vie* 90 (1980) 541–43.

[71] James J. McCartney, O.S.A., "The Development of the Doctrine of Ordinary and Extraordinary Means of Preserving Life in Catholic Moral Theology before the Karen Quinlan Case," *Linacre Quarterly* 47 (1980) 215–24.

his essay by wondering whether it is ever permissible to cease feeding (he refers to normal feeding) a patient who is terminal on the grounds that there is "no reasonable hope of success" or, to use the SCDF's terms, on the grounds that the means are disproportionate.

This is an interesting and extremely difficult question that occurs more frequently than it is comfortable to think. It is particularly thorny when the feeding is artificial. Some elderly and very senile patients, with associated complications, resist feeding, constantly remove their tubes, etc. It is situations like this that cannot be absolutely preprogramed and where prudence must combine with wisdom and courage.

John R. Connery, S.J., presents a study whose purpose is "to present and explain the traditional position on the obligation to prolong life and its limits."[72] Connery feels that there is a good deal of misunderstanding in present debates. He also regards the traditional position and language as still viable.

Connery first points out that the key element in distinguishing ordinary from extraordinary was the burden. "So if a particular means imposed a great burden on the patient either before, during or after its use, it would not be obligatory." The option belongs to the patient, for only the patient can gauge the burden he/she experiences.

Here Connery makes a key move. Many theologians today (following the late Gerald Kelly, S.J., and recently the Sacred Congregation for the Doctrine of the Faith) consider not only the burden; they consider the benefit. Thus, if a means causes no burden but offers no benefit, they would regard this as extraordinary or disproportionate. Connery rejects this because the notions of burden and benefit "deal with different issues—and usually apply to different types of cases." The question of benefit, he argues, is limited largely to terminal cases. Burden can be an issue even in nonterminal cases.

Connery very correctly argues that the option of refusing extraordinary measures is the patient's. If the patient is incompetent, the proxy must make the decision the patient would make. If there is no way of knowing this (e.g., the patient was never competent), "his [the proxy's] best option is to make the decision he would make if he were in the patient's place, or the decision that reasonable people would make for themselves in that situation."

Connery then turns to what is certainly one of the most difficult moral dilemmas in our time: the treatment of terribly defective newborns. Most people would feel very guilty, Connery believes, about allowing a defective person to drown were they able to save him/her. Conversely, there is no

[72] John R. Connery, S.J., "Prolonging Life: The Duty and its Limits," *Linacre Quarterly* 47 (1980) 151–65.

evidence to show that defective people consider death preferable to continued existence with their handicap. Connery continues: "If this is true, it is hard to understand how refusing help on the basis of a quality-of-life estimate is generally consistent with the duty of charity."

Robert Veatch and Paul Ramsey have both argued that we should abandon the ordinary-extraordinary terminology. For instance, Ramsey has suggested a "medical indications norm." According to this norm, if a treatment is medically indicated, it is obligatory; if it is not, it would not be obligatory. Thus useless treatment of a terminal patient would not be "medically indicated." Connery is dissatisfied here because he believes Ramsey's criterion would force burdens on incompetent people that the competent need not bear. Connery agrees with Ramsey that quality-of-life judgments are dangerous with regard to incompetents, but, he says, "I do not agree that in order to avoid them we should or have to make medical decisions final."

Connery's article is very carefully done and makes valuable distinctions about the obligation to *use* certain means and the obligation to *provide* them. But I want to put an important question to him in an effort to achieve greater clarity. He argues that burden and benefit are different issues and that traditionally it was the burden that was decisive in constituting a means extraordinary. He urges this as the basis for excluding quality-of-life ingredients in making decisions for those never competent.

But can we separate burden and benefit that sharply? Is not the benefit at times and in a sense identical with the burden? Connery gives the example of a quadruple amputation and says that because "it could certainly make life burdensome for its victim *afterwards*," it would be extraordinary. The very benefit we intend to provide (preservation of life) is also its burden and both are defined in terms of a kind of life. The life we save is the benefit; the kind of life is the burden.

Take the statement of the late Bishop Lawrence Casey in his *amicus* brief in the Quinlan case: "Karen Ann Quinlan has no reasonable hope of recovery from her comatose state by the use of any available medical procedures. The continuance of mechanical supportive measures to sustain continuation of her body functions and her life constitutes extraordinary means of treatment." Here treatment is burdensome (extraordinary) because of the quality of the benefit. In other words, it is impossible in some cases to determine what will benefit a patient without presupposing a standard of life. If the standard is bad enough (as in Connery's example of quadruple amputation), the benefit and burden coalesce.[73] Or

[73] Thus, Ph. Delhaye in his commentary on the document (cf. n. 70 above) of the SCDF notes that our task is to know if there is a proportion between the means used "and other aspects of the situation: the quality of the life one can prolong, the condition of the ill

again, what is a burden to the patient presupposes judgments about the patient's condition, and among the objective conditions to be considered one of the most decisive is the *kind of life* that will be preserved as a result of our interventions.[74] In cases like this, therefore, burden and benefit do not, as Connery thinks, "deal with different issues ... and usually apply to different types of cases."

In summary, I see no way out of *some* quality-of-life judgments[75] short of imposing survival on all defective newborns regardless of their condition and prognosis.[76] Is not our task rather to develop more detailed criteria to control and restrict the quality-of-life criteria which are unavoidably operative in our judgments—if, as Connery admits, the notion of burden can apply before, during, or *after* the use of lifesaving means?

Management of the critically ill and dying has become so confused that increasingly the cases are brought to court. Thus we have the well-known court cases involving Quinlan, Saikewicz, Spring, Fox, Dinnerstein, Becker. Connery reviews the first four of these cases.[77] When dealing with the incompetent patient, he fully endorses the notion of proxy

---

person," etc. It is interesting to note that Delhaye regards the notion of proportion as an "ouverture." It is not just the burden that is to be considered.

[74] Thus Tristram Englehardt, "Philosophy of Medicine," in *Social History of the Biomedical Sciences*, ed. Franco Maria Ricci (forthcoming), notes: "Physicians often justify withholding further care because such an intervention would be extraordinary or would involve heroic measures. However, the sense of ordinary and extraordinary does not appear to turn simply upon whether the treatment is costly or exotic, but upon whether it is likely to restore the patient to a quality of life acceptable to him, or should he be incompetent, to his family. In fact, such phrases are usually employed to indicate the result of various chains of reasoning that lead to the conclusion that treatment is obligatory or non-obligatory. Often the conclusion that a treatment is not obligatory or extraordinary will be made even when the treatment would not be costly or exotic, but because it would not achieve for the patient a quality of life that he would find tolerable." The questions I have put to Connery I would put to Joseph M. Boyle also; cf. "Quality of Life Standards and Withholding Life Saving Treatments," in *The Human Person*, ed. George F. McLean, 150–57 (this is Vol. 53 of the *Proceedings of the American Catholic Philosophical Association*).

[75] Of the use of such criteria, Connery states that I have shifted the emphasis from the nature of the means to the quality of life itself. "To this extent he departs from the tradition" (165, n. 15). Two points. The quality-of-life ingredient was always present in the very definition of burdensome means. Second, it is one thing to depart from a tradition, and in substance, not merely in formulation; it is another to extend this tradition into new problem areas. If such extension is true to the substantial value judgments of the tradition, it is a departure only in formulation. The distinction between substance and formulation is clearly proposed by John XXIII and Vatican II.

[76] I believe that this is what is logically entailed in James Burtchaell's response to Paul R. Johnson. Cf. Burtchaell, "How Much Should a Child Cost?" *Linacre Quarterly* 47 (1980) 54–63, and Johnson, "Selective Nontreatment of Defective Newborns: An Ethical Analysis," ibid. 39–53.

[77] John R. Connery, S.J., "Court's Guidelines on Incompetent Patients Compromise Their Rights," *Hospital Progress* 61, no. 9 (Sept. 1980) 46–49.

decision as "a hallowed Catholic principle."[78] He finds increasing resort to the courts, especially the guidelines set down by the court of appeals in the Fox case, a threat to the well-being of patients. This is true above all because they provide no way in which an incompetent person's rights can be exercised in a nonterminal case. Thus they compromise the incompetent person's rights to refuse disproportionate treatment.

Very much the same point is made in a fine article by Holy Cross's John J. Paris, S.J.[79] He faults the Mollen court in the Fox case for the cumbersome procedures it imposes, agrees with the Quinlan court that a proxy decision is appropriate, and insists that the decision be located within the family-physician group. I agree completely with Paris.[80]

Corrine Bayley, C.S.J., in an excellent summary article, agrees with Connery in the general lines of reasoning he has proposed.[81] But she regards the ordinary-extraordinary distinction as "an unfortunate use of words" since they are so easily misunderstood. "Emphasis is not on the means, but on how they will affect the patient." She rightly insists that the question of whether, e.g., to use or withdraw a respirator is an ethical question because "it deals with values, rights and obligation."

Bayley then notes that our first concern in decision-making for the incompetent is the patient's best interest, which means doing "what he or she would do if competent." Like Connery, Bayley argues that relatives and/or friends are best positioned to make this judgment. Furthermore, appeals to the courts, being cumbersome and drawn-out, are contrary to the patient's best interest. What is notable here is that Bayley is not a mere academician. She was for years a hospital administrator and was in a position to observe frequently and at first hand whether decisions left

---

[78] David E. Lee has challenged the use of substituted judgment in the Saikewicz case. He argues that (1) the notion of the right to refuse presupposes a decision-making capacity; (2) autonomy is such that it cannot be assumed by someone else without express authorization; (3) attempting to ascribe preferences to others apart from any expression of them is too tricky and dangerous ("The Saikewicz Decision and Patient Autonomy," *Linacre Quarterly* 47 [1980] 64–69). These objections can be met if we remember that (1) the autonomy appealed to is used in an analogous way when applied to the always incompetent; (2) determining what another would do is not simply determining his/her preferences (as Lee supposes) but roots in the "best interests" criterion. Best interests are, within a range and with some degree of risk, objectively identifiable. The vehicle for it is the "reasonable person criterion."

[79] John J. Paris, S.J., "Court Intervention and the Diminution of Patients' Rights: The Case of Brother Joseph Fox," *New England Journal of Medicine* 303 (1980) 876–78. See also his excellent article "Brother Fox, the Courts and Death with Dignity," *America* 143 (1980) 282–85.

[80] Richard A. McCormick, S.J., "The Fox Case," *Journal of the American Medical Association* 244 (1980) 2165–66.

[81] Corrine Bayley, C.S.J., "Terminating Treatment: Asking the Right Questions," *Hospital Progress* 61, no. 9 (Sept. 1980) 50–53, 72.

to families and physicians would or would not be to the patient's benefit.
It is significant, I believe, that many people in Bayley's position are
comfortable with proxy decisions (family-physicians) based on a best-
interests criterion, controlled by the "reasonable person standard."

I agree with the Connery-Bayley perspectives in the matter of proxy
decision. Indeed, Robert Veatch and I attempted to propose in these
pages a principle of "family self-determination" for such situations.[82] We
were uncomfortable with the original Fox decision, because it had proposed self-determination as the only way to get the dying, 83-year-old,
noncognitive, nonsapient Brother Fox off the respirator. Judge Meade
had argued that Fox could be relieved of the respirator because, though
incompetent, he had stated his opinion on the Quinlan case and similar
cases ("that extraordinary business"). Because he had done so, the
decision of Rev. Philip Eichner to remove him was really Brother Fox's
decision—an exercise of self-determination by anticipation.

Veatch–McCormick argued that these grounds were too narrow, that
they would leave most dying incompetents on respirators. Therefore,
beyond self-determination, we proposed the need of proxy judgments by
family/relatives, what we called a "principle of family self-determination." We argued that the state should intervene only when family
decisions "so exceed the limits of reason that the compromise with what
is objectively in the incompetent one's interest cannot be tolerated." This
is in full agreement with the principles laid out by Connery and Bayley
in their review of Catholic tradition.

In this issue of *TS*, Paul Ramsey challenges this view (*tolle et lege*). He
agrees with us that these decisions about/for incompetent dying patients
should not (at least generally) be adjudicated in the courts. There is no
need for this. However, neither should they be made by the families with
the physicians, as Connery–Bayley–Veatch–McCormick propose. Why?
Because these are subjective criteria, often subtly interpenetrated with
quality-of-life criteria that Ramsey rejects as allowable. So, as between
the courts and family self-determination, Ramsey argues that the appropriate and only *objective* criteria are "strictly medical criteria," "medical
indications," "clinical or physiological ones." By this he refers to the
"medical decision to cease to combat the dying of the dying . . . to cease
treatment when, and only when, to continue would only prolong the
dying of the dying." Unless we adopt criteria "in which physicians agree
to place their confidence," we will not keep these cases out of court. The
courts will preempt other "subjective standards" and the McCormick–
Veatch proposal will be counterproductive.

---

[82] "The Preservation of Life and Self-Determination," THEOLOGICAL STUDIES 41 (1980)
390–96.

The above is, I believe, an accurate summary of Ramsey's contribution. I say this because in the course of displaying a single flower Ramsey is wont to roam through a garden and pluck out and examine a whole scattering of weeds that too easily obscure his single display.[83] What is to be said of his argument and analysis? I speak for myself here, not for Veatch. Veatch will undoubtedly answer in his own way and time. I want to suggest three points.

1) Family self-determination (proxy decision) as subjective. Ramsey insists that allowing such determination of treatment for the incompetent exposes them to merely subjective criteria. I want to deny that. The standard for treating incompetents (if we have no living will or something similar) is to discover whether the treatment would be *objectively valuable for a patient in that condition.* In order to determine this, we have to resort to some empirical means. For me, that would be asking what is reasonably seen as *objectively valuable by a reasonable person.* It is the "best interests" standard as controlled by the "reasonable person" standard that Veatch and I proposed when we urged that the state should intervene "only when familial judgment so exceeds the limits of reason that the compromise with what is objectively in the incompetent one's interest cannot be tolerated." "Best interests" as controlled by the "reasonable person" standard may permit a range. But a range is not necessarily subjective.

2) Medical indications policy as objective. Ramsey argues that only a "medical indications policy" is objective and will keep these cases out of court by assuring best interests. By "objective" he clearly means "not influenced by personal value judgments." Thus "medically indicated" supposes that the judgment is not only objective but determined by *scientific evidence alone.* This must be denied. The "medical indications policy" of not prolonging a dying patient's dying contains a nonscientific value judgment. As Ramsey admits, some patients may want heroic measures to the moment of their death; others may not. These choices root in different subjective and value reasons. To say that "not to prolong a dying patient's dying" is a merely medical (scientific) indication is wrong. It is the acceptance of one value preference over another. It looks merely scientific (hence objective), but it is not. Clearly, therefore value judgments or preferences function in a "medical indications policy." And if they do, why refer to this as a *"medical* indications policy"? It is rather a policy that most reasonable people agree to, that conforms to their

---

[83] I agree that many of the weeds are indeed weeds (judicial obscurities and incoherences). In other cases, no. For instance, Ramsey says: *"Quinlan* was the right decision for the wrong reasons." I believe *Quinlan* was the right decision for the right reasons. Similarly, he believes *Saikewicz* was "a wrong decision for the wrong reason." I believe it was the right decision for the right reason—but with wrong procedures attached.

value preference, and therefore can be comfortably accepted as what most doctors think right and do.[84]

In summary: if a value judgment clearly underlies Ramsey's "medical indications policy," it is clearly not objective in the sense he proposes, sc., one distinct from personal value preferences and distinct from a policy based on best interests controlled by the "reasonable person" standard. Indeed, his policy is but a concretization of the "reasonable person" standard.

3) Incompetents who are not dying. Ramsey's policy simply does not touch these. Or rather, it mandates medical treatment on them all regardless of how heroic or extraordinary it is. For if a "medical indications policy" is merely scientific (clinical or physiological), it can contain no value judgments that might exempt us from using any and all treatments on the incompetent but not dying patient. Connery has caught this well. He asks: "Is it reasonable to make incompetent people bear burdens that competent people do not have to bear? Certainly the decision is more difficult . . . but the difficulty does not warrant retreat to a position which seems to compromise the rights of the incompetent."[85]

I agree with Connery. A "medical indications policy" leads straight to the violation of the rights of the incompetent nondying patients. It makes life-preserving treatment the only option regardless of the patient's condition. If this can be an assault on the best interests of the competent, it is no less so for the incompetent. The only way out of this cul-de-sac is to accept the validity of proxy judgments based on best interests—the very thing Ramsey denies because of the danger of subjective, quality-of-life judgments.

Connery believes, and I agree, that Ramsey has "canonized medical indications." This he has done in a laudable cause: to keep these cases out of court on the one hand, and to steer clear of possibly very subjective and discriminatory assessments of another's best interest. In doing this, he has, I believe, mechanized treatment decisions, paralyzed them for the nondying incompetent, and opposed himself to a very long tradition which insists that treatment of the ill, whether dying or nondying, is radically an ethical (value) decision, as both Connery and Bayley so

---

[84] That "medical indications" contain but hide a value judgment is clear from some of the facts revealed in the Fox case. Dr. Edward Kelly, the surgeon in the case, argued that once a respirator was employed, "it should not be withdrawn." Larry Kennedy, a spokesman for the Nassau Hospital, reinforced this by saying: "Our mission is to do all that we can to maintain life." I disagree with that, as does Ramsey. But our disagreement with Kennedy roots in a *value* judgment. Thus, when Ramsey uses phrases such as "useless prolonging of the dying process," he is not making a purely scientific or medical judgment. He is making a *value* judgment which *most physicians have made their own*; and for that reason it is easily conveyed by the phrase "medical indications."

[85] Connery, "Prolonging Life" 161.

correctly assert. To hide these value components under a "medical indications policy" will only delay the day when physicians must face up to the awesome task of sharing with families in difficult value judgments. In other words, I believe Ramsey is pedaling backwards.

It is important to stand back from these discussions to see their broader dimensions. On the one hand, there is widespread dissatisfaction with ordinary-extraordinary terminology for many reasons, not the least because it disguises the quality-of-life ingredient so often present in treatment decisions made by the competent dying patient, and frequently judged appropriate for the incompetent dying and nondying patient. On the other, there is legitimate and grave fear that quality-of-life considerations can be subjective discrimination against the incompetent which would violate their rights and undermine our own grasp on the sanctity of every human life. I sympathize deeply with both of these concerns. But in the face of such a dilemma, our task is not to deny the quality-of-life ingredient as a legitimate criterion but sharply to control it within the bounds of what we consider to be truly human and Christian.

THE FIFTH SYNOD OF BISHOPS

The fifth Synod of Bishops began September 26 and formally ended October 26. Treating of the family, the Synod raised, perhaps unrealistically, great expectations in an area swimming in problems. Any realistic treatment of the family is bound to touch upon several delicate and controversial areas, especially birth regulation and the pastoral problem associated with irregular second marriages.[86]

What did the Synod do? The available sources for a response to that question are four. First, there are the various interventions.[87] Second, there are the proposals (*De muneribus familiae christianae in mundo hodierno*) submitted to the Holy Father, though the actual vote on these proposals is unknown at this writing. Third, there is the "Message to Christian Families in the Modern World."[88] Finally, there is the closing speech of John Paul II.[89]

With regard to the two subjects mentioned above, it is clear what the Synod did. In their "Message to Christian Families in the Modern World,"

---

[86] Ph. Delhaye reports that when Paul VI acceded to the wishes of bishops to discuss the family in the Synod of 1980, he stated: "Yes, but it is necessary to avoid the burning questions." John Paul II did not take this attitude. It is amusing that Delhaye gives abortion as an example of the "burning questions" ("Le sens du synode 1980," *Esprit et vie* 90 [1980] 545–47).

[87] The interesting intervention of Archbishop Denis Hurley (Durban) was mysteriously omitted from the published synopses. It can be found in the *Tablet* 234 (1980) 1105–7. Hurley rightly wonders how "the act of artificially limiting the exercise of one faculty of life is intrinsically evil while the act of exterminating life itself is not."

[88] *Origins* 10 (1980) 321–25.   [89] Ibid. 325–29.

the synodal bishops stated that the "conjugal act itself, as the encyclical *Humanae vitae* tells us, must be fully human, total, and open to new life." Furthermore, in proposals 23, 24, and 25 the traditional doctrine of *Humanae vitae* is repeated, a pastoral approach of gradualism is suggested, and theologians are invited "to join forces with the hierarchical magisterium so that the biblical foundations and the personalistic reasons for this doctrine may be better brought out."

Speaking at the closing session of the Synod (Oct. 25), John Paul II stated that the irregularly remarried may not receive Communion unless they "live in a manner which is not opposed to the indissolubility of marriage, live in complete continence, that is, by abstinence from acts in which only married couples can engage."[90] In proposal 18 we read: "Nevertheless the Synod confirms the practice of the Church supported by Sacred Scripture (*Sacrae Scripturae innitentem*)[91] of not admitting the divorced and irregularly remarried to Eucharistic Communion. For they cannot be admitted to Eucharistic Communion since their state of life and condition objectively contradict the indissolubility of that covenant of love between Christ and the Church which is signified and realized in the Eucharist."

Thus, on the two most burning (not the only) issues to confront it, the Synod repeated traditional teaching.

This is theologically and pastorally disturbing, to say the very least. For two reasons. First, in both matters the synodal conclusions will not win sufficient theological support. Indeed, a heavy majority of theologians have drawn a different conclusion in both matters.[92] Second, it is disturbing because the papal and synodal statements were made at the very time

---

[90] Cf. ibid.

[91] It is often Scripture scholars themselves who, from the very perspectives of Scripture, point to a different possibility. The most recent study I have seen in this category is that of John R. Donahue, S.J., "Divorce: New Testament Perspectives," a paper delivered to the Midwestern Canon Law Society, April 21, 1980. Cf. also Raymund Schwager, "Inkonsequente Normfindung für Gewalt und Ehescheidung," *Orientierung* 44 (1980) 144–47.

[92] Cf. Normand Provencher, O.M.I., "L'accès des divorcés aux sacrements," *Studia canonica* 14 (1980) 89–106. Provencher argues that adherence to the doctrine of indissolubility need not imply negation of all reality to a second union. Rather, there is a reality and under certain conditions (he lists them, 105) divorced-remarrieds should be able to receive the sacraments. The conclusion of Provencher has been shared by a heavy majority of theologians during the past ten years. For a review cf. James H. Provost, "Intolerable Marriage Situations Revisited," *Jurist* 40 (1980) 141–96. Cf. also Pierre Benoit, O.P., "Christian Marriage according to St. Paul," *Clergy Review* 65 (1980) 309–21. As for contraception cf. F. J. Elizari, "A los diez años de 'Humanae vitae': Boletín bibliográfico," *Moralia: Revista de ciencias morales* 1 (1979) 235–53. Also *Theology Digest* 28 (1980) 33–37 and E. Chiavacci, "Valori di fondo e sistematica normativa," *Rivista di teologia morale* 10 (1978) 519–27. Chiavacci notes simply that the deontological argument (nature of the act) is no longer defended.

that several national episcopates in attendance were calling for a study of these problems at the highest levels.

Just a few episcopal interventions can be reviewed here to make the point just made. One of the most interesting interventions was that of Archbishop John R. Quinn.[93] He noted that many men and women of good will do not accept the "intrinsic evil of each and every use of contraception." This conviction is shared by a majority of priests and theologians, a conviction found among "theologians and pastors whose learning, faith, discretion, and dedication to the Church are beyond doubt." Quinn argued that this cannot be dismissed. He notes that the Church "has alw ays recognized the principle and fact of doctrinal development." Therefore he proposed three things: (1) a new context for the teaching; (2) a widespread and world-wide dialogue between the Holy See and theologians on the meaning of this dissent; (3) careful attention to the process by which magisterial documents are written and communicated. He then elaborated these three points.

The press reports of this careful, realistic, and courageous statement were somewhat misleading. Careful—because the problem was stated accurately. For instance, Quinn noted that the problem of many theologians is not that they view contraception as "simply something good, desirable, or indifferent." The problem is the usage "intrinsically evil" of *quilibet usus.*[94] Realistic—because Quinn is absolutely correct in saying that "this problem is not going to be solved or reduced merely by a simple reiteration of past formulations or by ignoring the fact of dissent." Furthermore, the way to face it is precisely through Quinn's suggested dialogue at the highest level. Courageous—because the suggestions were made *coram pontifice*, whose views on this matter are well known and who therefore could not be thought to have called the Synod to have them questioned. I say "questioned" because Quinn did refer to "doctrinal development" in areas such as biblical studies and religious liberty. In

---

[93] John R. Quinn, "'New Context' for Contraception Teaching," *Origins* 10 (1980) 263–67.

[94] Cf. the outstanding little essay by J. Dominion ("Open Letter to the Synod," *Tablet* 234 [1980] 840–42). Dominion makes any number of very telling points. One is that serious opposition to *Humanae vitae* "is not based on the assertion that infertile period methods do not work." Of course they do, for many people. The opposition is theological. Another is that those who oppose the encyclical's "intrinsically evil" formulation are accused of wanting abortion as well. Dominion asserts that "there is no evidence whatsoever that this is the case." Another fear is that the advent of contraception will become an attack on children. "There is not the slightest danger of this." Dominion's essay is strong testimony to the need of married experience in the formulation of the Church's convictions. See also Arthur McCormack, M.H.M., "The Population Problem and the Synod on the Family," *Clergy Review* 65 (1980) 328–38.

these contexts development meant change. I regard Quinn's intervention as outstanding.

The second intervention is that of Cardinal G. Emmett Carter of Toronto.[95] After noting that many theologians and Catholic couples have "moved beyond" *Humanae vitae,* he asked: Could this be a way the Holy Spirit is speaking to the whole Church? Could this be an expression of the *sensus fidelium*? Whatever the case, Carter concluded that "the magisterium must take account of this phenomenon or run the risk of speaking in a vacuum."

Next, Cardinal George Basil Hume.[96] He insisted that those who experience the sacrament of marriage constitute "an authentic *fons theologiae*." For some, the problem of *Humanae vitae* remains a real problem not because of their frailty and weakness. "They just cannot accept that the use of artificial means of contraception in some circumstances is *intrinsece inhonestum*." Hume concluded that "if we [the Synod fathers] listen to all the different points of view," a right way will be found.

Archbishop Derek Worlock (Liverpool), in his discussion of the divorced and remarried, asked: "Is this spirit of repentance and desire for sacramental strength to be forever frustrated?"[97] He noted that his own presynodal consultation would not accept the assertion that concession of the Eucharist to the irregularly remarried would scandalize Catholics and undermine the bond of marriage.

Archbishop Henri Legare (Grouard-McLennan, Alberta) stated that the problem of the divorced-remarried cannot be approached merely at the pastoral level.[98] The doctrine of marriage must be re-examined. To the present, the theology of marriage has been developed out of an "essentialist philosophy." Legare proposes that it must be rethought "in a more existentialist and personalist framework." He asked that we re-examine the relationship of the sacrament to the human institution of marriage.[99]

---

[95] D. Emmett Carter, "Spirit's Voice or Moral Decadence?" *Origins* 10 (1980) 276–77.

[96] George Basil Hume, "Development of Marriage Teaching," ibid. 275–76.

[97] Derek Worlock, "Marital Indissolubility and Pastoral Compassion," ibid. 273–75.

[98] Henri Legare, "Current Situations: Value, Risk, Suffering," ibid. 280–82.

[99] At least fifteen of the 162 Synod fathers spoke to this question, and most urged the Synod to find a way to readmit Catholics in irregular second marriages to the sacraments (*Catholic Chronicle,* Oct. 24, 1980, 10). Those who think this unthinkable and "in conflict with the basic nature of the Church" must reflect more deeply on current discipline. By policy (Decree on Ecumenism, Decree on Oriental Catholic Churches, and the *motu proprio* "Crescens matrimonium") Orthodox Catholics in good standing can receive the sacraments in the Western Catholic rite. Thus a divorced and remarried Orthodox person can receive the Eucharist in Catholic churches of the West. No one has argued that this is in "conflict with the basic nature of the Church."

Finally, the Canadian bishops, in a pastoral letter to Canadians at the end of the Synod, called attention to two things: (1) "The Synod fathers recommended that a new and far-reaching study be launched" on the pastoral care of the divorced and remarried. (2) In re *Humanae vitae*, "Many bishops recommended continuing research toward a new and fuller presentation of what is involved in this question." In a communication to Cardinal Joseph Ratzinger, the Canadian bishops had suggested that both matters be re-examined.[100]

Here we have synodal fathers acknowledging a problem, calling for further study and dialogue, admitting the need to consult the experience of the married as a *fons theologiae*, stressing the need to "listen to all the different points of view," yet repeating traditional formulations on the very issues regarded as problematic, as needing further study and dialogue.[101]

Furthermore, the disturbing character of these events is only deepened when we read the following concerning procedures from a reporter at the Synod:

The lay auditors were not representative of the Church, but were in fact firm promoters of natural family planning. The majority of Catholic families, which practice birth control, were not represented. Nor were dissenting theologians welcome at the Synod. As a result no true dialogue was really possible. Any criticism of *Humanae vitae* was considered scandalous. The final message ignored the population crisis. Some bishops were afraid to say what they really thought because they feared they would be misrepresented by the press or seen as challenging positions held by Pope Paul VI and John Paul II.[102]

Finally, on several occasions during the Synod, bishops intervened to say that the teaching of *Humanae vitae* was "certainly correct" but that "better reasons" had to be found to validate its conclusions. To maintain the certain truth of a formulation but admit that we must find "better reasons" is perilously close to saying that the formulation is correct regardless of the reasons. Catholic theological tradition will not support this, even though official Catholic practice has at times and still does. Such considerations raise the gravest doubts about the very freedom of the synodal process. And that brings us to the pastoral problems associated with the Synod.

[100] For the Canadian bishops' message, cf. *Origins* 10 (1980) 329–30. For their communication to Ratzinger, cf. *Catholic Chronicle*, Oct. 10, 1980, 5.

[101] It must be remembered that the Synod is not per se a teaching authority; it is advisory to the Holy Father (cf. the *motu proprio* "Apostolica sollicitudo" of Feb. 15, 1965, as in *Documents of Vatican II* [New York: Association Press, 1966] 720–24). Yet practically it will surely be viewed and used as a vehicle to communicate Catholic conviction.

[102] Thomas J..Reese, S.J., "The Close of the Synod," *America* 143 (1980) 281. Similarly, the *Tablet* refers to "foregone conclusions virtually imposed on a so-called consultative body" (234 [1980] 1059).

There is a single pastoral problem of great significance that is inseparable from the Synod and its outcome. It concerns the functioning of the teaching office of the Church, an ecclesiological problem with clear personal ramifications for both the theologian and the theologically informed pastoral minister. A word about each.

Theologian

How is the theologian to respond to the continuing "reaffirmation of *Humanae vitae*" when he is convinced of the inadequacy of some of its formulations ("intrinsece inhonestum ... semper illicitum") and when he knows that a majority of his/her colleagues share this view? Should he lapse into silence? Does loyalty demand this type of submission? Rahner's answer to this was noted above. How one answers these questions will depend very much on one's concept of the magisterium and how it relates or should relate to theological enquiry.

At this point I want to call attention to three very important articles that touch on this subject. The first is by André Naud and was presented at the 1979 meeting of the *Societé canadienne de théologie*.[103] Naud begins by noting that the responses to *Humanae vitae* and *Persona humana* show that there is a crisis. Adverting to the fact that theology and collective reflection are no longer in proper focus ("ne sont pas au point"), Naud organizes his thoughts around two themes: right of the Church to intervene and mode of intervention.

1) *Right of the Church*. Naud clearly accepts the right of the Church to intervene, even in a very practical way. So as between saying nothing (or remaining tautologously general) and settling definitively, there is settling *pro hic et nunc*, surely a prerogative of the sovereign pontiff. That brings up the heart of the problem, the mode of intervention.

2) *Mode of intervention*. Here Naud scores the fact that authoritative interventions leave the impression that they are changeless when this is not the case. He regards the text of *Lumen gentium* (no. 25 "adherence of mind and will") as "extrêmement ambiguës" when taken together with the type of freedom asserted by the German hierarchy (1968) in the face of noninfallible teaching. Finally, he wonders why bishops do not openly and honestly express their own doubts. For some this is custom ("one does not contradict the pope"). For others it represents the need for unanimity on the pastoral front. Naud sees this as artificial and ultimately deceitful ("mensongère"). "The mechanism of magisterial teaching finds itself, so to speak, distorted because no place has been allowed in the Church, as it should be, for doubt, hesitation, search."[104] The magisterium

---

[103] André Naud, "Les voix de l'église dans les questions morales," *Science et esprit* 32 (1980) 161–76.
[104] Ibid. 167.

is disabled when bishops become a mere echo of the pope.

Naud then turns more positively to the qualities magisterial teaching ought to have. First, it must present "motives and reasons." It is the guardian of the Christian message, not its autonomous creator. Second, as Rahner has suggested, it should state the degree of certitude with which a position is taken. Its very integrity ("honnêteté") is at stake here. Finally, we must advance beyond *Lumen gentium* 25. Citing the rather common theological rejection of Pius XII's approach in *Humani generis* (matters authoritatively settled by the pope are no longer a matter of free discussion among theologians), Naud continues: "The thought of the Church has, therefore, advanced in this matter. It must still advance. In my view, we should not repeat the text of *Lumen gentium* (25), even less brandish it to condemn, without clarifying its sense."[105]

Naud repeatedly emphasizes the need for bishops to speak freely on controversial questions, both *before* and *after* Roman interventions. To leave these matters (moral questions where revelation gives no definitive answer) entirely to the pope is abandonment of episcopal responsibility. There must be exchange. "Then, and then alone, will the ecclesial word correspond to the state of thought and certitude of the Church."[106]

Naud then turns to the role of pastors (those in pastoral ministry). Rahner had stated in 1968 that "in preaching and catechesis, one ought not in any case present teachings contrary to these provisional doctrines of the Church." Naud rejects this, as it is clear that Rahner himself would now. Naud calls it the "politics of silence" that "maintains a false evaluation of the true thought of the Church." Rather, the pastor's role must be redefined. The pastor of souls is no mere courier. "In the measure in which he has a share in magisterial activity, the pastor has not only the right to reflect, but the duty to do so. He has equally the right and duty to make his responsible contribution to the teaching of the Church."[107] Naud firmly rejects the old idea of an obedient or obsequious silence, and the apparent unanimity it presents. "It does not recognize sufficiently the right and the duty of each of those with a responsibility within the Christian community to participate in the communal search on moral questions that ought to be debated." Therefore he resolutely defends the right and duty of dissent, always, of course, with due reverence. Denials of this root in the urge toward a unity established on a false basis. As a result of this urge, he feels, we have tended unduly to expand

[105] Ibid. 168–69.

[106] Forthcoming in the *Way* (April 1981) is a fine article by Thomas E. Clarke, S.J., "Shepherding the Heritage: Bishops as Teachers." Clarke stresses the fact that Church teaching takes place through an interplay of the experience of the entire People of God, its creative testing and understanding by theologians, its validation by the episcopal college.

[107] Naud, "Les voix" 170.

the authority of the magisterium, especially of the pope, in matters not definitively decided by Scripture and tradition. He concludes his study as follows:

For all the questions which revelation cannot sufficiently clarify, my reflections point in the direction of a much greater reserve in the definition of the role of the Roman pontiff; of a more responsible sharing on the part of pastors (priests and bishops) in the magisterial function; of a diminished isolation of the critical role of the theologian; of a presentation of the thought of the Church which, in each instance, reveals adequately the qualities that give it credence; of an approach to the ecclesial community which considers each adult member of it as truly adult.[108]

This outstanding study has been presented at length because it out-spokenly represents the convictions of a large segment of the theological community. These convictions, basically ecclesiological in character, con-stitute the framework out of which many theologians feel obliged—and, I would add, in conscience—to think about and respond to the authori-tative noninfallible declarations of the Church on moral matters not definitively settled by the sources of faith. Thus it should be expected and pacifically accepted, even welcomed, that dissent will continue from some of the reaffirmations of the Synod.

Concretely, where theologians feel that they have convincing reasons for a position, they feel obliged in loyalty to the Church to say it, and say it publicly (since theology is a public enterprise). Naud argues that this must also be the case with bishops. This is one of the most important aspects of his study. I used to believe that closer co-operation between bishops and theologians might solve many of our pastoral problems and foster the credibility of the Church's teaching office. Such co-operation is nugatory, however, if the bishops do not speak their true mind after co-operation has occurred. If they do not, then we shall continue to experience in official documents the dominance of a theology emanating from those Walbert Bühlmann refers to as the "old guard."[109]

Next there is a fine essay by Bernard Cooke.[110] Cooke says some of the things stated by Naud. For instance: "What is needed—and has been needed for many years—is open and careful discussion that includes all the responsible voices in the Church." We need structures, Cooke argues, that allow bishops' collegial witness to apostolic tradition to openly interact with the reflection and research of scholars and both to be challenged by the life experience of devoted Catholics. Why so? Because,

---

[108] Ibid. 175–76.

[109] Walbert Bühlmann, "Chance zum Neubeginn in der Glaubenskongregation?" *Orientierung* 44 (1980) 196–97. This is a severe critique of "Roman centralism" in contemporary theology.

[110] Bernard Cooke, "The Responsibility of Theologians," *Commonweal* 107 (1980) 39–42.

although the bishops, together with the bishop of Rome, possess and pass on the truth upon which Christianity is grounded (Jesus' death and resurrection), still "when we move beyond this core reality to which the papacy and episcopacy witness, when we move to questions about the meaning and applicability of Christ's death and resurrection, other kinds of knowledge and experience enter the picture." A fortiori this would be true of concrete moral questions, a point both Naud and Cooke concede.

Third, in dealing with the pastoral problem of the theologian, it would be useful to study an excellent essay by Avery Dulles, S.J.[111] He first treats of the requisites for membership in either of the two (hierarchical, scholarly) magisteria. Where the theological magisterium is concerned, what is required is a group of factors such as advanced degree, distinguished career of teaching, noteworthy publications, esteem by one's colleagues. *Missio canonica* is not required. This notion, as applied to theologians, originated in Germany after the disturbances of 1848, when special measures were required to protect Catholic teachers from state interference. "This historically conditioned maneuver ought not to be the ground for redefining the concept of the Catholic theologian."

Dulles next reviews the functional specialties of each magisterium. The hierarchical magisterium is proclamatory, explanatory, promotional, judicial. Under this last category, Dulles believes that the position of Pius XII (*Humani generis*, DS 3885) about terminating a theological debate "still seems to stand." By this he means that it has not been officially abrogated; he does not mean that he agrees with the position. In summary, the functional specialty of the hierarchical magisterium is judgment about what is vital for the life and witness of Christian community. That of the theologian is understanding.

As for the relationship of the two magisteria, Dulles rejects reductionist (total identification) and separatist approaches. Instead, he proposes a "dialectical relationship of relative autonomy with mutual acceptance." Thus, while the hierarchy does not learn the Christian message from theologians, still the appropriate restatement of this faith does depend on scholarly work.

There is a certain tension that is normal and healthy in the relationship of the two magisteria; but in our time it has become explosive and has generated a "third magisterium." This refers to simple and devout believers (and their theological supporters) who have not been trained to distinguish the deposit of faith from traditional formulations and thus believe that liberal theologians are betraying the faith. Bishops are under great pressure from this "third magisterium" and this has sharpened the normal tensions between bishops and theologians. These two groups are

[111] Avery Dulles, S.J., "The Two Magisteria: An Interim Reflection," forthcoming in the *Proceedings of the Catholic Theological Society of America* 35 (1980).

being driven apart by forces that would put them in opposite camps.

Dulles believes—and I think accurately—that the hierarchical magisterium is tempted to identify traditional formulations too simplistically with the deposit of faith "and to appeal to authority of office as an excuse for not looking into new and complex questions." This attitude on the part of churchmen of the nineteenth century made it difficult for scholars to open up the biblical question, and Dulles asserts that "the same may be said in our time regarding recent developments in the morality of sex and family life." If the hierarchy is to regain influence with alienated Catholics, bishops cannot simply go by the book in condemning new ideas and their authors. Dulles then concludes as follows:

They must sincerely and evidently examine the issues on their merits. Before rejecting any new doctrinal proposal, they must assure themselves that they have really heard and appreciated the reasons and motivations of those who favor the proposal. Where there is widespread and persistent dissent on the part of committed Catholics, the hierarchy must carefully inquire whether something has gone wrong with the decision-making process. If the decision was not substantively wrong—a possibility we can rarely exclude—at least the way in which it was reached, expressed and imposed may have been deficient.

What is important here is that all three authors (Naud, Cooke, Dulles), and with them Rahner and many others, view dissent as (1) a normal, indeed indispensable, aspect of doctrinal progress, (2) and therefore as the right and duty of a theologian. In reactionary times in the Church it is all too easy to overlook this and define a theologian's loyalty in terms of adherence to a traditional formulation. We must remember that certain notions of loyalty and obedience are really encouragements to risk-avoidance and theological conformity. At this point "loyalty" betrays fidelity to one's vocation as a theologian and to those who have a right to expect more from the theologian. Similarly, it is all too easy to define the teaching role of the bishop too exclusively in terms of formal authority. It remains axiomatic that one of the great advantages of being a teacher is that it creates the possibility of learning.

Theologically Informed Pastoral Minister

Archbishop Quinn adverted to this problem in his synodal intervention ("grave personal problems for priests"). The priest has a dual role: representative of the Church's teaching authority, pastor of souls. Normally these two roles complement each other. But where contraception is concerned they are in severe tension and this causes grave personal problems. It can endanger the very identity of the priest in his ministry. In one role the priest is expected to set forth the teaching of the hierarchical magisterium as the remote objective norm for moral decision-making. On the other hand, the more theologically aware he is, the more he knows of the widespread disagreement with the substantive moral argument (*intrinsece inhonestum*) and the reasons for it.

The pastoral strategy constantly urged is compassion toward one regarded as a "habitual sinner" in need of time for conversion, or as one in a situation of *conscientia recta sed non vera*, but in either case as one who should receive the Eucharist. The problem of this pastoral strategy is two-dimensional. For the penitent or counselee it can appear to be a recommendation for hypocrisy. Purpose of amendment is clearly very problematical here and the penitent knows it better than anyone. For the priest it goes to the very marrow of his self-understanding. He is a man of the Church and as such is loyal to authority within the Church. But he also is aware that the intellectual foundations of the position he is asked to impose as counselor-advisor have been profoundly eroded. Thus he is split. And so split, he is asked to solve at a practical level the problem of dissent and nonconformity, a disproportionate burden for the average priest. In summary, the priest finds himself with no coherent theological grounding for pastoral strategy. All of these things Archbishop Quinn has realistically noted in his intervention.

Can anything be said to this problem at the present time? An interesting study by Philip S. Kaufman attempts an answer.[112] After reviewing the history of probabilism in the Church, Kaufman asks whether there is a probable opinion in this matter against *Humanae vitae*. He notes the "massive response of competent theologians" opposed to certain formulations of the encyclical. The standard answer is, of course, negative. According to this view, as Kaufman notes, "once the pope or a Roman congregation has taken an official position, there is no longer room for the legitimate doubt upon which probabilism is based."

Kaufman rejects this view and argues that it can be maintained only if the Roman magisterium has never been in error in its authentic moral teaching. He amply documents that this is not the case, citing especially but not exclusively slavery as an example. Kaufman concludes by insisting that widespread theological dissent is a theological source and "it should also be a valid and available source for the faithful in the formation of their consciences." He cites the remarks of Bernard Häring in a talk at Holy Cross Abbey: "Those who are doubtful whether they can accept it have to study it thoroughly, have to read it with good will, but they also have to accept other information in the Church. They cannot dissociate the pope from the whole of the Church." Kaufman argues that the faithful have a right to that "other information" and that it is "objectively immoral" to deny that right. In summary, he thinks probabilism is applicable.

[112] Philip S. Kaufman, "An Immoral Morality?" *Commonweal* 107 (1980) 493–97.

When we combine Rahner–Naud–Cooke–Dulles with Kaufman's essay, an important point emerges. When dissent occurs against an official formulation and becomes "massive" throughout the Church, it cannot be viewed as "isolated speculation" with no relationship to practical every-day living. That is exactly what Häring and Kaufman are underlining. To say anything different is to put truth in the service of authority and official formulations. It should be exactly vice versa.

And that is where this matter is, in my judgment, even after the Synod. There was neither the time nor the ability (cf. Reese's description of the synodal atmosphere and personnel) to engage in the serious dialogue and study suggested by Archbishop Quinn and the Canadian bishops. Such dialogue and study is required to maintain the presumption of truth certainly enjoyed by those possessing the *charisma veritatis*.[113]

[113] Cf. Bernard J. Cooke, "Contraception and the Synod," ibid. 648–50.

CURRENT THEOLOGY

NOTES ON MORAL THEOLOGY: 1981

RICHARD A. McCORMICK, S.J.

Kennedy Institute of Ethics and Woodstock Theological Center, D.C.

This version of the "Notes" will concentrate on three general themes: (1) methodology in moral theology; (2) the encyclical *Laborem exercens* and social morality; (3) pastoral problems (sterilization, hunger strikes, nuclear disarmament, divorce and remarriage).

METHODOLOGY IN MORAL THEOLOGY

Vatican II (*Gaudium et spes* 51) asserted that the "moral aspect of any procedure ... must be determined by objective standards which are based on the nature of the person and the person's acts" (*objectivis criteriis ex personae ejusdemque actuum natura desumptis*). The official commentary on this wording noted two things: (1) In the expression there is formulated a general principle that applies to all human actions, not just to marriage and sexuality. (2) The choice of this expression means that "human activity must be judged insofar as it refers to the human person integrally and adequately considered" (*personam humanam integre et adequate considerandam*).[1] Clearly this is utterly important to moral methodology. But what does it mean to use as a criterion "the human person integrally and adequately considered"?

Louis Janssens, in another of his helpful articles, answers: the human person in all his/her essential aspects.[2] He then lists and discusses eight such aspects. The human person is (1) a subject (normally called to consciousness, to act according to conscience, in freedom and in a responsible way). (2) A subject in corporeality. (3) A corporeal subject that is part of the material world. (4) Persons are essentially directed toward one another (only in relation to a Thou do we become I). (5) Persons need to live in social groups, with structures and institutions worthy of persons. (6) The human person is called to know and worship God. (7) The human person is a historical being, with successive life stages and continuing new possibilities. (8) All persons are utterly original but fundamentally equal.

Janssens then formulates from these characteristics a general criterion of the rightness or wrongness of human actions. An act is morally right

[1] *Schema constitutionis pastoralis de ecclesia in mundo huius temporis: Expensio modorum partis secundae* (Vatican Press, 1965) 37–38.

[2] Louis Janssens, "Artificial Insemination: Ethical Considerations," *Louvain Studies* 8(1980) 3–29.

if, according to reason enlightened by faith, it is beneficial to the human person "adequately considered in himself (nn. 1 and 2) and in his relations (nn. 3, 4, 5, 6)." He refers to this as an "ethic of responsibility on a personalist foundation."

Because of our limitations, however, our actions are characterized by ambiguity. That is, they are at times simultaneously both detrimental and beneficial to the human person, containing both values and disvalues. Thus, an amputation can be indicated to save one's life (value) but necessarily involves a burden for the person (disvalue). The key moral question for Janssens is: When is there a *ratio proportionata* "to perform an activity in a morally responsible manner which simultaneously results in values and disvalues?" Janssens insists that the answer must consider the action as a whole (exterior action, intention, situation or circumstances, consequences). "Only about this *whole* can it be said whether or not an action is worthy of man or appropriate for the human person."[3] He contrasts this with an approach he calls "Roman theology" which believes it possible to pass a judgment on the "external act alone." This belief is rooted in the contention that "the intention of nature was inscribed in the organs and their function," to use F. Hürth's words ("la volonté de la nature inscrite dans les organes et leur function").[4] Hürth's perspectives, Janssens argues, led to Pius XII's rejection of artificial insemination by husband (AIH) and they reappeared in *Humanae vitae* and "The Declaration on Certain Questions concerning Sexual Ethics." Janssens rejects this point of view as inadequate and inconsistent with Vatican II's personalist criterion. "From a personalist standpoint what must be examined is what the intervention as a whole means for the promotion of the human persons who are involved and for their relationships."[5]

Janssens' article is concerned with artificial insemination. With very many theologians he accepts AIH under certain conditions, as I would. He also approves AID (donor insemination) under carefully detailed conditions. This is a conclusion I am not able to share. Rahner's arguments—which are not unique to him—still seem to me to be persuasive.[6] Be that as it may, what is more important is the way Janssens formulates the question, and that is why it is presented in this section. He sees AID as involving both values and disvalues. "The moral question is whether there is a proportionate reason (*ratio proportionata*) to make this

[3] Ibid. 21.

[4] F. Hürth, S.J., "La fécondation artificielle: Sa valeur morale et juridique," *Nouvelle revue théologique* 68 (1946) 402-26, at 413.

[5] Janssens, "Artificial Insemination" 24.

[6] Karl Rahner, S.J., "The Problem of Genetic Manipulation," *Theological Investigations* 9 (New York: Herder and Herder, 1972) 225-52.

activity responsible or balance the positive and negative aspects according to the rules of priorities."[7] We learn this from experience and Janssens believes that the "results of serious research indicate that, with responsible selection, the positive aspects of the experience . . . supercede the lack of complete biological parenthood."[8]

Janssens' insistence on the "person adequately considered" as a normative criterion is absolutely correct, and his elaboration of what that means is very helpful. It is interesting to note that St. Thomas once wrote that "we do not wrong God unless we wrong our own good."[9] His "our own good" is identical with the "person adequately considered." This matter is of major methodological importance, because there are still some theologians who acknowledge this in theory but whose analyses and conclusions reveal different perspectives at work.[10] For this reason discussions of these matters quickly become discussions about authority, that is, that notwithstanding the inner reasonableness of an analysis or argument, official teachers have taken an authoritative position and that settles the matter.

Here a brief note. If *persona integre et adequate considerata* is the criterion for rectitude, it means that a different (from traditional) type of evidence is required for our assessment of human actions. For example,

[7] Janssens, "Artificial Insemination" 28.

[8] The reason for my doubts is that the criteria for the "results of serious research" are not mentioned and the existing reasons contra seem very powerful. Indeed, Janssens himself states my concern very clearly: "There is a fundamental difference between a deprivation which is forced by circumstances and a deficiency which is consciously caused" (27). Thus there is a fundamental difference between adoption and the asymmetry of relationship present in AID. This latter is "consciously caused," and ordinary circumstances would not seem to justify it.

[9] "Non enim Deus a nobis offenditur nisi ex eo quod contra nostrum bonum agimus" (*Summa contra gentiles* 3, 122).

[10] Thus Hürth emphasized biological finality ("une téléologie presque incroyable"). He wrote: "Man only has disposal of the use of his organs and his faculties with respect to the end which the Creator, in His formation of them, has intended. This end for man, then, is both the biological law and the moral law, such that the latter obliges him to live according to the biological law" (416). The criterion at work here is certainly not the "person adequately considered." A similar judgment must be made of those analyses that exclude all sterilization as intrinsically evil. Thus John Connery writes: "In the Judaeo-Christian tradition, the power to give life transcends the good of the person of its possessor and looks to the good of the person-to-be" ("Tubal Ligation: Good Medicine? Good Morality?" *Linacre Quarterly* 48 [1981] 112–14). To "transcend the good of the person" is to postulate criteria independent of the person. For this reason Connery rejects use of the principle of totality. He notes: "No doctor amputates a leg just to cripple a person. No doctor removes an eye just to blind a person. But doctors who do tubal ligations for contraceptive purposes do them precisely to destroy the power to procreate." To which the proper response is: neither walking *as such* nor seeing *as such* are threats to the good of the person. But actual procreating can be, as Pius XII acknowledged when he indicated the many justifications for legitimately avoiding it.

in the past the criteriological significance of sexual conduct was found in its procreativity. Thus sexual intercourse was seen as "the procreative act."[11] Deviations from this finality and significance were viewed as morally wrong and *the* decisive factor in judging conduct. It is to be noted that once the significance of our conduct is described in this way, there is very little room left for any evidence from the sciences in sexual morality.

However, *persona integre et adequate considerata* goes beyond such biological facticity. In my judgment, we have not successfully grappled with the task of integrating scientific studies into our moral assessments in this area. Indeed, our past categories and concepts have made it difficult even to know how to use other disciplines. This leaves a kind of vacuum in moral method, and in the recent past polls have moved in to fill it. Thus we are caught between false alternatives: mere authoritative statements (appeals to past assertions and present office) versus mere polls. If formally authoritative statements are no substitute for evidence, neither are polls. Our failure to take Vatican II seriously and flesh out the significance of *persona integre et adequate considerata* has left a vacuum and made it possible for certain authority figures to reduce scientific data to "mere polls" and dismiss them, or to collapse scientific studies into "scientism." Janssens' study has helped to fill the vacuum and overcome the false alternatives.

Another study of methodological importance is that of John Wright, S.J.[12] Wright interprets Paul VI (*Humanae vitae*) as formulating an "obligatory ideal" and sees this as the heart of that pontiff's teaching. An obligatory ideal is not just an exhortation; it binds our consciences.

Wright lists four different kinds of obligatory ideals. The first (love God with all our hearts and souls) is impossible of achievement; but we must never cease trying and ought to regret our failures. The second type is capable of realization but extrinsic circumstances make actual achievement impossible (e.g., feed the hungry, shelter the homeless, defend the helpless). The third type is fully achievable (e.g., persevering until death

---

[11] Daniel Maguire faults this author for referring to sexual intercourse as "the marital act" and therefore answering "the *what* question." He objects that in answering the *what* question one sets up all the subsequent answers (*The Moral Choice* [Garden City, N.Y.: Doubleday, 1978] 133–34). My intention was not to give a *what* answer but to elaborate a traditional value judgment: sexual intercourse will best preserve its viability as human language if it is used as the language of the covenanted relationship we call marriage. That is not exactly a *what* (meaning of the act) question as much as it is the conclusion of a teleological analysis. "Marital act" is a kind of shorthand to convey this assessment. There is nothing in the nature of such shorthand that prevents adaptation to different cultures.

[12] John H. Wright, S.J., "An End to the Birth Control Controversy?" *America* 144 (1981) 175–78.

in religious or marriage vows). Finally, there are ideals that considered abstractly make claims upon us, "but considered concretely with all attendant circumstances ought not to be achieved." Wright gives many examples here: not taking oaths, not paying debts by declaring bankruptcy, not keeping vows by getting a dispensation, not telling falsehoods, etc. There are times when these obligatory ideals ought not or need not be realized. Thus, speaking the truth at all times, never deceiving another, is an obligatory ideal. However, sometimes it must be set aside in the interests of a more urgent or higher good, e.g., to protect a third party against an unjust assailant. When that happens, "the ideal continues to make its claim on me. While I do not regret deceiving the would-be assailant, I regret having to deceive him."

Wright sees intercourse open to the possibility of conception as an ideal of this fourth kind. It always makes a claim upon married people, but "it may and sometimes should be set aside for reasons over which they have no control." Married people regret having to separate the unitive and procreative aspects of sexual expression, but not the separation itself. When is such separation legitimate? "Proportionate, objective reasons must be there for departing from the ideal, whether by choosing infertile periods or by rendering fertile periods unproductive."

Wright insists that this understanding does not undermine the "basic teaching" of Paul VI. Rather, "it places it in the same category as Jesus' prohibition of all oaths, the ideal of truthfulness in every situation, of paying all one's debts, of keeping one's promises and vows. . . . " To say anything else is to "suppose a kind of sacred structure to the physical act itself, a divine purpose in this particular activity that renders any attempt to control or interfere with it immoral." Wright rejects this—rightly in my view—on the grounds that "immediate finality is always subordinate to the total finality of a reasonable human life."[13]

Wright returned to the subject as a result of reactions ("most of them . . . favorable") to his original study. Among other things, he clarified the notion of obligatory ideal. But the most serious problem raised was that of fidelity to papal teaching. Clearly, Wright's proposal diverges from Paul VI's understanding ("intrinsece inhonestum . . . semper illicitum"). Here Wright distinguishes between faithfulness and fundamentalism. Faithfulness seeks to reveal the "essential intent and meaning," whereas

[13] Thus also Franz Scholz: "However, these natural ends are not the last word. They stand under the judgment of reason, as Thomas clearly emphasized" ("Innere, aber nicht absolute Abwegigkeit," *Theologie der Gegenwart* 24 [1981] 163–72, at 170). Brendan Soane writes: "Theologians seem to be generally agreed that the French hierarchy was right when it taught that the integrity of the marriage act is one value which can be balanced by others when couples decide what they should do" (*Clergy Review* 66 [198] 265).

fundamentalism simply fastens on "a particular verbal formula."[14] Wright concludes by adducing examples (freedom of conscience, separation of church and state, ecclesial status of separated brethren) where Vatican II modified earlier authoritative statements of Gregory XVI, Pius IX, and Pius XII without being unfaithful to their "essential intent."

Several aspects of this interesting presentation suggest comment. First, it is not new. Rather, it is a skilful and useful summary of much of the writing of the past ten years or so. Theologians such as Schüller, Fuchs, Böckle, and Janssens have been arguing an identical point for the past decade. Thus, when they refer to certain aspects of our conduct as involving disvalues (Janssens), nonmoral evil (Schüller), premoral evil (Fuchs), the very implication of the terms "disvalue" and "evil" is that they ought to be avoided insofar as compatibly (with other conflicting values) possible. This maintains an implicit mandate to reduce and overcome the conflicts that lead to the causation of such disvalues. It maintains the thrust away from the disvalue (Wright's "obligatory ideal"). This is identical with Wright's "regret having to do this, but not [regret] actually doing it," a point made in nearly identical language by Peter Chirico in 1970.[15]

Next, I believe it is important to underline Wright's contention that this understanding does not contradict Paul VI's. It simply inserts it into a framework consistent with our understanding of other "obligatory ideals." This framework is that of a conflict of values, a point also made by Chirico. An example from another area of concern may help. Paul VI made a prophetic statement to the United Nations: "no more war, never." Such a statement recognized the many evils inseparable from war and invited, indeed urged (obligatory ideal) us to create a world wherein war is no longer thinkable. Yet would such a statement invalidate the self-defense of a nation-state against an unjust aggressor? Would it invalidate for now the so-called "just-war theory"? Hardly.[16]

Similarly, we may say: "No more sterilization, never." The meaning: let us create a world where the causing of such disvalues is no longer

---

[14] John H. Wright, S.J., "The Birth Control Controversy, Continued," *America* 145 (1981) 66–68. Bernard Häring refers to the essence of the Church's concrete prohibition of contraception ("im Wesentlichen," "Grundanliegen," "das eigentliche Anliegen") as follows: "Not only the whole of married life but also each act must reflect and show a concern for openness for the parental vocation." The concrete norm is only a vehicle to make visible a basic concern ("Pastorale Erwägungen zur Bischofssynode über Familie und Ehe," *Theologie der Gegenwart* 24 [1981] 71–80).

[15] Peter Chirico, S.S., "Morality in General and Birth Control in Particular," *Chicago Studies* 9 (1970) 19–33.

[16] Richard A. McCormick, S.J., "Neuere Überlegungen zur Unveränderlichkeit sittlicher Normen," in *Sittliche Normen: Zum Problem ihrer allgemeinen und unwandelbaren Geltung* (forthcoming from Patmos Verlag).

necessary to achieve our legitimate or mandatory goals. But in the meantime would such a statement render invalid in a world of conflict a so-called "theory of justified sterilization"? Hardly.

Finally, Wright's distinction between "essential intent" and a "particular verbal formula" recalls the distinction of John XXIII and Vatican II between the substance and the formulation of a moral or doctrinal position. Rahner renders this by distinguishing between "a truth in itself and its abiding validity" and its "particular historical formulation."[17] I am convinced that this distinction, properly understood,[18] could reduce many tensions in the contemporary Church. More concretely, many of these tensions ("confusion of the faithful") are traceable to the insistence of some theologians on a basically fundamentalist interpretation of magisterial documents, one that is incompatible with history and, I believe, with the health of the contemporary magisterium. In this matter we need occasional reminders that faithfulness to tradition means not only remembering but forgetting.[19]

A perspective very close to Wright's but in different language is presented by Franz Scholz.[20] Scholz sets out to show that recent revisionist studies on moral norms within the Catholic community defy categorization into the polarities deontological-teleological. A proper appreciation of these currents[21] will reveal that both deontological and teleological elements are present in such studies.

[17] Karl Rahner, "Basic Observations on the Subject of Changeable and Unchangeable Factors in the Church," *Theological Investigations* 14 (New York: Seabury, 1976) 3–23.

[18] I have argued that the substance of the Catholic tradition on abortion might be said to be: "Human life as a basic gift and good . . . may be taken only when doing so is the only life-saving and life-serving alternative" (*How Brave a New World?* [New York: Doubleday, 1981] 194). John Connery, S.J., rejects this: "This simply does not do justice to the careful distinctions that have been worked out in course of history" (*Linacre Quarterly* 48 [1981] 276). Here Connery shows that he does not accept the distinction between substance and formulation, or does not understand it. For "careful distinctions . . . worked out in the course of history" are precisely formulations. If one cites them as that to which we must "do justice," one identifies substance and formulation. Another example is transubstantiation. Gabriel Daly insists that "it is possible to confess one's faith in the real presence of Christ in the Eucharist while having serious reservations about the theology of transubstantiation" ("The Pluriform Church," *Tablet* 235 [1981] 446). Yet "transubstantiation" is a term carefully "worked out in the course of history."

[19] Michael Richards, "The Tradition of Faith," *Clergy Review* 66 (1981) 307.

[20] Franz Scholz, "Innere, aber nicht absolute Abwegigkeit," *Theologie der Gegenwart* 24 (1981) 163–72.

[21] This is not always easily accessible because of apologetic caricatures in the literature. Scholz faults especially R. Spaemann, who in his most recent work ("Über die Unmöglichkeit einer universal-teleologischen Ethik," *Philosophisches Jahrbuch*, 1981, 70–86) puts Catholic teleologists in the category of "eudaimonistic utilitarianism." Scholz refers to "similar massive misrepresentations" in the United States. Francis X. Meehan confirms the existence of some rather robust strawpersons in this discussion: "My own fear is that the

Scholz borrows from W. D. Ross the notions of "prima-facie duties" and "actual duties," and "prima-facie rightness, wrongness." As has been noted in THEOLOGICAL STUDIES before,[22] the term "prima facie" indicates that certain features of acts have a *tendency* to make an act right or wrong. In so far as it has these features, it is right or wrong. But it is actually right or wrong only in terms of its wholeness and entirety. Scholz sees the features that create this tendency to rightness or wrongness as the deontological element. They establish a kind of presumptive duty to avoid (or perform) the action.

When in particular circumstances the features that constitute "prima-facie wrongness" are outweighed, these prima-facie elements continue to exert their claims. When, e.g., a person is prevented from making a promised visit to a friend because of an unforeseen emergency, the promise continues to exert its claim. The promisor ought to inform his/her friend as soon as possible of the emergency, send regrets, minimize the disappointment and damage caused by the omission, and make up for it according to his/her capacity. "In all of these gestures the 'claim' of the original duty exerts itself." This is virtually indistinguishable from Wright's "obligatory ideal" of the fourth kind.

When he turns to the traditional formulation of "intrinsically evil acts," Scholz argues that they should be understood (as Di Ianni understood them[23]) as "prima-facie evil acts," and therefore as intrinsically evil only "in the weak sense." He notes that the Polish theologian A. Szóstek ("from the Wojtyla school") provides for exceptions even for acts traditionally regarded as intrinsically evil.

Scholz concludes by noting two points. First, if one adopts the "prima-facie structure," it is possible to attribute to certain actions a minimal moral meaning (intrinsic wrongness, but "in a weak sense"). This introduces a deontological element that overcomes the ideal polarities deontological-teleological. Second, Scholz argues (much as Wright does) that this understanding is true to the substance (*Grundtenor, Grundkonzept*) of traditional formulations.

---

issue is beginning to be emotionally loaded with forms of code words that do not do justice to the complexities. If one wishes to react to his opponent captiously, one can then always reduce his point to absurdity" ("Contemporary Theological Developments on Sexuality," *Human Sexuality and Personhood* [St. Louis: Pope John XXIII Medico-Moral Education and Research Center, 1981] 173–90, at 190). Such a reduction can be seen in P. H. Hallett's reaction to John Wright's study: "Fr. Wright's theology of the ideal is in fact no different from Situation Ethics" (*National Catholic Register*, May 3, 1981).

[22] James Childress, "Just-War Theories: The Bases, Interpretations, Priorities, and Functions of Their Criteria," *TS* 39 (1978) 427–45.

[23] Albert R. Di Ianni, S.M., "The Direct/Indirect Distinction in Morals," *Thomist* 41 (1977) 350–80.

Totally out of sympathy with the teleological directions reported above (Janssens, Wright, Scholz) is Dario Composta.[24] He lists four types of "consequentialism." The first is biblical and he ascribes this to E. Schillebeeckx. The second type he calls "teleological consequentialism," insofar as it is founded on the "subject's ends or projects." Franz Böckle is his example here. The third is "intersubjective consequentialism," so called because the morality of the act is grounded in social consequences. William Van der Marck is the example of preference here. Finally, there is "theological consequentialism," which is constructed on a critique of various moral-theological theories. The author of these "Notes" is the honored champion of this type.

But these authors are used only as typical examples. By the time he is through, Composta manages to lock all of the following in his consequentialist prison: Marciano Vidal, E. Lopez Azpitarte, Peter Knauer, Joseph Fuchs, Bruno Schüller, Charles Curran, Louis Janssens.

"Biblical consequentialism" is the attitude that claims that each epoch must express that which is in conformity with the gospel according to the style of the times. Thus, the Middle Ages expressed this gospel fidelity through the mediation of the natural law. Our age requires a different mediation. The contemporary ethos becomes a *locus theologicus*. Composta sees this as a worldly relativism at odds with the gospel and the magisterium.

The "teleological consequentialism" he attributes to Böckle builds on the contention that "the morality of an act derives from the external consequences insofar as these are responsibly foreseen as ends." According to this analysis, Composta argues, there are no absolutely evil acts (*materia intrinsece absoluta*). "Neither killing of an innocent person, nor a direct lie, nor masturbation can be considered evil actions in all thinkable instances and without exception." Composta regards Böckle's analysis as "totally foreign to the ethical and normative values of the gospel," and therefore as "a process of decomposition of theology in general."

Van der Marck's "intersubjective consequentialism," Composta explains, is based on the contention that intersubjectivity is the essence of the human person and therefore of morality. Hence different epochs may pass different judgments on our actions depending on how they assess this intersubjectivity. Composta regards this as relativistic, "highly confused and bereft of any metaphysical foundations."

As for my own attempts to rethink the principle of double effect, Composta believes that it fails on a fundamental point: "fidelity to the

---

[24] "Il consequenzialismo: Una nuova corrente della 'Nuova Morale,'" *Divinitas* 25 (1981) 127–56.

Church's magisterium, which is never invoked as a demonstrative principle but only as an additional historical event."

Composta next lists three criticisms of "consequentialism." The first is that it is dualistic, treating persons as spirits who view their bodies as instruments. He sees this dualism in accusations of "biologism" leveled at formulations of the magisterium. Composta argues that biological nature manifests God's intentions.

Second, Composta accuses "consequentialists" of treating moral norms as pure creations of reason with no relation to objective reality. Thus: "if the body is an instrument separated from the spirit (as consequentialists teach), then each individual can make use of it indifferently for diverse purposes. These uses will be licit not because of any intrinsic finality but according to the options each individual agent imprints on them."[25] *Recta ratio* is indeed the norm but it is no longer "necessarily conformed to an immutable order." It is autonomous.

Third, Composta details his objections to "consequentialists'" notion of moral action. He claims that for them the basic goods (*ordo bonorum*) are neutral. Until the intervention of reason, they are not preferable or ends. Thus the arbitrariness of their morality. "If good and evil depend on the subjective 'preference' of the person . . . everything will depend on the decision of the agent."[26]

To avoid this difficulty, Composta asserts, "consequentialists" try to modify the understanding of norms. They deflate rigorous and concrete norms (e.g., against abortion) into parenetic (merely exhortatory) statements whose binding force awaits specification. Thus there can be "reasonable concubinage" or "licit, not immoral abortion when the interested agent foresees that advantages for the agent will derive from such an action."[27] This Composta calls "utilitarian laxism." But he is not finished yet. The use of "proportionate reasons" confirms the autonomous character of their so-called '*recta ratio.*'" Composta continues: "Thus, for example, by 'proportionate reasons' a Titius could 'reasonably' choose adultery because of advantageous consequences. In such a case the choice would not be condemned . . . because it was made with the intent of 'human' effects: the rescuing of a third party, or the reinforcement of the friendship of the two adulterers, or the prevention of suicide on the part of one of them."[28] Composta insists that the disorder involved here cannot be called premoral, nonmoral, or ontic evil. "An intention superimposed on a morally wrong object does not destroy the intrinsic malice." Those who deny this fall into "subjectivism, relativism, utilitarianism, and, in a word, the denial of morality."

[25] Ibid. 146.   [27] Ibid. 152.
[26] Ibid. 151.   [28] Ibid. 153.

Composta concludes this breath-taking account by noting that St. Thomas would not countenance the doing of an illicit act to achieve a good, "as Knauer definitely holds and with him all consequentialists." He ends by citing John Finnis to the effect that "consequentialism is not and cannot be anything more than a technique for justifying any decision."[29]

This is a remarkable article. In a relatively brief thirty pages it packages and displays virtually all of the distortions and misrepresentations of contemporary moral-theological discussion. It would be dreary to rehearse these distortions point by point. Over the years many of these issues have been engaged in these "Notes." For the record, however, a few points ought be to highlighted in a modest attempt to forestall their reappearance.

Item: To the best of my knowledge, no one holds—or can be forced in consistency to hold—that *recta ratio* is the arbitrary creator of the moral "ought," as Composta contends. Item: No one holds that the basic goods are neutral prior to the intervention of reason. That is precisely why contemporary theologians refer to nonmoral (premoral, ontic) *evil*. Item: No one holds that one may permissibly engage in adultery for "advantageous reasons." Nor does anything in the notion of *ratio proportionata* suggest this. Item: No one holds that one may engage in *illicit* acts for good ends, as Composta asserts. Item: No one holds or can be forced to hold that the body is a mere instrument to be manipulated dualistically for our purposes. What many do hold is that the *inclinationes naturales* may not be absolutized so that God's will is simply identified with biological facticity. Very few, if any, theologians indicted by Composta hold that moral rightness and wrongness are determined *solely* by consequences—if "consequences" refers to results beyond the moral object of the act. And so on.

At some point it is important to stand back from literature like this to detect its broader strategy. What I see happening is that theologians who often differ in significant ways are grouped under a single descriptive and misleading rubric ("consequentialism"). This rubric is then associated with some rather mischievous assumptions and conclusions. Then the entire analytic move is discredited with terms like "subjectivism, relativism, laxism." In his review of Finnis' *Natural Law and Natural Rights*, John Langan, S.J., protested this type of thing when he chided Finnis for not giving to other approaches "the careful and fair treatment that he rightly demands for natural law theories."[30]

---

[29] It is disheartening to see such loose language repeated at more popular levels. Thus, James Hitchcock refers to "proportionalism and consequentialism" as "ethical reasoning already broad enough to justify almost anything" (*National Catholic Register*, Oct. 18, 1981). A gentle reminder: *qui bene distinguit bene cognoscit.*

[30] Cf. *International Philosophical Quarterly* 21 (1981) 217–18.

The truly regrettable aspect of this type of writing is that it enlightens nothing. Anyone familiar with this discussion knows that there remain genuine unanswered problems and difficulties (e.g., the relevance and meaning of the principle of double effect) as we dialogue with our own tradition. These should be met honestly and serenely. Apologetics by incantation only delays such engagement. In this sense I would conclude that Composta simply has not understood the state of the question.

In several studies Norbert Rigali, S.J., has reviewed these developments. In one he concedes that "moderate teleology" is basically correct but that "moral theology must evolve beyond it."[31] Why? Because the model of human action basic to a teleological analysis is the human being as doer. Rigali believes that the "basic model of the human act is not a consequentialist but a relational model." There are certain ways of relating to other persons in the world that are immoral—which leads Rigali to conclude that there "may be more room in ethics for deontological considerations than the new consequentialism leads one to believe."

Rigali uses genocide as his example. Teleologists such as Fuchs, Schüller, Janssens, and Knauer cannot consider genocide "as immoral in principle." Like any other human activity, it "can be evaluated morally only in conjunction with its consequences in a concrete situation." Rigali rejects this as basically unchristian and concludes that "a more personalist Christian can understand genocide as a way of relating to the family of God that is simply incompatible with its authentic reality and meaning." Teleology, he says, cannot provide answers to these questions, even though it has served an excellent purpose in overcoming legalism and physicalism.

Several points. But before these points it is important to note that Rigali basically agrees with the analytic directions of much contemporary thought. He has different concerns. Now to his concerns. First, the word "genocide" is so close to a value term that it is a poor vehicle for Rigali's concern. In other words, I doubt very much that any contemporary theologians would describe it as a merely premoral or nonmoral evil.

Second, Rigali contends that those with teleological tendencies cannot say of genocide that it is "immoral in principle." They must evaluate it in relation with its consequences in a concrete situation. I really see no difference here. If an action in all thinkable situations is disproportionate, I would think one could say of it that it is "immoral in principle." What advantage that language achieves I do not know: Rigali does not tell us. Indeed, below Archbishop John Quinn's excellent statement on the arms

---

[31] Norbert J. Rigali, S.J., "After the Moral Catechism," *Chicago Studies* 20 (1981) 151–62.

race is cited. At the key point in his evaluation he states: "What good could be proportionate to such uncontrollable destruction and suffering?" If this is not saying it "is immoral in principle," I do not know what it is saying.

Third, as I understand recent literature, its teleological perspectives make no claim to be establishing a model of the human act. Rather more modestly, this literature is dialoguing with its own tradition and insisting that moral rightness and wrongness of an action cannot be concluded simply from a consideration of the *materia circa quam*, as this tradition does with actions such as masturbation, sterilization, etc. Other considerations (what traditionally were called circumstances, not excluding consequences) are morally relevant. This is a relatively modest undertaking simply because the moral life is far more than a series of conflict situations.

Finally, therefore, this teleology is not to be contrasted with Rigali's relational model, as if one had to choose between the two as competitors. It is rather a question of viewing this teleology within the broader context of human relationships—where these relationships themselves are part of the analysis.[32] In this sense the model of human action basic to this analysis is not the human being simply as a doer.

In another study Rigali, while again agreeing with the basic teleological dimensions of contemporary writing, asserts that it is inadequate because its concept of evil is restricted to the distinction between moral and premoral (ontic, nonmoral) evil.[33] Actually, the world is infected by the *mysterium iniquitatis*. To view evil merely in terms of moral and premoral evil "is to proceed without awareness of the Christian theology of original sin." Rigali traces this lack of awareness to the end-means structure indigenous to the teleological model. Furthermore, when this model is granted ultimacy ("a universal jurisdiction of teleology, by which the teleological model becomes fundamental and primary"), it tends to repeat the individualism of the classic moral manuals.

[32] Ph. Delhaye correctly notes that biblical morality is thoroughly relational ("Morale chrétienne: L'Objectivité de normes éthiques générales dans la morale bibliquement ressourcée," *Esprit et vie* 19 [1981] 88–93).

[33] Surprisingly, Rigali misinterprets these terms. Of moral and premoral evil he writes: "The first refers to subjective evil (evil of a moral subject as such, sin) while the second stands for objective evil (an evil other than that of the moral subject as such)." Thus he ties the terms to the objective-subjective distinction. But this is not their meaning in contemporary writing. The terms, in the context of their usage, refer to objective rightness and wrongness. Thus moral evil, in contrast to premoral evil, is understood in an objective sense—as harm (deprivation etc.) unjustifiably caused. Before we know whether it was justifiably caused, it is said to be ontic, premoral, or nonmoral evil. In this context the distinction has nothing to do with the sinfulness of the subject.

Rigali once again proposes a relational model.[34] This model views the person not as a being with ends and means, but as "a-being-in-the-world, a-person-in-relation-to-all-being." It is a model that takes account of "the manifold relations of persons to the reality which encompasses them." One of the practical differences Rigali sees in such a model is that "the prohibitions of indiscriminate bombing of noncombatants, of genocide, of using a bomb that would kill a million persons" are seen as simply absolute.

Once again three remarks. It has been noted that phrases such as "indiscriminate bombing of noncombatants" seem to me to contain their own condemnation in their very description. They are very close to value descriptions, much as is the word "torture." In this sense, even a teleologist could regard them as simply absolute—though I think a teleologist would have a more rigorous and intellectually satisfying analysis of this absoluteness than Rigali offers.

My second problem with Rigali's study is that he interprets recent teleological thought as seeing itself "up against *only* the premoral evils in individual decisions" (my emphasis). I know of no authors who would recognize themselves in that. To identify certain disvalues inseparable from individual decisions is not to deny other dimensions of evil. Nor is it to attempt to describe the whole of the moral life or the moral universe. One who sets out to describe a kitchen cannot be faulted for not describing the entire house.

Finally, Rigali contrasts the teleological model of norm- and decision-making with the relational, which he prefers as superior. As I suggested, this is a false contrast. It can succeed only if we first falsely deflate the teleological model so that it excludes "the manifold relations of persons to the reality which encompasses them." In other words, such a contrast must suppose that the evaluation of criteria based on "the person adequately considered" is a very narrow, individualistic one, cut off from much of the reality of the person. As far as I know, no one proposes this. No one proposes to understand the teleological model as Rigali describes it. Therefore, I believe he has created something of a strawperson. But it would be a mistake to miss what I believe is his substantial point: any assessment of the significance of our conduct leading to a moral norm must view the person in a truly adequate way.

John Connery, S.J., has recently addressed these problems at length.[35] Since his study appeared in this journal, a brief recall must suffice here.

---

[34] Norbert J. Rigali, S.J., "Evil and Models of Christian Ethics," *Horizons* 8 (1981) 7–22. For a discussion of various models in moral theology, cf. Pierre Daubercies, "Les présentations de la morale chrétienne: Comment les classifier?" *Esprit et vie* 91 (1981) 433–43.

[35] John R. Connery, S.J., "Catholic Ethics: Has the Norm for Rule-Making Changed?" *TS* 42 (1981) 232–50.

He first compares "proportionalism" with the traditional understanding of moral norms. In traditional terms, if the object, end, and circumstances were in accord with right reason, the act was morally right. "Proportionalists," by contrast, he says, "weigh all the good in the act against all the evil."

Next, against Knauer and Janssens, Connery denies that such a comparison (*ratio proportionata*) is necessary according to Thomas. All that is required is that damage associated with our actions (e.g., self-defense) be *praeter intentionem*. Third, Connery argues that the change to a proportionalist understanding of norms would mean that "such things as adultery, stealing, killing an innocent person are in themselves only ontic evil." Hence we would have to add a condition to every concrete rule ("unless there is a proportionate reason").

Finally, the article concludes with several critiques. For instance, for a proportionalist "a means has no independent morality of its own." Furthermore, this is a process of "demoralization" of all the good and evil in our actions. We can no longer say that "adultery, killing an innocent person, stealing" are morally wrong in themselves. Or again, the weighing of all the goods and evils (probable, possible, remote, etc.) is just too much to ask, whereas for the traditionalist "the main concern . . . is that the evil in the act be *praeter intentionem*." Connery concludes that shifting to a comparative standard "makes moral decision-making more difficult then is healthy for moral life."

I cannot possibly comment here on all the points raised in Connery's article. But I do want to respond extensively to several of them in the interests of clarifying the state of the question, a thing I do not believe Connery's study satisfactorily achieves.

1) *The notion of proportionate reason.* Connery conceives the term "proportionate reason" as synonymous with end or motive in the traditional sense. Thus he writes: an act "can be morally wrong by reason of its object and apart from an ultimate good intention." Or again: "an act can be bad apart from a good intention, i.e., a proportionate reason." Thus he interprets so-called "proportionalists" as saying that proportionate reason is something *in addition* to a clearly definable action. For this reason he can give as his example Thomas' example of the person who steals to commit adultery. The "to commit adultery" is seen as the end or motive and is identified by Connery as the proportionate reason. This is not, in my judgment, what this literature is saying. The proportionate reason is not in addition to an act already defined; it constitutes its very object, but in the full sense of that term. Take amputation of a cancerous limb to save a patient's life as an example. Connery would see amputation as the object and "to save a patient's life" as a motive. But the literature he is critiquing sees "to save a patient's life" (the proportionate reason)

as the object in the full sense of that term. In other words, proportionate reason enters into the very definition of *what* one is doing. If one conceives proportionate reason as *in addition to an act already definable by its object*, then one does indeed get into some mischievous results. For instance, it makes it possible for Connery to attribute to proportionalists the notion that a *ratio proportionata* can justify a *morally wrong* act.

Or again, what is the proportionate reason for forcefully resisting an attacker? It is clearly saving one's life. But that is *what* the action is, self-defense. It is not a motive superadded to an act with its own definition. By identifying proportionate reason with motive (in the traditional sense), Connery has inaccurately presented the literature and created a vulnerability that is not there.

2) *Value terms and descriptive terms.* Very close to the first point is the failure to distinguish these two. Connery repeatedly uses "adultery, killing an innocent person, stealing, etc." as examples of actions the tradition would judge "morally evil in themselves" but which "proportionalists might occasionally permit." Furthermore, he says that rules covering these actions "deal with moral evil." So they do—certainly, at least stealing and adultery. But these are compound value terms. They contain their own negative moral value judgment. For instance, tradition defines stealing as "taking another's property *against his/her reasonable will.*" That is always wrong and so-called "proportionalists" always would and do condemn it. But it is not the issue.

The issue is: What *materia circa quam* (object in a very restricted sense) should count as stealing or murder or lying? This is the issue as I read it in the works of Schüller, Fuchs, Janssens, J.-M. Aubert, W. Molinski, Chirico, John Dedek, F. Böckle, Charles Curran, Pater Knauer, Scholz, Helmut Weber, K. Demmer, F. Furger, Dietmar Mieth, Daniel Maguire, Henrico Chiavacci, Marciano Vidal, Walter Kerber, Timothy O'Connell, and many others. While these theologians differ in significant ways, they do share a certain bottom line, so to speak: individual actions independent of their morally significant circumstances (e.g., killing, contraception, speaking falsehood, sterilization, masturbation) cannot be said to be intrinsically morally evil as this term is used by tradition and the recent magisterium. Why? Because such concepts describe an action too narrowly in terms of its *materia circa quam* without morally relevant circumstances. This issue is confused by using value terms to describe the actions and then attributing this to "proportionalists" as if they are trying to justify adultery, stealing, lying etc.

3) *The morality of means.* Connery asserts that "to the proportionalist a means has no independent morality of its own. Its morality comes from its relation to the end of the act." As just noted, that depends on how the means is described. If it is described as "murder," "stealing," "lying," it

is already morally wrong by its very description. But if a means is described without all of its morally relevant circumstances, then clearly it has no morality of its own.

Connery admits that "there are means which receive their morality from the end of the act, e.g., violence, mutilations etc." But, he says, this is not true of all means. As suggested above, most authors of my acquaintance would not conceive mutilation as a means to the end (motive) of saving a life. They would say that the very meaning (object in the full sense) of the action includes the notion of "saving the patient's life." Furthermore, it is to be noted that Connery describes what is going on (violence, mutilation) merely in terms of its *materia circa quam*. Of course that yields no moral rightness or wrongness. But why is that not true of terms like "masturbation," "sterilization"? This matter was treated extensively in these "Notes" earlier.[36] At that time I noted of Joseph Fuchs: "He has tightened the relationship between the traditional object-end-circumstances and argued that it is only the combination of the three that yields the total object of choice. The good intended in one's choice specifies the object without smothering it out of existence, and thus, in a sense, becomes an integral part of the total object."

We are at the heart of the problem here. We can analyze it as follows. Connery's major objection is that certain actions are (and have been taught by the magisterium to be) morally evil *ex objecto*. But, he argues, the proportionalist does not and cannot say this. From this objection nearly everything else that he says follows.

What is to be said of this objection? I think it misses the point of what so-called "proportionalists" are saying. When contemporary theologians say that certain disvalues in our actions can be justified by a proportionate reason, they are not saying that *morally wrong* actions (*ex objecto*) can be justified by the end. They are saying that an action cannot be qualified morally simply by looking at its *materia circa quam*, or at its object in a very narrow and restricted sense. This is precisely what tradition has done in the categories exempted from teleological assessment (e.g., contraception, sterilization). It does this is no other area.

If we want to put this in traditional categories (object, end, circumstances), we can say that the tradition has defined certain actions as morally wrong *ex objecto* because it has included in the object not simply the *materia circa quam* (object in a very narrow sense) but also elements beyond it which clearly exclude any possible justification. Thus, a theft is not simply "taking another's property," but doing so "against the reasonable will of the owner." This latter addition has two characteristics in the tradition. (1) It is considered as essential to the object. (2) It

---

[36] *TS* 36 (1975) 86–89.

excludes any possible exceptions. Fair enough. Yet, when the same tradition deals with, e.g., masturbation or sterilization, it adds little or nothing to the *materia circa quam* and regards such *materia* alone as constituting the object. If it were consistent, it would describe the object as "sterilization *against the good of marriage*" as the object. This all could accept.

This consideration leads to a much broader one. It concerns the very usefulness of the traditional object-end-circumstances terminology. The major confusing element is the usage of "object." What is to be included in this notion? Sometimes traditional usage has included what really are morally relevant circumstances. Sometimes it has not and it has defined the object in terms of the *materia circa quam* (object in a very narrow sense). If this is unavoidable, then the terminology were better abandoned. I would think it better to speak of two characteristics of actions: (1) *materia circa quam* and (2) all morally relevant circumstances. These would include side effects, possible consequences, intentions, etc.

4) *Demoralization of good and evil in human acts.* Connery sees as a very "basic objection to proportionalism" the fact that it "demoralizes" the goods and evils in our actions. They are "only ontic or premoral." "It is not enough," he notes, "to judge that what one does goes against right reason to conclude that it is immoral." One must go a step further and balance the goods and evils in the action. This objection is virtually the same as that noted in no. 3 above, but in different language. Hence it deserves the same response. Take Connery's phrase "what one does." Suppose we describe this "what" as "mutilation." What is its morality? Clearly, we do not know, because no adequate human action has been described, only its *materia circa quam*. An action so described is neither in accordance with nor contrary to right reason.

Of course we must look to the goods and evils in the action, but we do that to find out "what one does." Only then can we determine whether it is against right reason or not. So, far from "demoralizing" the good and evil in our actions, contemporary authors are insisting that one cannot adequately describe a human action simply by presenting the *materia circa quam*. If the action is described as "adultery, stealing"—as Connery repeatedly does—this point is missed. No one to my knowledge is trying to discover whether such acts (adultery, stealing) "would produce more evil than good." Contemporary writers are trying to discover what should count as adultery. For instance, is every couple in an irregular second marriage living in adultery? We cannot know whether something is contrary to reason unless we know what it is. To miss the point is, in my judgment, a fundamental misunderstanding of the literature.

5) *"Praeter intentionem" and the tradition.* Connery states that the

"main concern of the traditionalist is that the evil in the act be *praeter intentionem*." No weighing or calculus of good and evil is required. He attributes this position to St. Thomas. I shall leave it to Knauer and Janssens to deal with Connery's understanding of Thomas. One can get almost anything from Thomas if enough texts are adduced. Still, several brief remarks are called for. First, while Thomas may not speak of a calculus of values and disvalues, I would further contend that he does not provide a true justification for violent self-defense. As Connery notes, "Thomas is satisfied with the simple explanation that it is natural for a person to defend himself." I think Connery is correct here. But to say that something is natural is hardly an adequate defense. Or if it is, it is arguably unchristian.

Second, if the main concern of the traditionalist is that the evil be *praeter intentionem*, and if "the requirement that the good effect be proportionate to the evil effect is meant to guarantee the proper direction of the intention" only, as Connery argues, then this reveals an unconcern with the evil effect. It looks very much like a "keep-the-hands-clean" morality, as Daniel Callahan has repeatedly noted. Franz Scholz has pointed out that looking evil in the eye avoids an "exoneration mentality" so easily associated with phrases such as "merely permitted, only indirectly willed."[37] In his lectures Joseph Fuchs constantly refers to *praeter intentionem* as a "psychological drug."

Finally, if one "does not have to weigh it [evil] against the good to be achieved to make a moral judgment about the legitimacy of self-defense," then any defensive reason could justify killing. I could kill my neighbor who is spanking my child. This reveals the inadequacy of a notion of agency centered solely on *praeter intentionem*.

6) *The novelty of proportionalism.* Connery notes that there is a history of exception-making in the Church. "One did not have to wait for proportionalism to provide for exceptions." Connery's presentation—as well as that of other discussants—makes it look as if we are talking about an entirely new system or method. Actually that is not the case. In nearly all areas of moral concern, whether prescriptions or prohibitions, whether of natural law or positive law, it was the notion of *ratio proportionata* that qualified the norm and established the possibility of exceptions.[38] One can see this at work in the restrictive interpretation of the prohibition

[37] Franz Scholz, "Objekt und Umstände, Wesenswirkungen und Nebeneffekte," in *Christlich glauben und handeln*, ed. Klaus Demmer and Bruno Schüller (Düsseldorf: Patmos, 1977) 243–60.

[38] As Daniel Maguire notes, "In a sense it [the principle of proportionality by which "we face the delicate challenge of balancing goods and bads"] may be said to be the master principle of ethics" (*The Moral Choice* [Garden City: Doubleday, 1978] 164).

against killing, in the exceptions established in the area of taking another's property, in the area of deceitful speech, of promise- and secret-keeping, of the Sunday obligation, of the duty of integral confession, of the obligation of the divine office, of the duty of fraternal correction, of the duty to procreate, and on and on. Of course, we did not have "to wait for proportionalism to provide for exceptions," because we always had it. That is why Schüller and Gustafson have noted that traditional Catholic moral theology in its understanding of norms is profoundly teleological.[39] As Schüller earlier put it, "The point of the above hypothesis . . . is that an ethical principle which in its more particular form has long been recognized and acknowledged is being widened out to include all the actions of persons except those that have as their immediate object the absolute value of salvation and the moral goodness of the neighbor."[40]

For instance, with regard to the duty to procreate, Pius XII referred to "serious reasons" (medical, eugenic, economic, social) that could exempt a married couple from this affirmative duty. Of these "serious reasons" Ford and Kelly write: "We believe that a careful analysis of all these phrases in the context would justify the interpretation that they are the equivalent of 'proportionate reasons.'"[41] Does this make Ford and Kelly purveyors of a new system called "proportionalism"? Hardly.

Indeed, even those norms which were regarded as exceptionless were analyzed within such a framework. Take the confessional secret as an example. Lugo defends the absoluteness of this obligation as follows:

If it [revelation of sins] were allowed in some circumstances because of some extremely important need, this alone would be sufficient to make sacramental confession always difficult. Penitents would always fear that the confessor would reveal their sins because he would think this is an example of the exceptional instance. To avoid this evil, it was necessary to exclude any exception. That rare evil which would be obviated by revelation of sins is *in no proportionate relationship to the perpetual evil and continuing harm* which would be associated with the difficulty of confession if an exception were allowed.[42]

Similarly, Lucius Rodrigo, S.J., in his massive *Theoria de conscientia morali reflexa*, argues that where doubts occur, probabilism must be excluded in dealing with the confessional secret. He argues as follows:

This *certain* obligation exists or continues as long as the basis of the prohibition against using confessional information continues—that is, the probable common

' James Gustafson, *Protestant and Roman Catholic Ethics* (Chicago: University of Chicago, 1978) 49.

[40] Bruno Schüller, S.J., "Zur Problematik allgemein verbindlicher ethischer Grundsätze," *Theologie und Philosophie* 45 (1970) 1–23, at 7.

[41] John C. Ford, S.J., and Gerald Kelly, S.J., *Contemporary Moral Theology* 2: *Marriage Questions* (Westminster, Md.: Newman, 1963) 425.

[42] *Tractatus de fide*, disp. 4, sect. 4, n. 57.

repugnance toward the sacrament traceable to the use of information that is certainly or probably sacramental in character, with the danger of the aforementioned annoyance [of the faithful]. For this repugnance is rightly judged to be such a huge common harm that even the danger of it is to be excluded *regardless of the inconvenience, because such inconvenience is rightly judged as the lesser inconvenience.*[43]

Rodrigo is arguing, just as Lugo had, that there is no *ratio* truly *proportionata* to the harm that would ensue if exceptions were allowed.

Considerations like these make it clear that we are not dealing with some new system of establishing exceptions, as Connery implies, when we use the notion *ratio proportionata*. The notion is utterly traditional. The only question, in my judgment, is: Why, if we are to be consistent, does not such utterly traditional moral reasoning apply to all areas where moral norms attempt to state the rightness and wrongness of human action? Specifically, there are two areas where this *Denkform* has been excluded. They are: (1) actions considered wrong because *contra naturam* (e.g., contraception, masturbation); (2) actions considered wrong *ex defectu juris* (e.g., direct killing of an innocent person). These actions were said to be intrinsically evil in the manualist tradition. Applying a new *Denkform* to these excluded categories does not necessarily change the conclusions, as Benedict Ashley, O.P., has noted,[44] and as Connery concedes—though I think it does in some cases. In fact, it might open us to a much richer analysis of the actions in question, and to a sharper insight into the Church's substantial concerns in these areas.

To call this fairly modest attempt "proportionalism" leaves the impression that one is abandoning a long tradition and introducing something entirely novel. That has apologetic advantages, for people are wary about "a whole new system." But it is historically inaccurate, as anyone familiar with Catholic moral tradition will realize.

7) *Proportionalism as dangerous.* Connery's final problem is that so-called "proportionalism" is dangerous. It calls for a continuous "calculus" and he sees this as unhealthy for the moral life "particularly in the area of sexuality."[45]

I disagree with that judgment and for several reasons. First, it supposes a notion of the moral-spiritual life as a succession of decisions about conforming (or not) to rules. Donald Evans rightly refers to the "sheer irrelevance of a formulated-rule morality in much of our moral life."[46]

[43] Lucius Rodrigo, S.J., *Praelectiones theologico-morales Comillenses* 4/2: *Theoria de conscientia morali reflexa* (Santander: "Sal Terrae," 1956) 635–36, n. 1760.

[44] Benedict M. Ashley, O.P., "The Use of Moral Theory by the Church," in *Human Sexuality and Personhood* (n. 21 above), 223–42, at 237.

[45] Cf. *TS* 42 (1981) 501.

[46] Donald Evans, "Paul Ramsey on Exceptionless Moral Rules," *American Journal of Jurisprudence* 16 (1971) 184–214, at 188.

There just is not that much of it. We do not live amidst crises as a regular way of life. The shape of most of our days is determined by vocation, employment, habit, family, etc.

Second, even when we get embroiled in conflict situations, there is often no calculus to be made for the simple reason that it has often already been made by the community. Being a Christian means being a member of a body, a *communio*, a people with experience, reflection, and memory. Just as our knowledge of the *magnalia Dei* is shared knowledge, so is our grasp of its implications for behavior. In other words, we form our consciences in a community. And not infrequently this community has made over its history certain value judgments that ought to instruct the individual, even though they are capable of being nuanced or even changed. For instance, Stanley Hauerwas has noted of abortion that it is meaningful to say that "Christians just . . . do not do that kind of thing."[47] I think something similar can be said about other conduct (e.g., premarital intercourse). In a sense, the very values one desires to achieve in such conduct have been judged disproportionate by the community to the disvalues inhering in it. One need not struggle through this calculus on every date. Therefore the danger Connery sees in this *Denkform* can reflect a lurking individualism of outlook.

Third, it can easily reinforce a kind of brinkmanship in attitude that is rather immature. One who is constantly concerned with rules, who needs rules to control life (especially absolute rules), was recognized by St. Paul as spiritually immature.[48] The mature do the just, fair, chaste thing by a kind of enthusiastic connaturality, without the coercive force of the law. That is what we should be aiming at in moral education.

Fourth, to regard personal conscience judgment (here the judgment of proportion) as dangerous is to perpetuate a kind of paternalism (let someone else make the judgment) in the moral life, the dependency syndrome. If anything is unhealthy and dangerous in the long run, it is that.

Finally, the objection seems to imply that conduct will be more chaste and consistent if rules are stated as unquestionable absolutes. And conversely, that suggests that cultural permissiveness is due to the theoretical rethinking of the meaning of norms in certain areas. There is no evidence that the rethinking of norms that Connery calls "proportionalism" has led to the permissiveness of our time. Such permissiveness is

---

[47] Stanley Hauerwas, "Abortion: Why the Arguments Fail," *Hospital Progress* 61, no. 1 (1980) 38–49, at 42. To say that such a statement is meaningful is not to say that it is a moral argument. It is rather the announcement of a finished moral argument, one that has grappled with the conflicting values.

[48] 1 Tim 1:9.

due to a whole host of cultural factors and would have occurred had all Catholic moral theologians been on vacation throughout.

I have devoted this large space to Connery's article for several reasons. First, he is thoughtful and careful. Furthermore, it is necessary to unpackage the jargon that all too often infects this discussion ("consequentialism," "proportionalism"). But another very important reason is that phrases in his essay such as "Church moral teaching," "Church's rules," etc. can leave the impression that the teleological tendencies of many contemporary moralists involve "going against the Church's teaching." Paul McKeever is correct, I believe, when he notes that "defending proportionalism is not directly contrary to the explicit teaching of the Church. There is no such explicit teaching."[49] Indeed, there is the contrary practice, if not the full-blown theory. So, rather than "going against the tradition," recent efforts are much more a dialogue with certain aspects of that tradition by adherents of the tradition.

A splendid article by Lisa Cahill in this journal makes this last point very well.[50] Since her study concerns the writings of the author of these "Notes," I shall leave detailed response to other and wiser heads—except to suggest that the clarity of her analysis of the state of the question is in direct proportion (if I may!) to the absence of the type of apologetical fervor we find in Composta and others.[51]

[49] Paul McKeever, "Proportionalism as a Methodology in Catholic Moral Teaching," in *Human Sexuality and Personhood* (n. 21 above) 211–22.

[50] Lisa Sowle Cahill, "Teleology, Utilitarianism, and Christian Ethics," *TS* 42 (1981) 601–29.

[51] Among these "others" William B. Smith must surely vie for the lead ("The Revision of Moral Theology in Richard A. McCormick," *Homiletic and Pastoral Review* 81, no. 6 [1981] 8–28). Smith's misuse of facts and his ideological innuendo are unrelenting. Just a few of the grosser errors can be noted here. (1) On abortion. Smith refers to my "studied silence" on the "Declaration on Abortion" of the Sacred Congregation for the Doctrine of the Faith. "It is strange," he writes, "that any moralist would be that silent about it. . . . " *False.* Cf. *TS* 36 (1975) 125–26, where I discuss it and refer to it as "this otherwise splendid Declaration." (2) On Hospital Directives. Smith states that our committee "so 'revised' the 1955 Directives that they were unrecognizable and so at variance with authentic Catholic teaching that the version was unacceptable to the Bishop Chairman of the USCC Department of Health Affairs." *False.* We (John Connery, Paul McKeever, and I) changed practically nothing in the Directives, a point that can be checked out with my colleagues or by consulting the doctoral dissertation on the subject by the late Clarence Deddens. (3) On the Ethics Advisory Board (DHEW), Smith writes: "When McCormick cast his vote with the unanimous recommendation of the EAB . . . he judged 'ethically acceptable' the Pierre Soupart proposal to initiate human life in a testtube for six days, study it, then destroy it." *False.* We never voted on the Soupart protocol. We returned it to Vanderbilt University for a rewrite. And if we had voted, I would have rejected it, a point well known to the members of the EAB.—In the good days of yore, Smith's recidivism would be an invitation to a duel. The postconciliar Church, however, suggests a gentler wrist-rapping, a reading of Genicot's treatise *De calumnia.*

LABOREM EXERCENS AND SOCIAL MORALITY

May 15, 1981 was the 90th anniversary of the encyclical *Rerum nova-rum*. This same year was also the 50th anniversary of *Quadragesimo anno*, the 20th of *Mater et magistra*, and the 10th of *Octogesima adveniens*. Not surprisingly, these anniversaries were not overlooked. On Sept. 15 Pope John Paul II belatedly issued his long encyclical *Laborem exercens* to commemorate the occasion.[52]

This encyclical, clearly in substance the work of the pontiff himself,[53] is in my judgment an outstanding piece of work. The early journalistic reception given it was extremely interesting. A few samples will set the tone. The irrepressible Malachi Martin sees it as the "most amazing papal document since Alexander VI sat down in the early 1500's and ... calmly disposed of one quarter of the globe."[54] Both the right and the left "recoiled" from the encyclical because "it contained stark rejections of both their positions." Martin feels that "with one stroke John Paul ... has severed the economic chain that has shackled Christendom to capitalism." Francisco Forte, a professor of economics, and historian Valerio Castronovo view the encyclical as a bit old hat ("una sorta di rerum vecchiarum").[55]

Quite the contrary, argued sociologist Pier Luigi Zampetti. "The real novelty of the encyclical escaped for the most part both supporters and critics of *Laborem exercens*."[56] He sees this novelty in the papal concept of work which can "modify the structure of capitalism." Michael Novak sees here a "text more philosophical and more experiential than any in this ninety-year tradition."[57] It "radiates with new and unusual angles of light." Arthur Jones asserts that "it further thrusts Church teaching as a weapon into the hands of those struggling for economic justice here and globally."[58] Peter Hebblethwaite regards it "more like a position paper for discussion than an authoritative statement."[59] The Holy Father is attempting to "breathe some new life into Catholic social teaching."

Harley Shaiken (Massachusetts Institute of Technology) argues that in the United States the Pope "would be viewed as among the more radical leaders," because "the teachings that are being stressed in the encyclical would require a profound change to implement."[60] Michel

---

[52] John Paul II, "On Human Work," *Origins* 11 (1981) 225–44.

[53] This becomes clear when we read Card. Casaroli, "La célébration de l'anniversaire de 'Rerum novarum,'" *Documentation catholique* 78 (1981) 626–30.

[54] *The Prince George's Journal*, Oct. 9, 1981.

[55] *L'Espresso*, Sept. 25, 1981.

[56] *Gente*, Oct. 2, 1981.

[57] *National Review*, Oct. 16, 1981, 1210.

[58] *National Catholic Reporter*, Sept. 25, 1981.

[59] Ibid.   [60] Ibid.

Schooyans believes that the encyclical "is without doubt the most important document ever devoted to the social teaching of the Church by a sovereign pontiff."[61] Bartolomeo Sorge, S.J., editor of *Civiltà cattolica*, proposes that the encyclical, distancing itself from both collectivism and capitalism, "is an invitation to elaborate together a new model for living together."[62] Flaminio Piccoli praises the document for its positive tone, "not lamentations and condemnations" but cogent proposals for social justice.[63] *Il Tempo* notes that while the reactions in Italy contain pros and cons, in Poland there was "broad and enthusiastic agreement."[64]

Bryan Hehir calls attention to the gradual development of Catholic social thought from national problems to international ones, and finally in *Laborem exercens* to transnational problems.[65] Nicholas von Hoffman underlines the difference in world view between John Paul II's encyclical and the economism of the Reagan administration, or, as he puts it, "between the Christian way and the American way, between social justice and the social models purveyed by Ron Reagan and Al Haig."[66] He says that "if the pope be inspired from on high, then it would appear that the late doggedly and dedicatedly liberal Hubert Humphrey sitteth at the right hand of the Creator with full permission to beam down the liberal agenda."

It will be some time, of course, before serious studies of the encyclical appear. But already the editors of *Civiltà cattolica* have some helpful remarks.[67] They note that *Laborem exercens* has a different methodology than *Populorum progressio* and *Octogesima adveniens*. John Paul II wanted to treat a single theme in depth,[68] whereas Paul VI's documents ranged over a whole host of social problems. Thus John Paul II underscores the point that "human work is a key, probably the essential key, to the whole social question." In approaching work, the Pope wants to provide an overall vision. Thus the positive tone of the encyclical.

The editors see as absolutely fundamental the principle that work is for man, not man for work. The encyclical is constructed on this foundation. Furthermore, the novety of the Pope's approach is that he rigorously remains on the ethical-religious plane, and this provides him

[61] *La libre belgique*, Sept. 23, 1981.   [63] *Il popolo*, Sept. 16, 1981.

[62] *Oggi*, Sept. 30, 1981.   [64] *Il tempo*, Sept. 17, 1981.

[65] Bryan Hehir, "A New Era of Social Teaching," *Commonweal* 108 (1981) 585.

[66] *New Republic*, no. 3486, Nov. 4, 1981.

[67] "Scoprire i nuove significati del lavoro umano: L'enciclica sociale di Giovanni Paolo II," *Civiltà cattolica* 132, no. 3151 (1981) 3–14.

[68] This is also noted by Oswald von Nell-Breuning, "Menschliche Arbeit," *Orientierung* 45 (1981) 195. Nell-Breuning calls attention to the fact that Leo XIII and subsequent popes, never having been workers, spoke of the subject "from above." John Paul II was a worker and could speak to the subject from his own experience.

with "exceptional clarity and freedom of judgment." But it also means fewer of the concrete pastoral judgments found in *Mater et magistra* and *Octogesima adveniens*. Far from being a step backwards—as some commentators stated—this simply indicates John Paul II's different purpose and method. He wanted, the editors assert, to offer a "gospel of work" (the Pope's words), a kind of profound meditation. He leaves to us the choices to be made "to safeguard the personalistic character of work, to overcome the mentality of economism and materialism, to change unjust economic structures."

Laborem exercens deserves careful reading and discussion. Rather than detailing and commenting further on its substantial content, I want to offer three remarks stimulated by this encyclical's style and content. First, the encyclical seems to represent a different type of teaching, one describable perhaps in terms of enlightenment and understanding rather than prescriptions and prohibitions. It is as if John Paul II is inviting us to share an ongoing philosophical meditation with him. This has not always been the style of so-called "authoritative teaching," and especially so in the areas of what might be called domestic morality. In this latter area, concrete prescriptions and proscriptions have played a central role.[69]

Second, the enlightenment occurs by identifying, analyzing, and constantly returning to certain basic and general notions. In the case of *Laborem exercens* there are two key notions. (1) Work is for the person (unfortunately, the rendering is constantly "man" in the English version), not the person for work. Hence the evil dimension of any system that reduces the person to a mere instrument. Work should bring about growth and a sense of accomplishment in the human person. It is, therefore, not primarily what is done but the person doing it (work in the subjective sense) that is primary. (2) The priority of labor over capital. Capital is for labor, not vice versa. Thus the error of an economism that considers labor only according to its economic purpose. Both capitalism and socialism are critiqued by these principles. John Paul II returns over and over again to these two principles, examines them from several points of view, and traces everything he subsequently says to these bases. This means that he provides an element of unity and simplicity in what could otherwise collapse into a confusion of details and of unrelated particulars.[70]

---

[69] Cf. Kenneth R. Overberg, *An Inconsistent Ethic? Teachings of the American Catholic Bishops* (Lanham, Md.: University Press of America, 1980).

[70] There is an interesting detail in the encyclical that is suggestive. When speaking of emigration (no. 23) John Paul II refers to it as "in some aspects an evil." But it is, as he writes, "a necessary evil." He continues: "Everything should be done ... to prevent this *material* [emphasis mine] evil from causing greater moral harm." This reflects the distinction between moral and nonmoral evil. That John Paul II is utterly familiar with this

Finally, such a procedure leaves room for specification by other disciplines and for disagreement about applications and tactics. The Pope is providing a prophetic vision, a way of construing the world theologically, rather than providing a series of concrete answers. The *National Catholic Reporter* referred to it as "philosophy and ground rules from which Catholics and others can begin forays in search for new answers."[71] That strikes me as an excellent direction for the magisterium to take, and for several reasons. For one, it is much more likely to persuade, and it is precisely persuasive analysis that commands assent in moral matters.[72] For another, it properly recognizes the competence and responsibility of others in the development and implementation of the Church's social teaching. Responsibility is to be underlined here. There is a gap between formulated social teaching and its practical implementation. That gap reflects the socially dormant conscience, and this notwithstanding Vatican II's statement: "Let everyone consider it his sacred obligation to count social necessities among the primary duties of modern man."[73]

If there are aspects of this encyclical that may provoke critical comment, I suspect that they may organize around four points. First, the treatment of management in *Laborem exercens* seems inconsistent, because in the papal categories it is a form of labor, yet a part of capital. Management and its dynamics and philosophy have a powerful, even dominating influence in contemporary times on work and workers.

Second, the political dimension of organized labor may be viewed by some as treated too uniquely with a view to the Polish situation. The Pope sees political activity as creating the danger that unions will "lose contact with their specific role, which is to secure the just rights of

---

language is clear from Andrzej Szostek's *Normy i Wyjatki* (Lublin: Katolicki Universytet Lubelski, 1980), for which dissertation the then Cardinal Wojtyla was a reader.

[71] *National Catholic Reporter*, Sept. 25, 1981, 10.

[72] As James Burtchaell, C.S.C., notes of a bishop who encounters things that grieve him in the Catholic press: "Better to exercise what authority one does have by becoming a more persuasive (and hence more authoritative) shepherd by becoming a more cogent teacher" ("The Catholic Press and Church Authority," *Origins* 11 [1981] 304–8, at 305). In this respect I recommend highly a little gem of an essay by Quentin de la Bedoyere ("Christian Disobedience," *Tablet* 235 [1981] 518–19). He notes: "What is required at the spiritual level ... is for the Church consciously to become the leader in the development of moral autonomy .... To her surprise she will, I believe, discover that her influence will become greater rather than less, and this influence will be effective not only among her own members but in a society which is looking for moral leadership." He asserts that the way the Church has exercised her authority in the past (and the way it still does exercise it) has "produced Catholics who have either been conformists or have broken away dramatically from the moral order."

[73] *Gaudium et spes*, no. 30.

workers." In many Western democracies union political activity is precisely the means of securing these rights.

Third, there appears to be some ambiguity about the role of women. Should they aspire to some role other than wife and mother? It is clear in the encyclical that they should receive equal pay, should not be discriminated against, etc. But is their very presence in the labor force a reluctant concession on the part of John Paul II?

Finally, there is the very composition of the encyclical. It seems clear that *Laborem exercens* is substantially the work of the Pope himself. But is that really appropriate? Philip Land, S.J., at a conference on the encyclical, suggested that "the day of a pope writing encyclicals by himself ought to be over. People in this room ought to be helping writing encyclicals."[74] At the same conference George Higgins, surely one of the nation's most expert persons in this area, stated that "there ought to be a more collegial way of writing these documents."

The Land–Higgins statements—which in no way derogate from the timeliness and power of *Laborem exercens*—bring to mind a very remarkable article that many may have missed. Though it appeared in 1971, it is still highly pertinent. It is Oswald von Nell-Breuning's account of his authorship of *Quadragesimo anno*.[75] Wlodimir Ledochowski, then the General of the Society of Jesus, was entrusted with the preparation of this commemorative encyclical. He in turn assigned the task to Nell-Breuning. "In strict secrecy.... Neither my local superior nor my provincial knew what work I had to do for the General." Nell-Breuning could consult no one and "was left wholly on my own." At the end of this absorbing article Nell-Breuning remarks: "When I think back on it today, it seems to me that such a procedure, that allowed the whole bearing of an official document to be determined by a consultant ... without any countercheck worth mentioning, seems frighteningly irresponsible." He finds it distressing that "even today [1971], apparently, if the occasion arose, they would proceed in a manner similar to that for *Quadragesimo anno*." His final paragraph reads:

Today people expect that announcements of the highest Church authorities—on questions in which the profane sciences also have a voice—be on just as high a level as that of scientific statements of the most qualified international bodies. This presumes that an international group of recognized specialists in the sciences participate in the elaboration and assume the technical cientific responsibility for such new statements.

[74] *Washington Post*, Oct. 24, 1981, C10.
[75] Oswald von Nell-Breuning, S.J., "Octogesimo anno," *Stimmen der Zeit* 187 (1971) 289–96.

Nell-Breuning's words point to the continuing interesting literature on the magisterium.[76] Just a single article will be noted here in passing.[77] Since everyone has a dream these days (e.g., Cardinal Hume at the Synod of 1980), Karl Rahner presents his. He is present at a meeting in 1985 where the pope is addressing leading representatives of the Christian churches from all over the world. The pope is attempting to put papal teaching authority in a more understandable context to still non-Catholic fears and misgivings. Rahner's pope has several interesting observations. One is that since the pope is, in his ex-cathedra decisions, defining the faith of the Church, "the pope must necessarily have recourse to the sense of the faith of the whole Church." An explicit recourse to the episcopate is "absolutely morally necessary," and a "moral obligation." An analogous "moral obligation" would seem to be the case in the situation of practical moral matters.

But what is of more interest is the statement of Rahner's pope on noninfallible teaching. He states: "Even the second Vatican Council did not speak clearly enough about such authentic but reformable Roman doctrinal decisions." The pope then adds: "Roman procedure after the council left something to be desired by way of straightforward clarity and modesty."

It is a well-known fact that Rahner refuses to believe that no. 25 of *Lumen gentium* is the last word on authentic noninfallible papal pronouncements. The matter is mentioned here for the record, so to speak. There are still theologians whose theology has no room for dissent. This overlooks the fact observed by Rahner's pope: "The ordinary magisterium of the pope in authentic doctrinal decisions at least in the past and up to very recent times was often involved in error and, on the other hand, Rome was accustomed to put forward and insist on such decisions as if there could be no doubt about their ultimate correctness and as if any further discussion of them was unbecoming for a Catholic theologian."

In the course of *Laborem exercens* John Paul II makes note of "a principle that has always been taught by the Church" (scil., the priority of labor over capital; no. 12). He also states that his reflections are "in

[76] B. C. Butler, "Ordinary Teaching," *Clergy Review* 66 (1981) 3–8; Pierre Grelot, "L'Eglise et l'enseignement de la morale," *Esprit et vie* 91 (1981) 465–76, 481–89; Karl Lehmann, "Lehramt und Theologie," *Internationale katholische Zeitschrift* 10 (1981) 331–38; Joseph A. Komonchak, "Research and the Church: A Theologian's View," *Living Light* 18 (1981) 112–20; M. Seckler, "Eine Wende im lehramtlichen Theologie-Verständnis?" *Theologische Quartalschrift* 161 (1981) 131–33; Ludiger Oeing-Hanhoff, "Ist das kirchliche Lehramt für den Bereich des Sittlichen zuständig?" *Theologische Quartalschrift* 161 (1981) 56–66.

[77] Karl Rahner, "Dream of the Church," *Tablet* 180 (1981) 52–55. Cf. also *Concern for the Church* (New York: Crossroad, 1981) 133–42.

organic connection with the whole tradition" of early social teaching. When one hears the phrase "the social teaching of the Church," the impression left is one of a coherent body of unified teaching. In an extremely interesting study, John Coleman, S.J., shows convincingly that this is not the case.[78] For instance, Leo XIII viewed private property as "an almost metaphysical right." This is in sharp contrast with *Mater et magistra* and *Populorum progressio*, where such a right is not absolute, and to John Paul II's noted phrase about "a social mortgage" on all property.

Similarly, subsequent tradition would not follow Pius XI when he asserted (*Quadragesimo anno*) that "no one can be at the same time a sincere Catholic and a true socialist." Indeed, more to the point there is Pius X's distorted interpretation of *Rerum novarum*, in which he asserted that the authority of capital over labor is as essential to the social organism as the authority of the Church, government, or family. John Paul II would certainly frown over that tenet. Then there is the heavy philosophical emphasis prior to Vatican II, but after that council "explicitly theological thought strongly informs the papal teaching." Coleman sees this as "a massive sea change," his only point being that history will not bear out the contention that in social teaching there is an unbroken coherent unity untouched by the waves of time.

To discover these waves of time or the historical context of encyclicals, we must attend to a whole variety of factors: the mind of the principal author (e.g., Nell-Breuning for *Quadragesimo anno*), the movements and disputed questions to which the pope was responding, the other writings of the papacy, etc.

Coleman's article deserves careful thought. Undoubtedly there will be some who will see in such historical exegesis a systematic undermining of the authority of papal statements. After all, the argument would run, what does it matter that Nell-Breuning wrote *Quadragesimo anno*? The pope "made it his own." *That* is what counts. I have heard this response many times before. An answer might be: "Of course it counts. But for what?" Certainly it does not purge the document of its limited perspectives and human ingredients. If one thinks so, then that person is attributing in a quite magical way a more unearthly, unhistorical character and authority to papal composition than we do to the composition of the Gospels. The recognition of limited, imperfect, even inconsistent elements in these magisterial documents should detract no more from their abiding value than do similar elements from the inspired word.

---

[78] John Coleman, S. J., "Development of Church Social Teaching," *Origins* 11 (1981) 33–41. For a comparison of the social teaching of Leo XIII and John Paul II, cf. Ph.-I. André-Vincent, "Pour le centenaire de 'Rerum novarum,'" *Esprit et vie* 91 (1981) 509–11.

In a long and thorough article Charles Curran amply documents the thesis of Coleman.[79] He shows that from Leo XIII to the present there have been important anthropological shifts, both personal and social, that ground Catholic social ethics. At the personal level, these changes have culminated in our contemporary emphasis on freedom, equality, participation, and historical consciousness. The methodological consequences of this are considerable. For instance, Curran sees in the early documents the formation of a social doctrine drawn out of a deductive reasoning process based on the immutable natural law applicable to all nations. Over the decades the approach has shifted to an "objective scrutiny of the present reality in the light of the gospel and of the teaching of the Church," a much more dynamic discernment process.

As examples of the social aspects of a shifting anthropology, Curran adduces private property and socialism. From the rather hardened attitude of Leo XIII, a certain relativizing characterizes magisterial statements on both these aspects. For instance, the right of private property is now seen as subordinate to the universal destiny of the goods of creation. Similarly now "with due prudence and discretion one could opt for a Marxist analysis of social reality provided that one recognizes the danger of its connection with Marxist ideology." Why? Because *Octogesima adveniens* acknowledges that there are various levels of expression in Marxism, even though it would be illusory to forget the link that binds them together.[80]

Curran's study is a fine synthetic overview of an important and still developing papal literature.

Before the publication of *Laborem exercens*, the editors of *Civiltà cattolica* published a study that makes many of the points noted by Curran and Coleman.[81] They note that in a sense *Rerum novarum* is a document that has to be "written on an ongoing basis" ("deve continuare ad essere scritta"). It is a kind of dynamic presence in all the social encyclicals that followed it. This dynamic presence and the real novelty of *Rerum novarum* is found not in its conclusions, many of which are dated, but in the fact that for the first time the Church's social concerns were given a systematic philosophical and theological justification. Thus its continuing relevance consists in the method in which it approached social problems.

---

[79] Charles E. Curran, "The Changing Anthropological Bases of Catholic Social Teaching," *Thomist* 45 (1981) 284–318.

[80] For critiques of Marxist analysis, cf. Pedro Arrupe, S.J., "Marxist Analysis by Christians," *Catholic Mind* 74, no. 1355 (1981) 58–64; Quentin Lauer, S.J., "Christians and 'Marxist Analysis,'" *Ateismo e dialogo* 16 (1981) 43–47.

[81] "Dalla 'Rerum novarum' ad oggi," *Civiltà cattolica* 132 (1981) 345–57.

However, that encyclical must be continually reworked, because the social teaching of the Church developed in stages. *Rerum novarum* represents the first stage. It was dominated by "Christian philosophy" and a "rigidly deductive" method, as Curran noted above. This had two shortcomings. First, it left no room for the relevance of the sciences (political science, sociology, economics). Second, and a consequence, doctrinal elaboration was seen as an exclusively hierarchical task, lay persons being merely "faithful executors."

The second stage covers the pontificates of Pius XI and Pius XII and might be called the stage of "social doctrine." Indeed, *Quadragesimo anno* used this term for the first time. It referred to an organic corpus of universal principles still rigidly deduced from social ethics and constituted a kind of third way between liberalism and socialism. However, there is greater emphasis on the historical moment and applications of principles to practice, hence the beginnings of a re-evaluation of the place of lay persons in the process. Pius XI distinguished "unchanged and unchangeable doctrine" from social action, this latter being the competence of lay persons.

The third stage began with John XXIII. John moved from the deductive to the inductive method, his point of departure being the "historical moment," to be viewed in light of the gospel. This led to a complete re-evaluation of the place of lay persons vis-à-vis social teaching, a re-evaluation completed by Vatican II. Lay persons do not simply apply the Church's social teaching; they must share in its very construction.

The novelty of this third stage is clear in the fact that the social teaching of the Church no longer refers to an immutable corpus of doctrine. Even the term "social doctrine" has fallen into disuse and is reserved for the period from Leo XIII to John XXIII. It is also clear in the new emphasis on the responsibility of the Christian community in the elaboration and application of the Church's social teaching, an emphasis most completely stated at Puebla (no. 473).

This extremely interesting and very realistic analytic chronicle suggests a question: Has such a development occurred in the area of the Church's approach to familial and sexual morality? The answer is rather clearly no. Perhaps the question were better worded as follows: Should not such a development occur in the approach to these other questions? If a clearly deductive method, one that left little room to the sciences and lay experience, prevailed in the elaboration of social teaching, it is reasonable to think that the same thing occurred in familial and sexual morality. And if this method has evolved and changed during the pontificates of John XXIII, Paul VI, and John Paul II, as the editors of *Civiltà cattolica* correctly note, it is reasonable to think that the same thing ought to happen in all areas of Church teaching. Yet two things seem clear about the Church's teaching on sexual and familial morality. First, earlier popes are invariably cited for their conclusions, not simply their systematic method. Second, the sciences and lay experience remain marginal factors in the continuing reflection of the Church on familial and sexual matters, as noted above.

Adverting to some of the changes mentioned by Curran and Coleman, Oswald von Nell-Breuning, S.J., asks if the Church's social teaching has not lost its identity.[82] Not surprisingly, his answer is a firm no. But one must distinguish between the changeless principles and their concrete application. These latter are conditioned by historical times and changes, and the perspectives of those living in such times. This happens even in our times. Thus, even Vatican II views the "Church in the Modern World" within a pronounced European-American (developed) perspective. For our social teaching to be freed from this narrowing of perspectives, we need the voice of the Third World bishops.

Nell-Breuning reviews the social teaching on the Church to highlight the distinction between abiding principles and time-conditioned and no longer valid applications. For instance, he cites two encyclicals of Leo XIII (*Diuturnum* [1881] and *Immortale* [1885]). Leo correctly recognized the basically different duties of church and state—and this assertion is timeless and unchanging. Here he breaks with the Middle Ages. However, he remained within the confines of *his* time and context. Leo grew up in a Catholic country and was familiar only with Catholic countries. Therefore for him the state is the political unity of a people united in the Catholic faith. Out of these perspectives he developed much of his teaching on the relation of church and state. But because these perspectives are time-conditioned, the normative conclusions he draws from them do not pertain to changeless principles. When this distinction is properly made and carefully applied, we will see that the Church's social teaching is a system of "open statements," what Nell-Breuning calls a "constant learning process."

He concludes the essay by insisting that most magisterial statements are not the best formulations of the matter, and that that which does get expressed is not an exhaustive account of objective reality, but merely a piece of it. Nell-Breuning's essay further confirms Wright's distinction between faithfulness to the magisterium and magisterial fundamentalism.

The distinction between abiding principles and time-conditioned application is also at work implicitly in Andrew Greeley's essay.[83] Greeley argues that Catholics have forgotten the fundamental social theory of

---

[82] Oswald von Nell-Breuning, S.J., "Hat die katholische Soziallehre ihre Identität verloren?" *Internationale katholische Zeitschrift* 10 (1981) 107–21.

[83] Andrew Greeley, "Quadragesimo anno after Fifty Years," *America* 145 (1981) 46–49.

Quadragesimo anno and "replaced it with a slightly baptized form of vulgar Marxism." The dominant social wisdom is concerned about the conflict between self and society. The individual strives for freedom; society strives to constrain this. Greeley sees this as a false picture of the relationship. There is an informal, intimate network of relationships that integrate self and society.

The common themes suggested by *Quadragesimo anno* are solidarity, decentralization, smallness, co-operation, respect for pre-existing networks of workers, families, and neighbors. This is the unique and still radical critique mounted by *Quadragesimo anno* in the face of both capitalism and Marxism. But Greeley despairs of its having any effects because "no one is even remotely aware" anymore of this Catholic heritage. Greeley seems to be suggesting that *Quadragesimo anno* is a relic because we never really did grasp its abiding substance.

An excellent article by David Hollenbach, S.J., represents a kind of contemporary footnote to *Laborem exercens*.[84] It points out that human rights are the central norms of social morality proposed by the Church. These rights, based on the dignity of the human person, concern essential *needs*, basic *freedoms*, and *relationships* with others. These needs, freedoms, and relationships are equally and integrally normative in the Church's approach.

However, the papal supposition that these values should be simultaneous and equally important is rejected by both the right and the left. Both Marxist socialists and authoritarian capitalists endorse a restriction of freedom for the alleviation of poverty. Both ideologies regard the Catholic "third way" approach (clearly that of John Paul II in *Laborem exercens*) as naive and moralistic in its failure to recognize genuine conflicts and the need for hard and nasty choices.

In his response to this criticism, Hollenbach distinguishes three distinct but related levels of analysis. (1) The foundational level (based on the dignity of the human person an an *imago Dei*). There is little disagreement at this level. (2) The level of social contexts most conducive to the realization of these fundamental values. (3) The level of analysis that proposes explanations of what causes the realization or destruction of these values. The sharpest and most heated disagreements occur at the second and third level.

For instance, one reading of the context and cause for the denial of human dignity sees imperialist capitalist governments and multinational corporations as the key driving force. Another reading would emphasize

---

[84] David Hollenbach, S.J., "Both Bread and Freedom: The Interconnection of Economic and Political Rights in Recent Catholic Social Thought," forthcoming in the bimonthly *Freedom at Issue* (Freedom House).

the deprivation of human rights as the context and cause. These models of interpretation can gradually get identified with the fundamental value of human dignity itself. When they do, they become ideologies that easily spawn blinding and misdirected passion.

Hollenbach argues that the Church is particularly, and rightly, sensitive to the dangers of identifying a model of social context and causality with the basic value of human dignity itself. She has a long memory about the injustices associated with both authoritarian regimes and liberal capitalism. Furthermore, living as she does in a variety of cultures and economic regimes, the Church is properly sensitive to their differences. Finally, her mission is particularly concerned with the fundamental values. These three considerations keep her alert to the dangers of competing ideologies and lead her to emphasize "the provision of *both* bread *and* freedom" as the appropriate goals of political economy.

As I read John Paul II's *Laborem exercens*, it is discussing above all Hollenbach's foundational level and from that level providing food for thought for the levels of context and causality. It constitutes a critique of any absolutizing at this second and third level.

PASTORAL PROBLEMS

Sterilization

Johannes Gründel of the University of Munich treats the very practical problem of sterilization in Catholic hospitals.[85] He first reviews official Catholic teaching on sterilization, a teaching that must be observed "as long as there are no correspondingly decisive reasons against it." This teaching is that direct sterilization is intrinsically evil. The reason for this conclusion, Gründel notes, is that "every marital act remains by its nature ordained to the procreation of new life" and hence that a sterilizing intervention is "unnatural." Thus Pius XI (1930), Pius XII (1951), Paul VI (1968), and the Congregation for the Doctrine of the Faith (1975). Of this teaching Gründel says: "If one proceeds in a fundamentalistic manner, if one relies only on the statements of Church authority, then there can be no doubt on this matter, no discussion. There is only a clear no."

Gründel notes that by no means can we exclude a further development of such teachings. "Precisely in this area many contemporary moral theologians have noted that the underlying argumentation is no longer convincing." It is the task of moral theology, as a science, to test these teachings. Just as John Wright did, Gründel adduces Pius IX's *Quanta cura* as an example where this testing led to change.

---

[85] Johannes Gründel, "Zur Problematik der operativen Sterilisation in katholischen Krankenhäusern," *Stimmen der Zeit* 199 (1981) 671–77.

Gründel next turns to the argument supporting traditional formulations and finds it unsupportable. "The biological-physiological integrity of conjugal intercourse does not represent an absolute value but is in the service of total personal well-being (*im Dienst des ganzheitlich personalen Vollzugs*)."[86]

Gründel then adverts to the document of the Congregation for the Doctrine of the Faith. The Congregation, while admitting broad dissent, asserted that such dissent does not have doctrinal significance so as to constitute a theological source. Gründel believes that this assertion questions the very nature of theology as a science, and he rejects it. "Regard for Catholic teaching means also, when the occasion arises, inclusion in the decision-making process of well-founded theological opinions at variance with official Church teaching."

He concludes that sterilization is a "physical evil" but it does not constitute a moral evil "if there are correspondingly serious reasons for its performance." He words his conclusion as follows: "If direct sterilization is not absolutely prohibited and immoral according to its nature, then there can be conflict situations in which such an intervention is morally responsible, and therefore may also be performed in a Catholic hospital."[87] In such conflict situations where procreation is absolutely counterindicated, "the fruitfulness of the couple has lost its function and meaning." Gründel's only remaining concern is that the intervention be strictly controlled against arbitrary abuse.

I cite this article by Gründel because he is representative of very many truly responsible theologians.[88] The article's very special value is that Gründel refuses to analyze the situation in terms of a juridical standoff between official teaching and theological opinion. In juridical terms, theologians are not official teachers as this term is ordinarily understood. Therefore, if the matter is couched juridically in terms of who is official, who is not, the traditional formulation wins out. It is a confrontation of unequals and eventually turns into a dialogue of the deaf. But, Gründel argues, to see the problem in this way is to rob theology of its scientific

---

[86] Similarly, Bernard Häring points out that many moral theologians judge the intervention "with a view to the whole good of the person and of healthy relationships in marriage." This is not the view of "influential theologians in the Congregation for the Doctrine of the Faith." However, Häring cites Cardinal Ratzinger's report to his priests on the 1980 Synod as supporting the possibility of exceptions: "Wherefore the criterion of *Humanae vitae*, clear as it is, is not inflexible, but open for differentiated judgments of ethically differentiated situations" ("Pastorale Erwägungen zur Bischofssynode über Familie und Ehe," *Theologie der Gegenwart* 24 [1981] 71–80).

[87] Gründel, "Zur Problematik" 675.

[88] Several theologians in Germany have informed me that there is only one theologian in that country (G. Ermecke) who still defends the formulations and conclusions of *Humanae vitae*.

character and in the process to paralyze doctrinal development *in principle.*[89] Were this the case, we would still have *Quanta cura* and not *Dignitatis humanae.* Therefore dialogue on these matters should occur on the merits of the argument, not solely on the respective juridical positions of the dialoguers. Otherwise authority is served, but not necessarily the truth.

Both John Wright and Johannes Gründel make reference to a kind of fundamentalism of procedure in the approach to statements of the magisterium. In this connection I should like to refer to three outstanding essays by the Irish Augustinian Gabriel Daly.[90] He describes the growth of two conflicting attitudes in the post-Vatican II Church. One is a fundamentalism that consists "in the rooting of one's entire faith in the pronouncements of authority." This is a kind of fideism, "the kind of religious faith which does not regard itself as in any way accountable to reason."

Daly observes that during the century preceding Vatican II there were three major attempts to open the Church to its critical responsibilities (Liberal Catholicism, Modernism, the "New Theology" of the 1940's). All were literally wiped out (*Tuas libenter* [1863], *Pascendi* [1907], and *Humani generis* [1950]) "by an alliance between fundamentalist attitudes and juridically centralized authority." These condemnations enshrined two constant features: (1) Neo-Scholastic supremacy over all other systems; (2) the use of papal power to impose Scholasticism, and Thomism in particular. These were the integral props of the "ultra-montane program." Daly sees a new ultramontanism developing, but without the former props.

The collegial ideal which might have been the queen of Vatican II's achievements is now a sleeping princess. Some day her prince will come; but on present showing he will need to be a man of unusual qualities not indeed in order to awaken her ... but to occupy the fortress where she has been placed in suspended animation.[91]

The essence of ultramontanism, according to Daly, "is the wish for *total* conformity with papal ideas and ideals in *all* things." It is the

---

[89] This is what the long pastoral of the Irish bishops actually does. Those who disagree with official formulations, they say, "very often advance as their reason for their conduct not their own ideas, but the authority of theologians in disagreement with the institution." This, the bishops note, involves a false notion of the role of theologians in the Church, "for their authority does not, indeed cannot, surpass that of the pope ...." The bishops go on to condemn actions like contraception and sterilization as "morally evil in themselves." Cf. "Conscience et morale," *Documentation catholique* 63 (1981) 31–40.

[90] Gabriel Daly, "Conflicting Mentalities," *Tablet* 235 (1981) 361–62; "The Ultramontane Influence," ibid 391–92; "The Pluriform Church, "ibid. 446–47.

[91] Daly, "The Ultramontane Influence" 391.

ultimate form of Roman Catholic fundamentalism. It becomes tyranny whenever it creates an atmosphere "in which open enquiry and honest dissent are arbitrarily construed as disloyalty or worse." Daly argues powerfully that "orthodoxy is meaningless and possibly immoral if it is not the answer to a genuine search for truth."

These simulating articles represent a passionate plea for the commercialism of ideas in the Church against what Daly sees as the oncoming crisis: "the danger that the Church's institutional influence and power may be invoked and used to stifle open discussion and to promote the aims of one school of thought to the exclusion of all others." Such attempts have not only failed in the past but have constituted self-inflicted wounds on the Church. As a matter of historical fact, much of what was put forward in the century before Vatican II and was suppressed was later adopted, but in what Daly calls a "haze of historical amnesia."

I mention these essays here because there is every indication that the problem of sterilization will be "solved," especially in this country, by repeated appeals to authoritative statements rather than by Daly's "normal commerce of intellectual life," the very condition for keeping Christian faith in the marketplace.

The Hunger Strike

1981 was the year of the hunger strike. Ten prisoners succumbed in the H-Block of Belfast's Maze Prison before the strike was terminated. Understandably, these dramatic events evoked a great deal of ethical comment. When Bobby Sands died, Bishop Edward Daly of Derry stated in a television interview:

Whilst I think the British Government has been intransigent, I find it very difficult—in my own conscience—to morally justify a hunger strike. I would not describe Bobby Sands' death as suicide. I could not accept that. I don't think he intended to bring about his own death. I think that he thought there was a possibility, that he hoped that something else would be achieved.[92]

The Irish bishops issued a statement after Bobby Sands' death saying that "the Church teaches that suicide is a great evil." However, they added that "there is some dispute about whether or not political hunger striking is suicide, or more precisely, about the circumstances in which it is suicide."[93]

The editors of the *Tablet* saw Bishop Daly's comment as "equivocal." They note: "It is the constant teaching of the Christian Church that hunger striking to death amounts to the serious sin of suicide."[94] They

[92] Cf. "Bobby Sands' Death," *Tablet* 235 (1981) 472.
[93] *New York Times*, June 8, 1981, B7.
[94] *Tablet* 235 (1981) 472.

fault the Primate of All Ireland for his silence. If a straightforward statement had been made, the bishops "might be regarded as reliable guides on other moral issues." There is no question where the *Tablet* editors stand on this matter.

Alberic Stacpoole (St. Benet's Hall, Oxford) traces such equivocation to the Church's desire to give people the benefit of the doubt.[95] "In this forgiving manner, it can speak of starvation-to-death as overplayed brinkmanship (without intent finally to take life); or as a political martyr process, where by double effect the witness-to-value, rather than the dying at the end of it, is of the essence."

Raymond E. Helmick believes that the different response of people to the hunger strikes means that they are responding not to the hunger strikes themselves "but to the context and purpose of these hunger strikes in particular ... in terms of their approval or disapproval of the hunger strikers' aims."[96]

Shortly after the *Tablet* editors had faulted the hierarchy for equivocation and silence, the Irish bishops issued a strongly worded statement.[97] On the hunger strike they wrote: "We therefore implore the hunger strikers and those who direct them to reflect deeply on the evil of their actions and their consequences." They deplored injustice and violence in Ireland and referred to the contempt for human life, the incitement to revenge, intimidation of the innocent, initiation of children into violence as "as appalling mass of evil." It is not clear whether their phrase "evil of their actions" refers to the strikes themselves or their violent repercussions. One might speculate that sensitivity to the plight of Catholics in Northern Ireland may have exercised a restraining influence on public statements by Catholic leaders.

In a letter to Bishop Edward Daly, Cardinal George Basil Hume repeated what he had said in an earlier pastoral: "The hunger strike to death is a form of violence." It "surely cannot be condoned by the Church as being in accordance with God's will for man."[98] Terence Cardinal Cooke shares this view.[99]

The H-Block strikers have, in a sense, resurrected a dispute that goes back at least sixty years (to 1920) to the hunger strike of Terence James MacSwiney, Lord Mayor of Cork. The lively moral discussion that surrounded MacSwiney's strike and death is detailed by Carroll Ed-

[95] *Tablet* 235 (1981) 473.

[96] Raymond E. Helmick, "Northern Ireland in Moral Focus," *Tablet* 235 (1981) 516–17.

[97] *Tablet* 235 (1981) 629. For the statement of four religious leaders (Archbishop Armstrong, Church of Ireland; Dr. Callaghan, Methodist; Dr. Craig, Presbyterian; Cardinal O' Fiaich, Roman Catholic), cf. *Tablet* 235 (1981) 436.

[98] *Catholic Chronicle*, May 15, 1981, 3.

[99] *New York Times*, June 8, 1981, B7.

wards.[100] The debate at that time centered on two key issues: whether the hunger striker intends his own death and whether there is a truly proportionate reason for such a drastic act. Thus P. J. Gannon, writing in *Studies*, argued that "no hunger striker aims at death. Quite the contrary; he desires to live."[101] Similarly, *America* appealed to the principle of double effect.[102] MacSwiney was not seeking to destroy himself but to live in a just society. Thus suicide is not an appropriate description of his conduct.

René Brouillard, writing in the Jesuit journal *Etudes* (see Edwards), noted that the striker must not choose death. His death is to be the result of his testimony, not a chosen cause of it. Brouillard concluded that the striker must be given the benefit of the doubt as long as respectable theological opinion was divided. Thus the discussion was conducted very largely in terms of MacSwiney's intention. Was he intending his own death? Or was it unintended? On more than one occasion he stated that he had no suicidal intent.

The shape of that earlier discussion can be gathered from five articles in the *Irish Ecclesiastical Record*.[103] There Canon John Waters and Dr. Patrick Cleary, then professor of moral theology at Maynooth, agreed that direct or intentional self-killing is suicide. But they disagreed sharply on what the hunger striker is actually intending. Waters argued that the men were aiming at death and that by dying (means) they intended to rally support for their cause. Cleary contended that they were simply refusing to co-operate with the regime even in a fast to death. Death was merely permitted.

In recent months this same discussion has been renewed. A few examples will suffice here. Denis O'Callaghan, professor of moral theology at Maynooth, notes that Irish moral theologians have classified hunger strikes in three categories. (1) The deliberate strike to death, morally equivalent to suicide. (2) The exercise in brinkmanship in which death, if it occurs, is accidental and not intended. (3) The case of the hunger striker who does not want to die but is prepared to tolerate his own death if the other side is not prepared to give in. O'Callaghan states that most moral theologians would regard this last category as indirect, not direct,

[100] Carroll Edwards, "Hunger Strike: Protest or Suicide?" *America* 144 (1981) 458–60.

[101] P. J. Gannon, "The Ethical Aspect of the Hunger Strike," *Studies* 9 (1920) 448–54, at 450.

[102] "Mayor MacSwiney's Hunger Strike," *America* 23 (1920) 495.

[103] John C. Waters, "The Morality of the Hunger Strike," *Irish Ecclesiastical Record* 12 (1918) 89–108; P. Cleary, "Some Questions regarding the Morality of Hunger Strikes," ibid. 265–73; John C. Waters, "The Morality of the Hunger Strike—Rejoinder," ibid. 13 (1919) 14–26; P. Cleary, "Some Further Questions regarding the Morality of the Hunger Strike," ibid. 219–29; John C. Waters, "A Further Rejoinder," ibid. 391–403.

self-killing.[104] As he notes elsewhere: "The suicide verdict turns on a question of fact—does the hunger striker intend his death (as the Czech student Jan Palach did when he burned himself to death in protest against the Russian invasion of his country), or is he prepared to accept death possibly as the inevitable side-effect of a protest action on which he has embarked?"[105]

O'Callaghan feels that attention to this aspect of the problem ("amounting almost to an obsession") has obscured consideration of the motives and circumstances of the hunger strikes. On these grounds he judges the strikes to be "morally unjustifiable."

Joseph Farraher, S.J., is quite emphatic on his stand. "I have always held and still hold that to kill oneself or seriously threaten to kill oneself, even for a noble cause, is a usurpation of God's dominion over life and is objectively gravely sinful."[106] Farraher clearly believes that a "hunger strike to death" is killing oneself. He thinks that O'Callaghan's third category is not indirect killing but "direct killing in intention, even if only conditionally." Farraher is convinced that the pseudonymous writer (Carroll Edwards) in *America* completely confuses the notions of direct and indirect "in saying that since death was not the strikers' desire or aim, it was not directly intended, while at the same time making it clear that death is intended as a means even if not desired for itself."

Responding to a rather fuzzy letter in *The Times*, moral theologian John Mahoney, S.J., of Heythrop College, asks: Is death from a political hunger strike suicide?[107] He admits that during the prolonged and progressive nature of the action there is room for bluff and brinkmanship. However, "it is difficult to avoid concluding that, as far as it is humanly evident, the hunger-striker who dies has at some stage deliberately and irrevocably chosen to do so." It is clear that Mahoney regards this as morally wrong.

Herbert McCabe, O.P., is not so sure.[108] He begins by supposing (*dato non concesso*) that the strikers' cause is just (i.e., that they are unjustly imprisoned). If the hunger striker is determined to discontinue the strike as soon as his just demands are met, "it does not seem plausible to describe the hunger striker who dies as a suicide." However, if he threatens to take his own life if his demands are not met, then that is different. If it is wrong to intend one's death, it is wrong to threaten to do

---

[104] *Catholic Chronicle*, May 15, 1981, 3.

[105] *Irish Times*, June 15, 1981.

[106] Joseph Farraher, S.J., "Are Hunger Strikes Moral?" *Homiletic and Pastoral Review* 82, no. 1 (1981) 67-68.

[107] *The Times*, May 6, 1981.

[108] Herbert McCabe, O.P., "Thoughts on Hunger Strikes," *New Blackfriars* 62 (1981) 303-10.

so; for a threat "is nothing but the announcement that under certain conditions he will do this thing that is wrong." A person who proposes to commit adultery if the weather is not good enough for tennis intends to do what is wrong just as much as the person who intends to commit adultery whatever the weather. Interestingly, McCabe remarks as an aside that this argument is not available to anyone who believes in the moral acceptability of the nuclear deterrent.

In the final analysis, McCabe does not believe that the hunger striker need be threatening suicide. He need not be intending to discredit authorities *by his death.* In the case of the Czech student, the student's intention would be thwarted if he did not die. McCabe is unable to say whether factually this is what the hunger strikers were doing.

This is a sampling of how the recent discussion has proceeded. The heavy emphasis is on the intention and there is virtually unanimous agreement that the hunger strike is morally wrong if it must be said that the striker at some point intends his own death. Thus the key assumption is that it is always wrong to intend to kill an innocent person, including oneself. This reflects the quite traditional teaching summarized by Zalba twenty-five years ago: "It is permissible for one fasting for a public cause . . . to extend the fast to the point of great danger of death and *therefore with the intention of taking food when the stomach permits.*"[109]

Now enter Walter Kerber, S.J.[110] Kerber considers the hunger strike in itself, that is, in abstraction from the circumstances of any particular strike. He notes that traditional moral theology must condemn the hunger strike as a threat to kill oneself. This is judged to be intrinsically evil.

However, certain characteristics of the hunger strike suggest questions about the plausibility of this absolute condemnation. Our sensitivities do not always equate the hunger strike with suicide. Furthermore, the public regards some hunger strikers (e.g., Gandhi) as moral heroes. There is often expressly Christian motivation present. Finally, only Catholic theology uses the double-effect principle to judge such actions, a principle borrowed from philosophy, not the gospel.

Such "plausibility considerations," however, do not suffice. We must get a true picture of what a hunger strike is. Kerber sees it as a form of nonviolent protest, a political strategy that is far better than its alternative, war. When compared to war, it uses a minimum of physical force. It provides less occasion for hate and it respects the human dignity and

---

[109] M. Zalba, S.J., *Theologiae moralis summa* 2 (Madrid: Editorial Catolica, 1957) 62, no. 149; emphasis added.

[110] Walter Kerber, S.J., "Zur moraltheologischen Beurteilung eines politisch motivierten Hungerstreiks," *Theologie und Philosophie* 57 (1982) forthcoming in Heft 1. The final manuscript was kindly forwarded to me by the author.

ethical responsibility of one's opponent. It distinguishes more clearly between the person and the injustice. Thus it is a strategy aimed at doing away with violence.

The hunger strike is at one with the just-war theory in holding that force cannot be completely avoided. It differs from such a theory in its claim that force against *another* is not always the best means. Sufficient is a means involving less evil than war. Indeed, when the actual use of force in most wars is submitted to rigorous ethical scrutiny, it cannot be justified.

Kerber argues that the hunger strike cannot be seen as a matter of individualistic ethics. It must be viewed "in conjunction with a more general political ethic of violent confrontation." Thus it should be seen as an alternative to war, and when it is, it is unintelligible how it can be absolutely forbidden. Kerber argues that, as long as it cannot be shown to be evil in itself, the hunger strike can be justified as the lesser evil.

Kerber then adverts to an interesting paradox provoked by his reflections. On the one hand, traditional theology (especially its doctrine of double effect) would have to view the hunger strike as suicide, as *actio intrinsece mala*. On the other hand, the hunger strike can under certain conditions represent a more humane means, one that is in closer conformity with the gospel. This paradox, he suggests, is not traceable to a poor application of basic principles, but to the principles themselves, scil., *actio intrinsece mala* and the double effect.

He then turns to the notion of *actio intrinsece mala*. There are very few of these in traditional theology, and direct killing of self or an innocent third party is one of them. In other cases, he notes, "ordinarily Catholic moral theology judges the ethical character of an action according to a weighing of premoral, but morally important consequences, therefore 'teleologically.' " So why not also with direct killing of self or an innocent third party?

The standard justification for calling such killing *actio intrinsece mala* is that "God alone is the Lord of life." But, Kerber argues, the only conclusion that follows from that formulation is that we may not dispose of human life at our pleasure ("beliebig"). What gives the conclusion (*actio intrinsece mala*) plausibility is that we can think of very few goods that take precedence over an individual life.

As a way of approaching the hunger strike, Kerber next takes up capital punishment as an exception to the prohibition of killing. Capital punishment certainly represents a direct killing. In traditional teaching, only the state has the right to enact it. But where did it get the right directly to dispose of human life? The ordinary explanation is that God established the order of basic human rights as the unconditional presupposition of a life worthy of human beings and that the death penalty is a necessary means to this. In other words, "the maintenance of the civil order is so important, so unconditioned a good, that it can be concluded that God has given the power of the death penalty to the state." This grant of power in no way detracts from God's lordship over life, because the decision about the licitness or illicitness of capital punishment is not arbitrarily made but "from considerations touching what best corresponds to God's plans for the life of human beings in society."

Kerber suggests that the same form of reasoning can throw light on the hunger strike. Under certain very detailed conditions, the taking of one's life could represent the avoidance of the terrible evils of war and represent an intervention in the service of a just order and the common good. In this case, too, God's lordship over life is not diminished, "because the hunger striker does not arbitrarily dispose of his own life, but seeks the plan of God, namely, peace and justice." Just as with capital punishment, the conclusion about the hunger strike is drawn from "considerations touching what best corresponds to God's plan for the life of human beings in society." In the circumstances it would represent the lesser evil.

Kerber concludes his analysis by noting that it is a first tentative attempt that needs further discussion by experts. As for the H-Block strikers, he suggests that they lack ethical credibility because the responsible organization is not committed solely to nonviolence.

This is an interesting and important article. It is basically providing grounds for questioning the two handles that we have grasped to analyze hunger strikes (*actio intrinsece mala*, double effect). Kerber clearly opts for a teleological understanding of the prohibition against killing, specifically the direct killing of self or an innocent third party. What he does well is to show that abandoning the notion of direct self-killing as intrinsically evil does not derogate from God's lordship over life and need not open all kinds of doors onto slippery slopes.

Kerber makes it very clear that one's analysis of a relatively rare and marginal happening like the hunger strike is inseparably bound up with and transparent of one's methodology. He explicitly notes that he is drawing on the works of Schüller *et al.* From my own comments in these "Notes" over the years, it is clear that my analysis would follow the lines of Kerber's. Concretely, it means that I would judge the H-Block hunger strike in terms of the circumstances Kerber mentions. From all I know (and it is not all by any means), that particular political strategy in those circumstances would not survive moral scrutiny. That is to say nothing about the good will or culpability of the strikers. It is simply to take seriously an analysis that finds justification of the hunger strike only as an alternative to war.

Nuclear Disarmament

"The most historic change in late 20th-century U.S. history." That is the way veteran journalist Arthur Jones referred to the ground swell within the Catholic community against U.S. militarism and the nuclear-dominated national security mentality.[111] Bishop Thomas Gumbleton, president of Pax Christi, has been urging this "no" for many years in a crusade that must have been lonely and was at times misunderstood. But this courageous and thoughtful bishop should be seen for what he truly is—a prophetic voice.

The perceptions of many others have caught up with Gumbleton's foresight. Thus there has been a veritable outpouring of episcopal statements against nuclear buildup and proliferation.[112] Elden F. Curtiss (Helena) and Thomas J. Murphy (Great Falls) repudiated the MX, declaring that "continued stockpiling of arms, in a world already capable of destroying itself, is a false and precarious means of assuring lasting peace." Thomas Grady (Orlando) asserted that "nuclear war should be opposed as an unjust war. Nuclear weapons should be banned." Raymond Lucker (New Ulm) wrote: "Nuclear weapons may not be used for attack or for first strike. They may not be used in defense. They may not be threatened to be used. Therefore it seems to me that even to possess them is wrong." Twenty-nine American bishops signed a statement saying just that.

Anthony Pilla (Cleveland), in a pastoral letter, declared that it is "imperative that we take action now to end proliferation of nuclear arms, the reliance on militarism and the use of war to alleviate international problems." Michael Kenny (Juneau) declared himself "categorically opposed not only to the use but to the possession of nuclear weapons." Walter Sullivan (Richmond) told a largely military audience that it is "immoral to be associated with the production or use" of nuclear weapons.

John R. Roach (St. Paul-Minneapolis) argued that Reagan's decision (announced Aug. 8) to build and stockpile neutron warheads was simply fueling the arms race. He was supported by Frank J. Rodimer (Paterson) and Phillip F. Straling (San Bernadino). Undoubtedly in the days ahead (I write in November 1981) there will be continuing additions to these statements. A few years ago Pax Christi counted only three bishops; now the number is fifty-four.

Three episcopal statements attracted special attention. The first was

---

[111] Nicholas von Hoffman wrote that while the mass media focus on allegations against Cardinal Cody, "the real news about the American Roman Catholic Church is its swinging toward a resolutely anti-bomb stance" (*Philadelphia Daily News*, Oct. 3, 1981).

[112] The following episcopal citations are from NC releases.

that of Raymond Hunthausen (Seattle).[113] In a speech to the Pacific Northwest Synod of the Lutheran Church of America (June 12), Hunthausen referred to "our willingness to destroy life everywhere on this earth for the sake of our security as Americans" as the root of our problems. He referred to the basing of Trident submarines in his territory as the "Auschwitz of Puget Sound." They, together with MX and cruise missiles, are to be understood as "a buildup to a first-strike capability. The common element in all political analyses to check this buildup is despair." Therefore, Hunthausen concludes, taking up our cross with Christ in the nuclear age means unilateral disarmament. To the objection that this is to encourage risk, Hunthausen replies that it is a "more reasonable risk than constant nuclear escalation." He concludes by suggesting that "our paralyzed political process" needs a catalyst and that catalyst is tax resistance.

Hunthausen's statement was backed by sixteen leaders of nine denominations in Washington State. Rev. Loren Arnett, executive minister of the Washington Association, stated that the response of other religious leaders to Hunthausen's statement was "bravo."[114] He continued: "We've been waiting for someone in our group to have the courage to forthrightly state the commitment that the archbishop declared that day in Tacoma." The Catholic Biblical Association, meeting in Seattle at the time, unanimously passed a resolution supportive of Hunthausen.

The impact of this dramatic speech was enormous. Its twin suggestion (unilateral disarmament, tax resistance) has been both praised and criticized. In this latter category there have been allegations that Hunthausen does not represent Catholic teaching, that his position is naive and emasculates the nation's right to security, that it is incompatible with the just-war theory, etc.

I believe that such responses (often emanating from the archconservative community) miss the point and purpose of Hunthausen's intervention. He referred to the "paralyzed political process" and "despair" at the political analysis of the nuclear buildup. There is an independent and uncontrollable dynamic of escalation in nuclear buildup in our time. It seems that nothing we think or do can stop such madness. And that incapacity can lead to public apathy. And where there is apathy, there is no serious wrestling with moral issues. As Volkmar Deile, a leader of West Germany's Action for Reconciliation, worded it: "There is an increasing feeling in Germany that talking to the superpowers about disarmament is like trying to persuade drug dealers to stop deliveries of dope. The feeling is that they are hooked on armaments."[115] That is a

---

[113] Raymond Hunthausen, "Faith and Disarmament," *Christianity and Crisis* 41 (1981) 229–31.

[114] *Inside Passage*, Sept. 18, 1981.   [115] *Time* 118 (Oct. 19, 1981) 52.

pervasive feeling in the United States and it was in that atmosphere that Hunthausen's statement makes eminent good sense. The sheer madness (to use a phrase frequently used by Bishop Walter Sullivan) of what is going on and what the Reagan administration intends even to increase, calls for a symbolic response, a gesture whose very radicalness alone is capable of disturbing apathy and making people think about ethical issues they have too often left to the political process and the armaments industry. That is what Hunthausen has provided.

In this spirit Archbishop Francis T. Hurley (Anchorage) wrote that the Hunthausen "proposal forces the conscience of Christians who profess Christ and His teachings to make some judgment about the arms race."[116] Similarly, the *National Catholic Reporter* editorialized that Hunthausen's remarks "should have the effect of causing more Christians, including other bishops, to confront themselves on this question."[117]

The second incident involves Leroy T. Matthiesen (Amarillo) and the Texas bishops. On Aug. 21, Matthiesen, in whose diocese final work on the neutron bomb will be done (Pantex Corporation), denounced the decision of the Reagan administration to build neutron warheads. "The announcement of the decision to produce and stockpile neutron warheads is the latest in a series of tragic, anti-life positions taken by our government."[118] He then asked those involved in production of neutron weapons to quit their jobs and seek "employment in peaceful pursuits." On Sept. 10, all twelve Catholic bishops of Texas joined Matthiesen. "We his brother bishops of Texas share Bishop Matthiesen's concern and fully support his appeal to those involved in the manufacture of these weapons in every nation to consider seriously the moral and ethical implications of what they are doing."[119]

The third statement of note is that of Archbishop John R. Quinn.[120] To respond in a Christian way to the arms race, we must "change our very ways of thinking." We have already stockpiled enough nuclear weapons to destroy every major Soviet city forty times over. When he considers the vast and indiscriminate destructiveness of nuclear weapons, he concedes that "a 'just' nuclear war is a contradiction in terms." He asks, interestingly, in the light of the discussion above on method: "What good could possibly be proportionate to such uncontrollable destruction and suffering?" Quinn admits that no one can preprogram the response of another to the "madness." Some might be called to a "radically prophetic response." Whatever the case, Quinn invites all to a day of prayer a month to gain grace "which can change our hearts in this critical time of

[116] *Inside Passage*, July 17, 1981.
[117] *National Catholic Reporter*, July 3, 1981, 12.
[118] *New York Times*, Sept. 13, 1981, 37.
[119] Ibid.
[120] John R. Quinn, "Instruments of Peace, Weapons of War," *Origins* 11 (1981) 284–87.

need." He further urges broad-based educational programs to heighten awareness of the ethical horrors our policies imply. And he concludes by recommending practical expressions of concern in the political and social arenas.

What is interesting about these statements is that they emanate not from a handful of pacifists but from an increasingly large number of mainstream religious leaders who are in some other respects quite self-effacing and even in some areas conservative. Religious leadership in the United States, especially Catholic, is on a collision course with the U.S. Government. That just may be the best thing to happen to both in a long time.

As I read the episcopal statements, in varying degree and with different emphases they display several characteristics. (1) There is a straightforward moral condemnation of the use of nuclear weapons. (2) There is, in addition, a condemnation of the arms race ("stockpiling toward annihilation") to the neglect of more basic needs. (3) There is a pervasive sense of frustration at the insensitivity and intransigence of the processes responsible for this policy of a race toward death. (4) There is a deep desire to alter the consciousness of people to the moral dimensions and implications of nuclear weaponry. Thus we hear phrases such as "change of heart" and "conversion" being frequently used. Bishop Matthiesen remarked in the aftermath of his statement: "On the whole I accomplished what I wanted to by bringing an issue to the consciousness of people. It's amazing how people have begun to live with the unlivable."[121]

This remarkable spate of episcopal statements in one sense should not be surprising. The Church's official teaching has for decades condemned indiscriminate force. This teaching was clearly summarized by Vatican II (*Gaudium et spes*, no. 80).

Yet several things have converged to bring the individual bishops out of the nuclear closet. Patty Edmonds mentions four.[122] (1) Current events, and the direction our government is taking. (2) Personal experience. A number of bishops have been exposed to Pax Christi literature and talk of their own conversion. (3) John Paul II's very strong statements on the arms race. (4) Fellow bishops' statements.

Leroy Matthiesen's suggestion that persons working on the neutron warhead leave their jobs and seek "employment in peaceful pursuits" reflects the analysis made by Francis X. Winters, S.J., in a seminal article.[123] Winters first describes the grave doubts beginning to emerge about the wisdom of SALT agreements as a way of limiting the dangers

[121] *New York Times*, Sept. 8, 1981, 20.

[122] *National Catholic Reporter*, Oct. 30, 1981, 19.

[123] Francis X. Winters, S.J., "The Bow or the Cloud? American Bishops Challenge the Arms Race," *America* 145 (1981) 26–30.

of nuclear war. For instance, there is the dilemma of negotiating with the Soviets at the very time we are punishing them for aggressive international behavior.

Winters next turns to the teaching of the American bishops personified in Cardinal Krol. This teaching can be summarized in three steps. (1) It is immoral to use the strategic nuclear arsenal of the United States. (2) It is immoral to threaten to use such weapons as part of a strategy of nuclear deterrence. (3) Mere possession of nuclear weapons can be tolerated as the lesser of two evils "while negotiations proceed."

Winters underscores the radical character of this testimony. It demands of us that we deny ourselves the option of certain strategies (targeting cities). "With this imperative, the Church rejects the essential capstone of all U.S. deterrent strategy." Furthermore, the use of any nuclear weapons against any targets is rejected "precisely because it runs the risk of escaping human control." Thus there is a moral obligation of unilateral renunciation of the right to use and the threat to use nuclear weapons. If arms control means that a nation is constrained to observe limitations only insofar as its adversary admits the same duty, it "is alien to the moral teaching of the Church." As Winters summarizes it, "Unilateral obligation to forego nuclear threats and attacks, yes; unilateral disarmament, no."

Winters concludes this well-informed study by noting the dilemma this poses for Catholic government officials. On the one hand, they have assumed a constitutional obligation to execute and/or articulate our nuclear deterrent policy. On the other, if their consciences are formed by Catholic teaching, they may not do this.

Why have the bishops been moved to embrace such a radical stance? Winters surmises that the very security of the nation demands this renunciation. National security is not compatible with the use of nuclear weapons, though it may be agonizingly and arduously compatible with what most Americans shudder to contemplate: military defeat. Winters notes that here "the generals will bolt" and many officials will probably ignore the teaching. "But the debate will have begun. A seed will have been sown, a tension created in American society."

Winters has, I believe, captured beautifully the essence of the problem as many of us experience it. We are pursuing a deterrent policy (if there is serious resolve ever to use these weapons) which no acceptable moral principles can justify. Several points merit comment. The Winters study argues that no use, whatever the target, of nuclear weapons can be justified, because on all accounts any use will necessarily involve civilians indiscriminately. As Winters puts it, he has "yet to meet a U.S. defense official, civilian or military, who argues that strategic nuclear war will allow any meaningful shelter for civilians." This is doubly important at a time when we hear talk of a "limited nuclear exchange" and of "winning" such an exchange.

Second, it is important to pinpoint just why this conclusion must be drawn. Archbishop Quinn has, I believe, done this very well. As noted above, he asks: "What good could possibly be proportionate to such uncontrollable destruction and suffering?" That is not only an evaluative calculus, and a correct one at that; it implies a methodological approach, one I also believe to be correct.

Third, some contrasts are to be noted in the statements of Krol (who claimed to be speaking for "the great majority of the bishops") and other bishops. (1) Krol did not condemn mere possession of nuclear weapons. A good number of bishops do condemn such a possession (e.g., Raymond Lucker: "It is immoral to possess nuclear weapons"). (2) If it is permissible to possess them, according to Krol, then presumably it is not immoral to make them. Yet Leroy Matthiesen, and with him many other bishops, request those working at Pantex to leave their jobs for more peaceable pursuits. (3) Krol does not believe unilateral disarmament is a moral demand. Hunthausen does, and with him all those who believe mere possession of nuclear weapons is immoral.

These are interesting differences and point to the single area where problems and questions still haunt us: possession of nuclear weapons. It is clear to nearly every ethical commentator that we may never morally use strategic nuclear weapons. If that is so, most would agree that it is seriously wrong to threaten to use them. But what about mere possession?

On the one hand, they do seem to deter. Vatican II seemed to acquiesce in this contention.[124] On the other hand, many believe that any war between the superpowers begun with conventional weapons is likely to end in nuclear war. It is this danger that leads some to argue that mere possession is immoral. The deterrent effect leads others to an opposite conclusion.

Whatever the proper answer to this question is, two things must be remembered. First, the danger that nuclear weapons might ever be used creates the serious and immediate moral imperative to work for their abolition. Second, we must remember that bishops and academics do not make policy. We can have clear and distinct ethical ideas (e.g., the distinction between the threat to use and mere possession). By and large, I believe these distinctions are regarded as quaint by policymakers. Therefore we must interpret the possession of nuclear weapons in terms of what policymakers actually think and intend about them. Nothing

---

[124] I say "acquiesce" because the document certainly did not endorse such deterrence; nor did it condemn it. It simply acknowledged that "many regard this state of affairs as the most effective way by which peace of a sort can be maintained."

that I have seen or heard offers great confidence here. Are not our policymakers ready to use nuclear weapons "if necessary"? This means that there is no such thing, at the present time and realistically, as having nuclear weapons with no intention to use them. It is this that makes the case against mere possession of such weapons so powerful.

What is possibly responsible for these differences is underlined in a very thoughtful study by Francis X. Meehan.[125] Meehan identifies two different approaches to the nuclear problem, that of the liberal and that of the activist. The analytic detachment of the liberal can end in affirming the reigning militarism. Catholic teaching does not clearly condemn nuclear deterrence and this "manages to deprive Catholic teaching of the clear and unequivocal condemnation of weapons-building. Thus, it also impedes consensus in moral evaluation." In the face of this ambiguity, the rational realism of the liberal can become "absorbed in the militarist's own ground of reasoning." By contrast, the activist does not shy away from application, criticizing this weapon being made at this time in this place. Thus it is different methods and different emphases that are responsible for different conclusions. Meehan is eminently fair but his sympathies lie with the "activist's instinct for the meaning of the concrete as a special theological source of wisdom and insight for the whole Church."

I cannot close this brief roundup without references to three interesting studies. One is William F. Wolff's indictment of the wishy-washy, issue-evading stance of the hierarchy (up to that time) on deterrence.[126] Another is Alan Geyer's splendid description of the social characteristics of militarism.[127] Finally, there is Thomas Powers' presentation of eight reasons for getting rid of the bomb.[128] These articles, together with Meehan's helpful analysis, provide the background for reading what Vincent Yzermans refers to as "a Catholic revolution."[129]

The Divorced-Remarried

What is the situation of the divorced and (irregularly) remarried in the Church today? May they ever receive the sacraments? As everyone knows, at the end of the 1980 Synod Pope John Paul II repeated the "traditional practice" as the norm of the Church. But nearly everyone also knows that the papal statement headed into rather heavy weather—

[125] Francis X. Meehan, "Disarmament in the Real World," *America* 143 (1980) 423-26.
[126] William F. Wolff, "The Church and the Bomb," *America* 144 (1981) 11-13.
[127] Alan Geyer, "Some Theological Perspectives on Militarism," *Nexus* 59 (Summer 1980) 34-44.
[128] Thomas Powers, "Principles of Abolition," *Commonweal* 108 (1981) 424-26.
[129] *New York Times*, Nov. 14, 1981, 23.

a virtually unanimous theological opinion that some divorced and remarried may be admitted to the sacraments.

Rather typical of the literature of the past ten years is the study of Gonzalo González, O.P.[130] González considers the place in the Church of those who have remarried after divorce. He observes that "there are increasing theological voices that demand a new treatment of the problem" and a pastoral practice "contrary to the established one." Using a comprehensive background of theological and ecclesiastical literature, he looks at the reception of the current practice and concludes that the present discipline "has not been received, although it has been obeyed, in many communities."

González then reviews several key emphases that must structure a new pastoral approach, an approach he believes calls for courage (*audacia*). Among these emphases are the recognition that a first marriage has failed irreparably and that not infrequently the couple now have the obligation to maintain and nurture the second union. He rejects their situation as "a state of sin," critiques the usual arguments about full integration as a condition for reception of the Eucharist, and calls for a modification of present discipline. We must maintain the radical nature of the permanence of marriage, but also the radical character of mercy in the faith community.

In the context of full integration in the Church, he discusses those who are incapable of believing that God does not want them to remake their lives, and those who accept the ideal but consider themselves incapable of achieving it in real life (hence the title of the article). Here the Church should display in its attitudes and policies the mercy of God so central to its teaching.

There is little that is new in this study. It repeats themes common in the literature for over ten years. What is interesting is that it appeared after the Pope's closing statement at the 1980 Synod.

Helmut Krätzl, the auxiliary bishop of Vienna, notes that the problem under discussion here has become one of the most discussed in all of pastoral practice.[131] On Nov. 15, 1978, there was a meeting of the Senate of Priests of Vienna. A kind of basic working paper on this problem was the vehicle of discussion. Later on, this basic working paper was distributed to all priests in the diocese and to other dioceses for further discussion. Krätzl puts together in the form of ten theses the results of these discussions.

---

[130] Gonzalo González, "Incapacidad para entender, impossibilidad de cumplir: Sobre la situación eclesial y la pastoral de los divorciados que han contraído nuevo matrimonio," *Ciencia Tomista* 108 (1981) 327–46.

[131] Helmut Krätzl, "Thesen zur Pastoral an wiederverheirateten Geschiedenen," *Theologisch-praktische Quartalschrift* 129 (1981) 143–54.

Some of the theses read as follows. "The Church stands under the clear radical demand of Jesus for unconditional fidelity in marriage." "The Church, after the example of Jesus, must show a special care for those who have failed, therefore also for those who have failed in marriage." "The divorced-remarried are not excommunicated—they are simply not in full possession of all rights." "Internal-forum solutions do not change the legal situation for the external forum." "Pastoral care of marriage must not restrict itself to crisis situations, but must have in view the entire problem of marriage." Krätzl discusses all of these in a balanced and compassionate way.

Thesis 5 reads: "There exists in the Church an official consensus that the divorced-remarried may be admitted to the sacraments; but there is no consensus about the required presuppositions for such admission." Krätzl notes that there is a consensus in the Church that those who are in an irregular second marriage but are convinced in conscience that their first marriage was invalid—without the ability to establish this legally—may be admitted to the sacraments.

But what about those whose first marriage was valid? Krätzl reports accurately that even here a broad consensus had grown up in the past ten years that under certain conditions even these persons could responsibly be admitted to the sacraments without living as brother and sister. Josef Ratzinger, then professor at Regensburg, had stated this clearly.[132] Since then, many theologians have agreed with Ratzinger. Krätzl mentions studies by Häring, Böckle, Hörmann, Fuchs, Gründel, Rotter, Lehmann, and Kasper among others. The most recent study to draw this conclusion was that of K. Forster, professor of pastoral at Augsburg.[133] Forster sees his solution not as a denial of official practice but as "a new and deepened interpretation of it." Bishop Krätzl does not deny this but says that theological developments must be placed on a broader and more official basis. To do this, the traditional arguments against the practice must be carefully compared to the newer arguments. "Just how great is the distance between the two kinds of argument appeared before the Roman Synod of Bishops, in the course of the interventions at the Synod itself, and in the reactions to it."

The synodal fathers were aware of this and knew that they had not said the last word on the subject. Indeed, after the Synod, Cardinal Ratzinger, in a letter to priests, noted that the "Synod desired that a new and even more searching investigation—including even consideration of the praxis of the Eastern Church—be undertaken to make our pastoral

[132] Josef Ratzinger, "Zur Frage nach der Unauflöslichkeit der Ehe," in *Ehe und Ehescheidung* (Munich, 1972) 54.

[133] K. Forster, "Möglichkeiten einer Bussordnung für wiederverheiratete Geschiedene," *Herder Korrespondenz* 34 (1980) 462-68, at 466.

compassion even more all-embracing."[134]

Krätzl ends his article by citing the Austrian bishops after the close of the Synod. After stating that the divorced and irregularly remarried deserve understanding, compassion, and acceptance as brothers and sisters in Christ, and that they can count on God's grace, the bishops conclude: "According to the traditional practice of the Church, they cannot share fully in the sacramental life of the Church, unless there are special conditions that need greater clarity in conversation with an experienced priest."

Bishop Krätzl has accurately summarized the German theologians on this matter (a "broad consensus"). As I read the theological literature of the past ten years, a similar consensus had formed elsewhere also, a consensus not exactly in full agreement with the "traditional practice" restated by the Pope. Where does that leave us? Krätzl seems very reluctant to fly in the face of such a consensus. The spirit of his study is to urge more conversation and prudence in the interim. Furthermore, the Austrian bishops clearly seem to be saying that the "traditional practice" repeated by the Pope is not a hard and fast rule but must take into account "special conditions."

Similar conclusions are drawn by Bernard Häring.[135] Häring explicitly excludes discussion of the theoretical arguments pro or con the "traditional practice" or even of a modification of it. There is a proper and necessary place for these. He wants to show that even the strict norm asserted by John Paul II at the Synod's end needs prudential interpretation.

Häring begins by reminding readers of several overarching general principles. First, we mislead the faithful if we make an unqualifiable dogma of what is an application in need of ongoing refinement. Next, history teaches us that the consciences of the faithful often discover solutions that the Church comes to recognize as correct only at a later date. Finally, the pastoral guide must always be aware of the law of growth.

Häring next insists that it is clear from the synodal interventions as well as the reports of the smaller discussion groups (with the sole exception of the "Latin group") that the basic concern of the Synod was a pastoral of healing. The whole Church and especially its pastoral leaders must be for the divorced a sacrament of God's healing and merciful love. Concrete rules such as that excluding the divorced from the sacraments are subordinate to this basic concern, because concrete rules are precisely vehicles for this basic concern. Furthermore, a sudden change in this

---

[134] Krätzl, "Thesen" 152.

[135] Bernard Häring, "Pastorale Erwägungen zur Bischofssynode über Familie und Ehe," *Theologie der Gegenwart* 24 (1981) 71–80.

practical norm without previous change to a more healing attitude would only make things worse.

Häring also insists that the requirement to live as brother-sister should not be made if foreseeably it will lead to disastrous results: decisive alienation from the authority of the Church, disturbance of family harmony, dangerous conscience conflicts, harm to the education of the children, etc. A medicinal measure (*poena medicinalis*) is not to be used when it causes more harm than good in the overall life of the Church.

Häring then turns to the notion of *oikonomia*. As noted, the synodal participants had asked John Paul II if the Western Church could not learn something from the Eastern practice. Häring describes beautifully the meaning of this *oikonomia*. It is founded in a therapeutic view of redemption. Christ came to heal the sick. Christ, who celebrated the messianic meal with sinners and tax collectors, is the basic symbol of *oikonomia*. Thus healing is a kind of "household principle" in the Church ("Heilshaushaltsprinzip"). The Church must organize her policies and practices as a reflection of this symbol, and for Häring this clearly means that the divorced-remarried should not, under appropriate conditions, be excluded from the sacraments. But before this can happen, the faithful must be deeply imbued with the spirit of *oikonomia*, with the spirit of healing love which is its theological foundation.[136] Häring obviously thinks that this is the future of pastoral practice in the Western Church. Indeed, he mentions a letter of the late Patriarch Athenagoras to a trusted friend in which Athenagoras insists that reconciliation of the Eastern and Western Churches could not occur unless Rome gives assurances that it understands and acknowledges *oikonomia*.

Häring concludes with the hope that his reflections can pave the way for future doctrinal development.

Häring's article is pastorally insightful, as his writings always are. His distinction between a basic concern ("Grundanliegen") and a concrete directive, and their relationship, provides him with the opening to give a rather broad interpretation (as he says, "less rigorous") to the rule itself.

However, there is a limit to what merely pastoral considerations can achieve, as Häring himself would admit. By treating the matter pastorally, Häring is implicitly accepting the present rule excluding the remarried from the sacraments, though I think it is clear that this is not his own conviction. By doing so, he implicitly accepts the notion of indissolubility that stands behind it. That notion is a profoundly juridical one. It regards

---

[136] Interestingly in this respect, Johann B. Metz observes that if the Church were more radical in the gospel sense, it would not have to be so rigorous in the legal sense. "The Church could then, to take just one example, admit to the sacraments those whose marriages had failed and who were seeking forgiveness for this without having to fear that the floodgates would be opened" (*The Emergent Church* [New York: Crossroad, 1981] 8).

the bond of marriage as still in existence even though any semblance of a human relationship is irretrievably dead and gone. It is that notion of permanence that generates the rule excluding the remarried from the sacraments. Hence any well-founded and lasting modification of the rule will have to grapple systematically and theoretically with the underlying notion of permanence or indissolubility.

That is done in a tentative but fruitful way by William Cosgrave.[137] His notion of permanence as a serious moral obligation is virtually identical with suggestions made earlier in these "Notes."[138] And on that not disinterested but cheerful note this version of the "Notes" were well advised to grind to a halt.

[137] William Cosgrave, "Rethinking the Indissolubility of Marriage," *Catholic Mind* 79, no. 1352 (April 1981) 11-25.

[138] *TS* 36 (1975) 112-17.

CURRENT THEOLOGY

NOTES ON MORAL THEOLOGY: 1982

RICHARD A. McCORMICK, S.J.

Kennedy Institute of Ethics and Woodstock Theological Center, D.C.

Much interesting literature of the past year has gathered around four areas: (1) intrinsic evil, moral norms, and the magisterium; (2) moral reasoning and storytelling; (3) nuclear deterrence and nuclear war; (4) women, newborns, and the conceived.

INTRINSIC EVIL, MORAL NORMS, AND THE MAGISTERIUM

The past year will be remembered for many turbulent events (e.g., the invasion of Lebanon, the Falklands war, the steep economic recession). Not least among the turbulences was what Agatha Christie might call "this recent unpleasantness." I refer to the tensions between the Holy See and the Jesuits. Some of these tensions were, so it was said, doctrinal, and specifically moral, in character. Whatever the case, whenever the matter was mentioned publicly, it was generally accompanied by reminders of the "traditional loyalty of the Society of Jesus to the pope." This loyalty is underlined by the fourth vow of Jesuits. The impression was not infrequently left that Jesuits were in violation of their most treasured traditions when they dissented from certain policies or formulations of the Holy See.

For this reason a study by historian John W. O'Malley, S.J., is highly topical.[1] The Spanish Jesuit José García de Madariaga has recently argued that "matter which is doctrinal can form part of the proper object of the fourth vow; and . . . therefore the pope can impose an order which is strictly or purely doctrinal in virtue of that vow."[2] In other words, Madariaga proposes an understanding of vowed allegiance wherein Jesuits can be obliged by vow to a special defense of *Laborem exercens*, *Populorum progressio*, or *Humanae vitae*.

In a carefully documented and utterly persuasive way, O'Malley shows that such a thesis rests on highly questionable presuppositions and is untenable. For instance, Madariaga refers to the "papal magisterium" in Ignatius' time. O'Malley shows that the use of this term to describe a sixteenth-century reality is "to read back into the sixteenth century a reality that came into existence only in the nineteenth." The popes of

---

[1] John W. O'Malley, S.J., "The Fourth Vow in Its Ignatian Context: An Historical Study," *Studies in the Spirituality of Jesuits* 15, no. 1 (1983).

[2] José García de Madariaga, S.J., "The Jesuit's Fourth Vow: Can It Extend to What He Teaches?" *Review for Religious* 41 (1982) 214–38.

that time simply did not teach in the way they do now. The first encyclical dealing with doctrinal matters was issued in the nineteenth century.

Another false supposition is that Ignatius identified the Church with the pope, an identification that lacks any solid evidence. Furthermore, this skewers the discussion by placing interpretation of the vow primarily within Ignatius' esteem for the papacy rather than within the context of the apostolic aim of the first Jesuits. This false start leads to a "totalism" that is not historically verifiable.

O'Malley concludes this excellent study by rejecting Madariaga's assertion that the pope "can command the defense of any Catholic truth whatever, even if it is not infallible." In O'Malley's words, "Such commands have never been given, there is no evidence that Ignatius ever considered such a likelihood or even possibility, and there is no solid indication from any word or deed of the early Jesuits that they had that understanding of the vow."

The fourth vow is rather a symbol of the universal mission of the Society and a guarantor of the mobility and disponibility to achieve this. It shows a fundamental concern of the Society that the members of the order be persons "on mission" under the pastoral guidance of the pope.

O'Malley's rich and balanced study should quiet some of the expansive allegations aimed at theologians who are doing nothing more than their theological and ecclesial task when they receive authentic teaching both docilely and critically. Furthermore, I believe that the thesis O'Malley defends from a historical view can very likely be established theologically. Is it possible for a theologian to vow to defend a formulation that *ex hypothesi* could be in need of qualification, or could even be in error? Would that not be a vow that in some rare instances would undermine the truth, perpetuate error? How is that in any sense the *melius* traditionally demanded for the validity of a vow? O'Malley raises this issue from the viewpoint of a papal command and rightly contends that "such a command would at least border on the immoral." It would in effect be a "command to violate the criteria for 'true' interpretation, which we must assume any pope wants."

One final point. O'Malley notes that Ignatius did bequeath to his followers a pastoral principle: "the greater good of souls." In Ignatius' time this translated into the avoidance of all public criticism of authority. But O'Malley rightly argues that such a translation on the grounds of pastoral prudence is hardly valid for all times.[3] As he notes, "The faithful continue to prove themselves tougher than their clergy sometimes give them credit for, and they rightly seem more scandalized when abuses or

---

[3] Cf. the interesting article by Miguel Mᵃ. Garijo-Guembe, " 'Reception' and Its Place in Theology," *Theology Digest* 30 (1982) 49–53.

dissent are brought to their attention by outsiders than they are when these are dealt with straightforwardly by those properly qualified within the church."[4]

A recent study by Joseph Fuchs, S.J., constitutes a kind of companion piece to O'Malley's essay.[5] Fuchs asks: In what sense are moral truths "truths of salvation"? The question arises because it has been traditionally stated by some authors[6] that the Church's moral teachings are truths of salvation. For this reason they are said to be the object of the charism of infallibility.

Fuchs argues that the term "moral truths" must be carefully distinguished. One level concerns the moral goodness of the person. This refers to the acceptance of God's enabling love into our persons, to a person's "being decided for God" (*optio fundamentalis*). In this sense "salvation is the moral *goodness* of the *person*, given by grace." We might call this the vertical dimension of moral truth. "Moral goodness is both effect and sign of the grace of salvation. What we can say about the moral goodness of the person is therefore a *truth of salvation*."[7]

Another level is the horizontal, the realization in concrete behavior of what is promotive for human persons. We refer to this as the rightness (or wrongness) of human conduct. This innerworldly activity we sometimes call "moral" rightness (or wrongness), but it is moral only in an analogous sense. That is, moral goodness contains an inclination, an intention, a goodwill, a readiness to do what is right. It is because of this relationship between personal goodness and material rightness that this rightness is called "moral." But this rightness is not directly and in itself concerned with personal moral goodness. Salvation (as in "truths of salvation"), therefore, does not have a direct relationship to right behavior, but to personal goodness. Concrete moral norms, therefore, are truths of salvation only in an analogous sense.

---

[4] In an interesting article Heinrich Fries touches on theology's responsibility to the magisterium. He notes that theology must have the courage to keep alive problems once consigned to silence: the admission of the divorced to the sacraments, *communicatio in sacris*, mixed marriage, celibacy, the place of women in the Church. "Theology," he insists, "must assume the suspicion and the objection of disturbing the peace occasionally. But the question is not one of disturbance but of responsibility in the community of believers. Calm [*Ruhe*] is by no means the primary Christian duty" ("Die Verantwortung des Theologen für die Kirche," *Stimmen der Zeit* 200 [1982] 245–58, at 255).

[5] Joseph Fuchs, S.J., "Sittliche Wahrheiten—Heilswahrheiten?" *Stimmen der Zeit* 200 (1982) 662–76.

[6] Thus G. Ermecke, "Die Bedeutung von 'Humanwissenschaften' für die Moraltheologie," *Münchener theologische Zeitschrift* 26 (1975) 126–40. Cf. also "Zur Bestimmung der Lage in der Moraltheologie," *ibid.* 30 (1979) 33–44, where the teaching of *Humanae vitae* is called "a truth of salvation that obliges under sin" (35).

[7] Fuchs, "Sittliche Wahrheiten" 665.

It is the failure to distinguish the pairs good-bad and right-wrong that has led to an uncritical notion of the Church's competence in moral matters. Fuchs argues that the widespread notion that the Church is equally competent in all moral questions is neither easily understandable nor founded on the text of the councils. What is the right way of acting in different areas of human life is determined by human experience, human evaluation, human judgment. "The Catholic lay people as Catholics, the priests as priests, the bishops and the pope as such do not have a specific Christian or ecclesiastical competence in regard to these matters."[8]

This does not mean that the pastors of the Church should not offer guidance on right-wrong activity. It merely suggests appropriate caution and tentativeness; for horizontal activity in this world does not belong to the Church's competence in the same way as the *depositum fidei*. In this sense we may say that the Church enjoys the assistance of the Spirit in offering concrete moral guidance, "but this assistance does not necessarily mean the specific assistance that, according to Vatican I and Vatican II, is promised to her and guarantees infallibility under certain conditions."[9]

Fuchs concludes that the formula "moral truths are truths of salvation" is unnuanced and runs the risk of oversacralizing the teaching office into a kind of "administrator of moral truths."

Fuch's study is important and much needed. There is still a deep-seated hankering in the Church to "infallibilize" the ordinary activity of the magisterium.[10] The ambiguity about the Church's competence is partly due to official statements themselves. They (Vatican I, II) speak in a very general way of the Church's competence in faith and morals. Vatican II clearly states the Church's competence on questions of natural moral law.[11] On the other hand, as Fuchs notes, infallibility is coextensive with the "deposit of divine revelation."[12] Furthermore, Vatican II noted

[8] Ibid. 670-71.
[9] Ibid. 673.
[10] Thus K. D. Whitehead states of past controversies: "What was better understood in the past, however, that is not so well understood today, is that when the teaching authority of the church stepped into these controversies to *decide* some aspect of them, any further 'dissent' from the points decided meant that one was henceforth placing oneself in the ranks of the heretics" (*New Oxford Review* 49, no. 8 [Oct. 1982] 26). To this the proper response is: what is better understood today is that Whitehead has fallen into serious theological error by lumping any dissent from a decision of Church authority with heresy. Moreover, such expansiveness only heaps ridicule on the teaching office of the Church. In the same category is the absolutely stunning hilarity delivered by Cardinal Luigi Ciappi that the absolution of a priest who disagrees publicly with *Humanae vitae* is invalid (*National Catholic Register*, Sept. 26, 1982).
[11] *Gaudium et spes*, no. 89.
[12] *Lumen gentium*, no. 25.

that "the Church guards the heritage of God's word and draws from it religious and moral principles, without always having at hand the solution to particular problems."[13] It further reminded lay persons to "not imagine that their pastors are always such experts that to every problem which arises, however complicated, they can readily give them a concrete solution, *or even that such is their mission.*"[14]

These and similar statements lead to the conclusion that the term "competence" when applied to the teaching office of the Church is an analogous term. The Church has a definite mission to provide concrete moral guidance; for "faith throws a new light on everything, manifests God's design for man's total vocation, and thus directs the mind to solutions which are fully human."[15] But this mission with regard to concrete moral guidance (rightness-wrongness) is not precisely and directly concerned with "truths of salvation" and hence is not buttressed by the certainty and stability such truths can rightly claim. This is clear from the history of moral teaching in the Church.

The point Fuchs is making is suggested in the Pauline corpus. For instance, in Galatians Paul refers to the good news that he has directly from the Lord. It is not "human knowledge." There are other matters that are indeed "human knowledge" (e.g., in 1 Cor 7, whether to live in virginity or not). The moral rightness-wrongness of concrete actions is in this latter category.[16]

This discussion takes a specific and practical turn in some recent documents of the magisterium. From the time of *Casti connubii* the term "intrinsic evil" is no stranger in official documents (e.g., *Persona humana, Humanae vitae*). While the term has a variety of possible understandings (e.g., intrinsic evil = *prohibitum quia malum*, not *malum quia prohibitum*), the most common contemporary understanding refers to actions judged morally wrong independently of further circumstances, consequences, or goals; for instance, speaking a falsehood, masturbation, use of contraceptive agents. It is obvious that discussion of this matter opens on the larger question of the moral norms that articulate such prohibitions.

A recent international conference approached some of these questions from a variety of viewpoints. Joseph Fuchs presents an excellent report on the state of the question.[17] Certain deontologically understood prohi-

[13] *Gaudium et spes*, no. 33.

[14] Ibid., no. 43, emphasis added.

[15] Ibid., no. 11. Cf. also J.-M. Aubert, "L'Objectivité de la morale chrétienne et la philosophie de l'être," *Revue des sciences religieuses* 56 (1982) 52–66.

[16] Fuchs pursues this extensively in his *Essere del Signore* (Rome: Gregorian Univ., 1981).

[17] Joseph Fuchs, S.J., " 'Intrinsece malum': Überlegungen zu einem umstrittenen Begriff," in Walter Kerber, ed., *Sittliche Normen: Zum Problem ihrer allgemeinen und unwandelbaren Geltung* (Düsseldorf: Patmos, 1982) 74–91.

bitions (e.g., speaking falsehoods) have been based on the nature of the acts and their violations called "intrinsic evils." Fuchs, with Schüller earlier,[18] rejects this as failing to distinguish between the creative will and the moral will of God. One cannot conclude an "ought" from such psychological or biological givens, even though they must be considered.[19] Others have been grounded on a lack of right (ex defectu juris). For instance, with regard to human life, it is asserted that God alone is the Lord of life. But from such statements, Fuchs argues, one can conclude only that arbitrary disposal of human life is excluded. One cannot derive a deontologically understood intrinsic evil.

The discussion of intrinsic evil necessarily brings into play the distinction between premoral and moral evil. Moral evil refers to those evils that render the person as a whole bad: e.g., the desire of and will to injustice or unchastity. But such evils do not tell us what concrete acts count as injustice or unchastity. That is, they do not tell us what concrete acts are morally right or wrong. Premoral evils do not touch directly the moral goodness of the person, but only the person's well-being. But they are relevant to moral goodness. How? The morally good person will avoid causing them unless there is a correspondingly serious reason. Fuchs emphasizes the fact that no premoral evils or goods are absolute. Therefore they cannot be the grounds for intrinsic evils as this term is commonly understood.

Fuchs concludes with three summary assertions. First, norms touching personal goodness are not in question in the discussion of intrinsic evil. Clearly, actions that render a person bad are intrinsically evil. Second, the discussion concerns only moral rightness and wrongness. In this area it is much more intelligible and defensible to understand norms as stating "prima-facie duties" or as binding ut in pluribus. Finally, one can speak of intrinsic evil only in instances where the action is fully and exhaustively defined with all of its morally relevant elements (with its object, circumstances, goals, consequences). For instance, it is morally wrong to kill a person only to provide pleasure to a third party.

The rest of the essays in this study share the general teleological direction of Fuchs's thought, without the concentration on the notion of intrinsic evil.[20]

This development has not gone unchallenged. In a long study Servais

---

[18] Bruno Schüller, S.J., "Neuere Beiträge zum Thema 'Begründung sittlicher Normen,'" in Theologische Berichte 4 (Einsiedeln: Benziger, 1974) 145–46.

[19] This point is also made by Hubert Windisch. Cf. n. 36 below.

[20] Authors include Franz (Lucern), Karl Hörmann (Vienna), Wilhelm Ernst (Erfurt), Walter Kerber (Munich), Heinz Schürmann (Erfurt), Alfons Riedl (Linz), and the compositor of these "Notes."

Pinckaers, O.P., passes in review what he calls "proportionalism."[21] He uses especially the writings of Knauer and Louis Janssens as his show-pieces, but basically he includes in his analysis all "proportionalists" and mentions specifically Fuchs, Schüller, and this author. One of the basic critiques these "novateurs" make is against the idea of acts and effects evil in themselves as often understood, and therefore against the tradi-tional principle of the double effect. That being the case, what remains of the double-effect principle is the last requirement (*ratio proportionata*). Pinckaers sees this as a "kind of revolution at the very heart of post-Tridentine morality." It means, Pinckaers mistakenly states, that "there are no acts intrinsically evil, or evil in themselves, absolutely."[22] In contemporary philosophical language the authors Pinckaers engages are, he says, teleologists. For them moral laws bind only *ut in pluribus* and he believes that this "establishes a practical separation between the order of concrete norms and the order of virtues," practically excluding the theological and moral virtues from the moral life. This he sees as the reduction of morality to laws and obligations, and its divorce from any nourishing influence by the Scriptures.

Pinckaers finally lists three essential points where he faults "propor-tionalists": the notion of finality, objectivity, and the relation to revela-tion. As for finality, Pinckaers asserts that "proportionalists" reduce all values to that which is useful to the end. True moral finality is determined by the nature of things, some of which (e.g., human persons) are ends in themselves that can never be reduced to means. Moreover, God is the ultimate end, a finality very different from the "technical" finality one finds in teleological writing. Teleologists reduce the *honestum* to the *utile* and thus compromise the objectivity of true moral finality.

As for objectivity, Pinckaers continues his veritable onslaught by objecting to the terms "ontic" and "premoral." After all, health "is already moral in itself by the fact that it is the health of a person." Similarly, taking the life of a person is not just "premoral and neutral." It is the very moral nature of goods, established by their relation to the human person, that grounds the objectivity of the moral order. To see such goods as "simply premoral" is to destroy the objectivity of the moral order.

[21] Servais Pinckaers, O.P., "La question des actes intrinsèquement mauvais et le 'pro-portionalisme,'" *Revue thomiste* 82 (1982) 181–212.

[22] Pinckaers' statement is too broad, as is clear from Fuchs's essay reviewed above. He should have added, as I did above, "as often understood." There are many acts that could be called "intrinsically evil" if their circumstances are exhaustively included in the descrip-tion of the actions. I have similar problems with the essay by John Hill, "The Debate between Frankena and McCormick," *Irish Theological Quarterly* 49 (1982) 121–33.

Finally, "proportionalists" reduce morality to a purely natural and rational exercise with no room for the gospel. This further isolates morality from exegesis, dogmatic theology, and patristics, and puts the theological virtues at the margin of the moral life without any real operative influence.

It is difficult to know where to begin in commenting on this seriously flawed article. Key concepts are repeatedly misunderstood and misrepresented. Let just a few examples suffice. Item: Pinckaers states that the principle of finality in the writing he criticizes relativizes all intangible and stable values.[23] What this means I have no idea; for the discussion is not about "intangible and stable values." At any rate, I recognize this in none of the writings he cites.

Item: the author asserts that persons are to be loved for themselves and are never to be used as means—as if his adversaries held the contrary. He seems unaware that the Kantian maxim is largely parenetic, as Schüller has shown,[24] and does not tell us what it means to treat a person as a means only.

Item: Pinckaers contrasts the "technical finality" asserted by "proportionalists" with true moral finality, which involves a conscious and voluntary tending toward God as one's final end—as if these were somehow competitive and mutually exclusive.

Item: he asserts that one is on the moral level only when one "detaches oneself from the useful"—as if what is useful for persons had nothing to do with morality. Here, as elsewhere, Pinckaers mysteriously fails to distinguish *benevolentia* and *beneficentia*. Of course there is a priority of the *honestum* over the *utile*; but that is not the question. The question raised by the authors he critiques is: What *utile* (concretely) does the *honestum* require of us?

Item: Pinckaers misunderstands the notion of premoral (nonmoral, ontic) evil and good. He states of health that it is "already moral in itself from the fact that it is the health of a person." Also, of human life he states that it is "already in itself a moral object that as such provokes in one moral sentiments and responses." Of course it does; no one denies this. Indeed, it is clearly asserted by Fuchs, Janssens, Schüller, and others. But this is not what is meant by saying that certain evils or goods are premoral. Being a "moral object" says nothing about the rightness or wrongness of concrete responses to such an object. Similarly, no author I know of would identify premoral with neutral as Pinckaers does.

Item: Pinckaers accuses "proportionalists" of failing to accord to the

[23] Pinckaers, "La question" 198.
[24] Bruno Schüller, S.J., "Die Personwürde des Menschen als Beweisgrund in der normativen Ethik," *Theologie und Glaube* 53 (1978) 538–55.

virtues (including the theological) any real significance in moral judgment. This, he says, is the result of the separation of concrete norms from the virtues. Here he fails to realize that "proportionalists" are dealing with a different problem, one he fails even to recognize.

Item: Pinckaers asserts that "proportionalists" locate morality on a purely natural level and that the gospel is only a kind of afterthought "injection."

I could continue this chronicle almost endlessly. But nothing is achieved by that. There is a single error which seems to me to provide the clue to Pinckaers' misunderstandings and which reduces his study to an example of a common error, *ignorantia elenchi* (missing the point). He fails to distinguish the pairs good-bad, right-wrong. Never in his study does he mention this latter pair. The moral life is absorbed into goodness-badness (involving intention, inclination, goodwill, etc.). However, the entire discussion of moral norms is concerned with the moral rightness or wrongness of our concrete conduct. To miss this point is to fail to understand the issue.

This failure is responsible for Pinckaers' mistaken assertion that agape is not functional in "proportionalist" thought. Agape is simply not the issue under discussion. It is responsible for his misleading assertion that faith and the gospel must have first place in Christian morality. Of course they must; but that is not the issue. The question is: What do the faith and the gospel concretely demand of followers of Christ, and not merely in terms of sentiments and desires? The answer to that is a question of rightness and wrongness. Nowhere does Pinckaers address this serious question. Or better, he seems to think he can solve it by parenesis.

This single error is responsible for Pinckaers' erroneous idea that "proportionalists" reduce the moral life ("pour l'essential") to the rational level and to external acts. It explains why he can accuse Louis Janssens of neglecting interiority, "where St. Thomas places the source of morality." His moral categories are good-bad, these only. But these categories, as Fuchs (with many others) has repeatedly emphasized, apply to the person as a whole. A good person will strive to perform right actions. But what makes a person good does not enlighten the criterion for what makes an action right or wrong. Not making this distinction, Pinckaers has only confused the entire discussion of intrinsic evil and the theological foundation of norms.

I respectfully invite my friend and colleague to discuss in detail when abortion is justified and why, whether nuclear deterrence is morally tolerable and why, whether *in vitro* fertilization is justifiable and why, whether business bribes can sometimes be justified. When he does this in a disciplined way, he will be discussing the rightness and wrongness of human conduct, not the goodness or badness of intentions, desires, dispositions. He would not be discussing the interiority of the moral life, the primacy of charity, or the person as a moral object—unless he chose to remain at the level of parenesis. He will move from exhortation to moral argument. He will then see that "proportionalists" are not "elaborating their conception of morality in a way that blocks any real and living contact with Scripture." To discuss concrete moral norms is not to discuss a "conception of morality." It is much more modest. Pinckaers' authors are but dialoguing with their own tradition on a relatively narrow issue. St. Thomas noted: "God is not offended by us except when we act against our own good."[25] Deciding at a very concrete level of interhuman relationships what is "against our own good" is the question of the rightness or wrongness of human action. To miss this is to miss the point of the discussion.

M. Zalba, S.J., presents a more accurate picture of what many theologians have been writing.[26] He reviews the "principle of compromise" proposed by Charles Curran and finds it Protestant at root. When dealing with intrinsically evil acts, Zalba notes that many theologians regard interventions such as sterilization as premoral or ontic evils.

His response to this is interesting. He believes that this is a gratuitous assertion. It supposes that killing, speaking falsehoods, taking another's property, sterilization are premoral and get their moral character from a supervening intention. But this is not so, says Zalba. These actions never occur in the abstract.

These actions... are concerned with a concrete person, either innocent or not... with regard to goods which the neighbor rightly protects as his own or not, with regard to truth to which the hearer has a right or not.... Therefore any intervention against innocent life, against legitimate private possessions, against fidelity (in speech) owed to one's conversation partner, against the generative faculty *as such*, freely actuated (not as a member—e.g., cancerous— subordinate in the subject to the principle of totality) is fundamentally always immoral by reason of the object.[27]

Now what has Zalba done here? He has introduced into the object the very moral qualifiers (circumstances) that make the action morally wrong (e.g., the truth *to which the hearer has a right*; *innocent* life). And that is the problem with speaking about things intrinsically evil *ex objecto* as these terms are often used. These qualifiers were introduced over the

[25] "Non enim Deus a nobis offenditur nisi ex eo quod contra nostrum bonum agimus" (*Summa contra gentes* 3, 122).

[26] Marcelino Zalba, S.J., "Principia ethica in crisim vocata intra (propter?) crisim morum," *Periodica* 71 (1982) 25–63, 319–57.

[27] Ibid. 40.

years for obviously teleological reasons. Otherwise any falsehood would constitute a lie, any killing a murder. Therefore, far from negating the teleological reasoning that leads theologians to distinguish premoral (ontic) evil from moral evil, these examples rather confirm and strengthen the distinction.[28] Of course actions always occur with regard to concrete persons. But that did not prevent Thomas from distinguishing *homicidium* (always wrong) from *occisio hominis* ("aliquando liceat").[29] Indeed, Thomas referred to actions "absolutely considered" as having a deformity but being justified in certain circumstances ("aliquibus circumstantiis advenientibus bonae efficiuntur").[30] This is exactly what the terms nonmoral, premoral, ontic are meant to convey when applied to killing, falsehood, etc. My question to Zalba, then, is: If such a distinction (between *occisio hominis* and *homicidium*) is legitimate where life, the most basic of human values, is concerned, must it not be also where less urgent values are concerned? Or may we sometimes take life but never the physical integrity of sexual intercourse?[31]

This question is raised clearly and precisely in an excellent study by N. Hendricks, O.S.B.[32] He approaches the matter from a slightly different point of view: the very meaning of "intrinsece inhonestum" and the doctrine of double effect. He reviews the manualist teaching on the conflict of duties (better, conflict of values). In a conflict of values, one should choose the more important, or the lesser evil.[33] Hendricks correctly notes that the manualist tradition solved these conflicts in a teleological manner, "that is, by means of a comparison of values in conflict, or, in other words, in terms of the effects that the act or omission would produce."[34] However, this teleological solution was limited by the principle that a good end does not justify an evil means. Thus, if the conflict involved an act with a double effect, the evil effect had to be indirect.

---

[28] Zalba himself refers to particular situations "in quibus ipsius normae applicatio esset nociva propter circumstantias particulares" (32). Here exceptions are justified because failure to make the exceptions would be "nociva." Similarly, he refers to "libertatem ab urgentia legis propter incommodum illius momento proportionatum." The only thing that separates such phrases from Fuchs, Janssens, Schüller, and others is Zalba's refusal to apply it in the sexual sphere (contraception), a refusal I do not believe he has persuasively argued in this study.

[29] *Quodl.* 8, a. 14.

[30] *Quodl.* 9, a. 15.

[31] Zalba's study is chiefly concerned with defending the teaching of *Humanae vitae* on the intrinsically evil character of contraception.

[32] N. Hendricks, O.S.B., "La contraception artificielle: Conflit de devoirs ou acte à double effet," *Nouvelle revue théologique* 104 (1982) 396–413.

[33] Thus Noldin-Schmitt: "Regulae ad solvendam collisionem. Supremum in hac re principium est: Praevalet obligatio oriens ex lege quae spectata natura et fine maioris momenti est" *Summa theologiae moralis* 1 [Regensburg: Pustet, 1931[21]] 203).

[34] Hendricks, "La contraception" 401.

He then applies this to contraception, noting that it is in a sense an action with a double effect (prevention of conception, physical expression of love). Since it has such a twofold effect, one cannot simply apply the lesser-evil principle but must also apply double effect. Concretely, the contraceptive effect is justified only when it is indirect, and not the means to the end. So much for the traditional understanding.

Hendricks then turns to the usage "intrinsece inhonestum." Certain manuals understand this to mean *ex natura sua* in contrast to *ex lege positiva*. In this sense, to kill a person is "intrinsically evil" because it is not an evil simply by positive law. But it is not necessarily at all times a *moral* evil. In the tradition, if it occurred indirectly it was not a moral evil. Thus "intrinsically evil" is not the same as "morally evil."

Hendricks argues that *Humanae vitae* uses "intrinsic evil" in this sense, since it speaks of "suapta natura" (no. 13) and "ex propria natura" (no. 14). Thus contraception can remain "intrinsically evil" but morally licit if indirect (as in some sterilizing interventions). However, it is precisely here that the problem with *Humanae vitae* occurs. All traditional moralists consider some acts that are evil *ex natura sua* (in this sense "intrinsically") to be justified even though they are means to an end.[35] Hendricks offers as an example the harming of a donor in an organ transplant. This makes the assertion that direct contraception is always a *moral* evil very problematic.

Hendricks has stated the problem of the notion of "intrinsic evil" and the double effect very well.[36] The principle of double effect is a necessary

---

[35] Cf. J. Aertnys–C. Damen–J. Visser, *Theologia moralis* 1 (Turin: Marietti, 1967[18]) 88: "Sic ablatio rei alienae, homicidium, famae laesio, sunt intrinsece mala; aliquando tamen licita evadunt." Thus also M. Brunec, "Mendacium—intrinsece malum—sed non absolute," *Salesianum* 26 (1964) 659–60: "Laesio integritatis corporalis, e.g., supponitur in theologia morali esse actio intrinsece mala. Nihilo minus omnes moralistae admittunt liceitatem occisionis aggressoris in casu justae defensionis; admittunt liceitatem operationis chirurgicae qua aufertur aliqua pars corporis, quando haec ablatio necessaria esse videtur ad conservationem vitae."

[36] He notes that even if one concludes that direct deprivation of procreativity is only a nonmoral evil, there still remains the argument about the inseparability of the two senses of sexual intimacy (unitive, procreative). Two points. First, what kind of evil would such a separation constitute? The logic of Hendricks' presentation (as well as previous writing) would suggest that the evil is premoral. Second, *Humanae vitae* itself contains what appears to be an inconsistency. Of infertile acts it states (no. 11) that they are legitimate "since their ordering (*destinatio*) toward the expression and strengthening of the union of the spouses does not cease." The rather clear implication is that any *destinatio ad procreationem* ceases. Otherwise why did the encyclical not say "since their ordering toward procreation does not cease"? The unstated but obvious reason is that any *destinatio ad procreationem* is absent in infertile acts. If it is absent, clearly the unitive and procreative dimensions are most often separated. This point is sharply made by Hubert Windisch. He argues that the message of *Humanae vitae* and *Familiaris consortio* is prophetic in the sense that it discloses a future state of affairs more becoming to human persons but not necessarily possible for

conflict-solvent only if certain actions are intrinsically evil (= *morally* evil). But (1) if that term means rather *ex natura sua* and (2) if other actions are said to be intrinsically evil (= *ex natura sua*, not *ex lege positiva*) but still justified at times, then the double-effect principle is no longer necessary. I think Hendricks is right and his logic impeccable.

Fernando Citterio presents a long review essay of recent developments in Catholic moral theology.[37] He concentrates especially on the work of Fuchs, Knauer, Schüller, and Scholz. Much of this material has been reviewed previously in these "Notes." Citterio is not persuaded by these "novatori," as he calls them.[38] For instance, where Fuchs's thesis is concerned (denial of *intrinsece malum* in the traditional sense), he believes that this denies "the proper structure of an action." As for Schüller and Knauer, he is not convinced that an evaluation of the consequences of an action can be the determining element of the moral character of the act. He also believes that in such teleological theories far too much power ("potestà illimitata") is conceded to human beings.

---

all now. Prophecy and norm are not identical. Prophetic statements open new horizons. They urge people not to settle for what is possible now. The difference between NFP and other (nonabortifacient) methods is morally *significant* but not morally decisive. Windisch regards no. 32 of *Familiaris consortio* (which condemns the separation of the unitive and procreative in artificial methods but denies that it occurs in NFP) as unintelligible ("unverständlich"), because there is such a separation in NFP. Three elements must be considered in assessing the ethical character of birth regulation: the intention, the method, the circuumstances (479). Individually, these elements in themselves are premoral or "morally meaningful" but not decisive. Cf. "Prophetische Moral: Moraltheologische Anmerkungen zu lehramtlichen Aussagen über Empfängnisverhütung," *Stimmen der Zeit* 200 (1982) 473–82. A similar point was made by John Wright, S.J., as reviewed in these "Notes" last year (TS 43 [1982] 74) and by this author (cf. ibid. 75–76).—In a similar vein Patrick Verspieren, S.J., gives cautious approval to *in vitro* fertilization even though it involves separation of the unitive and procreative in the sense rejected by *Familiaris consortio*. Of this separation he says that "it represents an intrusion (regrettable from certain points of view) of technology into the domain of profound intimacy. . . ." It is clear that Verspieren would regard this as a nonmoral evil, and the action morally wrong only if it involved "insémination artificielle intra-conjugale mise en oeuvre sans raison proportionée" ("L'Aventure de la fécondation in vitro," *Etudes*, Nov. 1982, 479–92, at 482). Cf. also J. G. Ziegler, "Extrakorporale Befruchtung: Ein moraltheologischer Beitrag," *Theologie der Gegenwart* 25 (1982) 254–60. Ziegler sees such a separation as justified by the principle of totality. Cf. also Jörg Splett, "Natur: Norm oder Prinzip? Philosophische Überlegungen zu einer personal verantworteten Sexualität," *Lebendiges Zeugnis* 37 (1982) 58–72, at 68–69.

[37] Ferdinando Citterio, "La revisione critica dei tradizionali principi morali alle luce della teoria del 'compromesso etico,' " *Scuola cattolica* 110 (1982) 29–64.

[38] Two points. Citterio states (46) that the "novatori" declare moral the "Caiphas principle" whereby it would be permissible to kill one innocent person to prevent the unjust slaughter of many more. One of his references is to my 'Il principio del duplice effeto," *Concilium* 120 (1976) 129–49. In that article I reject the "Caiphas principle" (146). Second, Citterio continually supports his assertions by ample quotations from traditionalist critics without citing the many responses made to them.

But his basic reservation is that this analytic development downplays the importance of the object.

This discussion is almost stalemated by now. It is growing repetitious, arid, and fruitless, especially so when carefully crafted positions are summarily dismissed with terms such as "consequentialism" and "proportionalism" (cf. Finnis, Grisez, and now Pinckaers). One has to wonder why. Is there a term (or terms) that is being used but is variously understood by the participants? Is there somewhere a fundamental misunderstanding that could dissolve the standoff? Has the whole question been misstated? I am not sure, but let me make a stab at clarification here. The attempt brings together the notions of consequence, object of the act, and intrinsic evil.

I detect an ambiguity in the literature about the meaning of the term "consequences of the act." This ambiguity affects one's notion of the terminology "premoral" and "ontic" as well as one's notion of the object of an act. The term "consequence" can refer to the immediate implications of our activity, or to later-on effects, as William Van der Marck has noted.[39] Those who oppose contemporary teleological tendencies interpret the term "consequence" as later-on effects of an action one performs here and now. Thus they argue that teleologists must hold that one may perform morally wrong actions to achieve a good end. For example, an abortion now could be justified because it will later spare the family the crushing price of an additional college education.

Those who espouse teleological tendencies most often interpret the term "consequence" as applying to the immediate intersubjective implications of an action. Thus, by "consequence" they mean that the physical reality of killing (death = consequence) can be, as intersubjective reality, murder, waging war, self-defense, the death penalty, or resisting insurrection, depending on the circumstances, especially depending on the reason (ratio) for which the act is done. Taking something from another can be intersubjectively stealing, borrowing, satisfying dire need, or repossessing one's property.

The teleologist's contention is that too often the meaning of an action is identified with a single form of intersubjectivity; then all actions sharing similar generic features are called by the same name, regardless of the reason for which they are done. For instance, Persona humana states (of masturbation) that "whatever the motive for acting in this way, deliberate use of the sexual faculty outside normal conjugal relations essentially contradicts the finality of the faculty."[40]

[39] William Van der Marck, Toward a Christian Ethic (New York: Newman, 1967).
[40] The Pope Speaks 21 (1976) 60–73.

In this reductionist *Denkform* every killing would be a murder, even killing in self-defense or in a just war. If, however, every killing is not murder, but occasionally can find moral justification, then that means that the immediate implications of the action (consequence)—the reason the act was performed—are different, and this difference makes a different action, a different object.[41] Before this difference, this *ratio*, is considered, there is no final moral character of the action, because there is no human action as yet. Thus one may refer to the generic features (killing) as premoral or nonmoral. This is utterly traditional. Otherwise, how could Thomas say that not every *occisio* constitutes *homicidium*, even though abstractly considered it remains a "difformity"?

The distinction, then, between consequence as immediate implication (*ratio*) and as later-on effect seems very important. For instance, it is sometimes popularly but simplistically stated that the teleologist judges actions by their consequences, but that the deontologist prescinds from them. But that is false, because it is impossible to define an action independently of its consequences (understood as immediate implications). "To act" means intentionally to bring into being certain effects, or to refrain from doing so. If we prescind from effects, we can no longer speak of an action. In this sense everyone judges actions by their consequences.

In this light the concern of some traditional theologians that revisionist thought would do away with the notion of the object of an act and lead to extrinsicism is misplaced. It is, I believe, not so much a matter of abandoning this notion; it is much more a matter of what is to determine the object of an action. It is the contention of many of us that the traditional understanding (e.g., as in *Persona humana*) of this term excludes elements essential to the very meaning of the action (consequences in the sense of immediate implications) and narrows the significance to physical realities, the *materia circa quam*. Knauer, Fuchs, and others have insisted on this for many years, and it is one of the emphases

---

[41] Jacques Maritain notes: "The moral law must never be given up, we must fasten on to it all the more as the social or political environment becomes more perverted or criminal. But the moral nature or specification, the moral *object* of the same physical acts, changes when the situation to which they pertain becomes so different that the inner relation of the will to the thing done becomes itself typically different. In our civilized societies it is not murder, it is a meritorious deed for a fighting man to kill an enemy soldier in a just war. In utterly barbarized societies like a concentration camp, or even in quite particular conditions like those of clandestine resistance in an occupied country, many things which were, as to their moral nature, objectively fraud or murder or perfidy in ordinary civilized life cease, now, to come under the same definition and become, as to their moral nature, objectively permissible or ethical things" (*Man and the State* [Chicago: Univ. of Chicago, 1952] 73).

underscored in a recent review of these discussions by Philip S. Keane, S.S.[42]

It is the great merit of Hendricks' essay to state this problem with utter clarity where the term "intrinsic evil" is applied to an action or its object. Essentially Hendricks makes three moves. (1) He shows that in traditional thought (Pius XII) a contraceptive effect is regarded as intrinsically evil but can be justified, but only when indirect. Therefore this effect cannot be called a moral evil. (2) He shows that in traditional teaching certain other actions considered intrinsically evil (that is, *ex natura sua*, not *ex lege positiva*) may occasionally be justified even though directly done. The evil caused in such actions must also be called nonmoral or premoral. (3) Therefore he raises the absolutely unavoidable question: Why is this not true of all actions said to be intrinsically evil? If certain areas are excepted from this analysis, it must be for special reasons. But it has been shown that the reasons traditionally adduced are not sound arguments. In other words, the tradition itself, if we are to be consistent with it, calls for the adjustments Hendricks suggests.

What Hendricks is arguing, and in my judgment has established, is that when there is a different *ratio* (immediate implication or consequence) for performing the action, then that action is different. It has a different object, to use traditional terminology. That means that the sharp contrast Citterio and others are trying to establish between teleology (in the sense explained) and morality *ex objecto* simply does not exist; for it is precisely teleological considerations that tell us what the object is.

Does this clarify matters? I shall await the reactions of my kind and gracious critics.[43]

---

[42] Philip S. Keane, S.S., "The Objective Moral Order; Reflections on Recent Research," *TS* 43 (1982) 260–78.

[43] Further interesting literature in the area of general moral theology would include: L. P. Gillon, O.P., "Charité et amour universel de l'être," *Angelicum* 59 (1982) 37–44; Peter H. Van Ness, "Christian Freedom and Ethical Inquiry," *Calvin Theological Journal* 17 (1982) 26–52; Theodore R. Jungkuntz, "Trinitarian Ethics," *Center Journal* 1 (1982) 39–52; Douglas A. Knight, "Old Testament Ethics," *Christian Century* 99 (1982) 55–59; Günter Virt, "Epikie—ein dynamisches Prinzip der Gerechtigkeit," *Diakonia* 13 (1982) 241–47; Dietmar Mieth, "Brauchen wir Gott für die Moral?" *Freiburger Zeitschrift für Philosophie und Theologie* 29 (1982) 210–22; Wilhelm Ernst, "Gewissen in katholischer Sicht," *Internationale katholische Zeitschrift* 11 (1982) 153–71; *Journal of Ecumenical Studies* 19 (1982) 1–267, the whole issue being on authority in the Church; Edward V. Vacek, S.J., "Scheler's Phenomenology of Love," *Journal of Religion* 62 (1982) 156–77; Robert L. Hurd, "The Concept of Freedom in Rahner," *Listening* 17 (1982) 138–52; Josef Blank, "Aspekte des Bösen," *Orientierung* 46 (1982) 44–47; François Marty, "Loi universelle et action dans le monde sensible: L'Universel et le particulier dans la morale de Kant," *Recherches de science religieuse* 70 (1982) 39–58; Jean Remy, "Sociologie de la morale," *Recherches de science*

MORAL REASONING AND STORYTELLING

The intense concern of the past decade with moral norms and their grounding can lead to a one-sided view of the moral-spiritual life and to a one-dimensional perspective on moral reasoning. For this reason three essays that address this subject are both timely and extremely interesting. Ronald Green examines Genesis 22 in Soren Kierkegaard and rabbinic writings.[44] Kierkegaard had claimed that the biblical episode of Abraham's near-sacrifice of Isaac represents a kind of suspension of the ethical. There is a chasm between Abraham's conduct and any possible justification of it. That is, it is antirational.

Green surveys a variety of classical Jewish sources and concludes that Kierkegaard's interpretation has almost no resonance within the Jewish tradition. Rather than involving a suspension of the ethical, this episode is viewed by Jewish writers as involving a moment of supreme moral responsibility on the part of both God and man. It is the lesson of obedient self-sacrifice, not an enjoined violation of the ethical. Green notes that this midrashic treatment of the biblical episode points up a central fact about the Jewish tradition: although the Jewish ethical tradition is unquestionably based on the divine command, it is also a tradition of reason and human autonomy. If Jews have regarded God's commands as absolute, they have also found it unthinkable that they would ultimately defy our sense of right and wrong. Reason and revelation cannot disagree.

Daniel Maguire treats practical moral reason from a Catholic point of view.[45] It is Maguire's thesis that there is an "intellectualistic fallacy" rampant in contemporary ethical deliberation, an analytical and rationalistic approach that assumes that morality becomes intelligible in the same way that mathematics and logic do.

Maguire first shows that *ratio practica* in St. Thomas is profoundly shaped by an affective component. While Thomas did not systematize this notion, it is undeniably present in many of his treatises: on prudence, wisdom, the gifts of the Holy Spirit, delight, and faith. For example, where prudence is concerned, that virtue perfects reason by being conjoined with the moral virtues. But the moral virtues attune a person to the morally good so that it becomes connatural to judge correctly about

---

religieuse 70 (1982) 75–108; Joseph Moingt, "Moralité de la morale," *ibid.* 195–212; Douglas Sturm, "Two Decades of Moral Theology: Charles E. Curran as Agent of Aggiornamento," *Religious Studies Review* 8 (1982) 116–24; Helmut Weber, "Eine neue Wende in der Wertung des Gewissens?" *Trierer theologische Zeitschrift* 91 (1982) 18–33.

[44] Ronald Green, "Abraham, Isaac, and the Jewish Tradition: An Ethical Reappraisal," *Journal of Religious Ethics* 10 (1982) 1–21.

[45] Daniel C. Maguire, "*Ratio practica* and the Intellectualistic Fallacy," ibid. 22–39.

the good. This connaturalizing effect of virtue affects the manner of knowing and perceiving the good. "The way of knowing is affectively qualified." This same is true of the gift of wisdom, which has its essence in the intellect but its cause in the will, so that the resultant knowledge involves a kind of tasting. Or again, where delight is concerned, its first effect is a broadening or expansion of the soul. This results in a heightening of the awareness of the good. As Maguire words it, "the good delighted in is experienced more expansively and thus is better known."

After showing that the affective component in moral knowledge is more explicit and systematized in John of St. Thomas, Maguire presents his own formulation of the matter. How do we know that promises ought to be kept? He rejects as inadequate a host of answers given to such questions (noncognitive answers, naked rationalism, custom, the promotion of survival). Maguire argues that moral knowledge is born in the awe and affectivity that characterize "the foundational moral experience"—the experience of the value of persons and their environment. This experience is not the conclusion of a syllogism, even though it can be supported by human reasoning. Maguire points out in illuminating ways how this knowledge differs from metaphysical and mathematical abstractions. For instance, it is partitionable ("experienced, but then barbarically limited to one's own tribe"), universal ("universally available to all persons"), but constantly in process of growth or recession. It is specially related to faith, mysticism, and religious awareness. Thus Maguire notes that the fundamental moral experience is not complete in its intelligibility "unless a deeper Preciousness underlies the preciousness that gives birth to moral awareness." In this sense ethics is naturally religious. This fine study concludes with the assertion that we can know much of what is right and wrong but that we should be a bit more modest about the claims of reason.

Maguire's insistence on the affective shaping of moral knowledge is certainly correct. It suggests many things. One thing I want to highlight is the expansive and deepening role of affect in moral knowledge. From the Christian point of view, faith creates sensitivities in the believer beyond the reach of natural vitalities. It bestows sensitivity to dimensions of possibility not otherwise suspected, or what Thomas Clarke, S.J., refers to as "distinctive habits of perception and response."[46] This is no call to a new obscurantism, nor is it an invitation to authority to press unsupportable claims. It is simply an acknowledgment of the depth and beauty of the spiritual life, the complexity of reality, and therefore of the many-faceted ways of discovering moral truth. Or, as Maguire nicely

---

[46] Thomas E. Clarke, S.J., "Touching in Power: Our Health System," in *Above Every Name* (New Jersey: Paulist, 1980) 252.

words it, "Through love the person is rendered more subtle and open to knowledge of things divine and created." This should paradoxically make the theologian both more tentative and more confident: more tentative because he/she knows the depths of love still to be achieved; more confident because he/she knows that this achievement is, thank God, not entirely or chiefly our own doing.

John Howard Yoder presents a different perspective on practical moral reasoning.[47] It is not so much a matter of asking how ideas work but how the community works. Therefore he enumerates the functions of the community that have an immediate and irreplaceable contribution to make to practical moral reasoning.

First, the community will have "agents of direction," a term Yoder uses to describe prophecy (a statement of the place of the believing community in history). Next, the community will be aided by "agents of memory" who bring from the storehouse of tradition the memorable and identity-confirming acts of faithfulness and failure. Third, the community will be guided by "agents of linguistic self-consciousness"—teachers or *didaskaloi*. Yoder has some edifying things to say about such persons. For example, the teacher "will scrutinize openmindedly, but sceptically, typologies that dichotomize the complementary and formulae that reconcile the incompatible." They will resist the tyranny of language, and because few of us do that teachers ought to be few in number. Fourth, the community will be guided by "agents of order and due process." These are the overseers (bishops) whose task is to enable the open conversational process, to make sure that all are heard.

Having stated the importance of community as the context for moral reasoning, Yoder next specifies the distinctive way such a community will go about moral analysis. The first characteristic he highlights is shared decision-making. In this process the teacher will teach the community the pitfalls of methodological dichotomies (e.g., duty vs. utility) and insist that "every decision includes elements of principle, elements of character and due process, and elements of utility."

Yoder then engages Daniel Maguire. Yoder agrees with Maguire's conclusion about affectivity in moral knowledge but argues that the importance of this emphasis is that it better highlights how moral personality is formed, that is, in community. The intellectualistic fallacy Maguire had attacked becomes possible by abstracting from community.

Yoder concludes with a statement of ethical perspective which we have learned to associate with him, especially distrust of ethical approaches that appeal to commonly knowable and broadly shared values. "Practical

---

[47] John H. Yoder, "The Hermeneutics of Peoplehood: A Protestant Perspective on Practical Moral Reasoning," *Journal of Religious Ethics* 10 (1982) 40–67.

moral reasoning, if Christian, must always be expected to be at some point subversive. Any approach which trusts the common wisdom enough to make specifically subversive decisions unthinkable has thereby forfeited its claim to be adequate." Yoder argues that the search for a public moral language "is motivated ... by embarrassment about particularity." When we focus on the generalizability of ethical demands, we forget that "we confess as Lord and Christ the man Jesus." To abstract from this particularity to get at the general is a denial of faith.

Yoder's great emphasis on community as the conveyor of ethics leads naturally to a consideration of the place of narrative in moral theology; for a community is defined and specified by its story. The importance of story to ethics has become synonymous with the name of Stanley Hauerwas, most notably in his acclaimed book *A Community of Character*.[48] In a recent study Hauerwas argues that the renovation of moral theology called for by Vatican II has not occurred because of a lack of appreciation for the narrative character of Christian ethical reflection.[49] Rather, the new "liberal" moral theologians continue to use the basic natural-law methodology of Neo-Scholasticism but with the language of "human experience." This methodology of "universalistic laws," desires, tendencies fails to take as fundamental the community and thus its narrative context. This failure leads to a failure in pastoral practice.

Hauerwas then points out the direction of a true Christian ethic. Narratives are essential for our understanding of God, ourselves, and the world. The central claim of Christian ethics is that we know ourselves truthfully only when we know ourselves in relation to God. Our participation in God's life is a participation in the history He creates, His story. And that story is particularistic, that is, it deals with Israel, Jesus, and the ingathering of disciples we name the Church. "Christian ethics is, therefore, not an ethic based on universal presuppositions that can be known separate from these particular peoples' tradition." Rather, it is "the discipline that attempts to remind us of the kind of skills, linguistic, conceptual and practical that are necessary to be such a people."

In this perspective Christian ethics is not primarily concerned with doing. "Its first task is to help us rightly see the world" with Jesus (his life, death, and resurrection) as central to its meaning. This seeing is not just looking but involves our personal initiation into the narrative, learning to grow in that story.

[48] A recent study, which owes much to Hauerwas and Alasdair MacIntyre, is Harold Alderman's "By Virtue of a Virtue," *Review of Metaphysics* 36 (1982) 127–53. Alderman argues that the ultimate moral appeal should not be rights, goods, or rules but the "character of the paradigmatic individual."

[49] Stanley Hauerwas, "Story: Ethics and the Pastoral Task," *Chicago Studies* 21 (1982) 59–71. The entire issue is devoted to the place of narrative in a variety of contexts.

How does this perspective affect practical problem-solving? Hauerwas insists that its effect should be to direct our attention away from "dilemma ethics." The first question in pastoral care is not "What should I do?" but "What should I be?" Furthermore, this perspective helps to make the Church's stance about marriage and divorce more intelligible in itself. This stand as absolute is not intelligible in itself. It must be seen as an aid to help us live more nearly faithful to the story that forms the Christian community. It functions as a reminder of what kind of "virtues are necessary to sustain a Christian people to carry on the story of God." Christian ethics, understood in this narrative way, is deeply antithetical to the natural-law method of Catholic moral theology. It does not pretend to be based on a universally valid stand applicable to all persons irrespective of their story. In this sense it may be called sectarian.

Hauerwas, like Yoder, who has clearly been a strong influence on him, is fresh and provocative, and with others I am constantly instructed by him. What he is doing is very important. I agree with John C. Bennett when he refers to Hauerwas' work as "rich, moving," and "mind-changing."[50] It is also easy to agree that Catholic moral theologians have overstressed decision-making to the neglect of virtue and character. But I am constrained to agree with Bennett when he states of Hauerwas—and one could say this of Yoder also—that he "neglects decision-making too much and gives no help to the members of the Christian community in their capacity as citizens of the larger society."[51]

Because Hauerwas has contrasted his narrative approach with the methodology of Catholic moral theology and because his analyses are so enriching (particularly as a critique of liberalism), I should like to append a few glosses here. First, there is the emphasis on being rather than doing, virtue rather than decision-making. This represents an appropriate redressing of an imbalance. After all, the moral-spiritual life is primarily and properly a manner of being (good-bad, to use the language used earlier) and only by analogy taken up with rightness-wrongness of action. However, if one overpresses this emphasis to the neglect of considerations of rightness-wrongness, even to the point of declaring such considerations irrelevant, then that would be dereliction of responsibility. It would leave

---

[50] John C. Bennett, "John C. Bennett on Stanley Hauerwas' Social Ethic," *Review of Books and Religion* 10, no. 3 (1981) 1–2.

[51] Kenneth Himes, O.F.M., has made this same point in his review of Gerard Fourez's book *Liberation Ethics*. He notes: "Setting normative ethics and calling [story] ethics in opposition is mistaken because they are not mutually exclusive but complementary. Calling ethics highlights certain dimensions of moral life—vision, character, metaphor—but does little to assist in the task of moral justification" (*National Catholic Reporter*, Oct. 15, 1982, 10).

rightness-wrongness considerations untouched by the very narrative that should nourish them.[52]

Second, there is Hauerwas' contrast between an ethic built on a particular narrative and one of "universalistic laws," as he puts it. This is also explicit in Yoder's study. That cuts reality too sharply. If one asserts that certain basic obligations or duties apply across the board to persons as persons, that is not an indication, as Hauerwas maintains, that one has failed to take community and its narrative context as fundamental. Nor is it, as Yoder asserts, "motivated . . . by embarrassment about particularity." It is to argue something about the human condition that we think is generally knowable if our story is to include, for example, Romans 1.

The root of the dichotomy Hauerwas and Yoder assert between narrative and "universalizing" morality is the particularizing and exclusive character they give the story—as if the Incarnate Word of God had nothing to do with or to say about those persons who never lived that particular story. Thus I would guess—possibly erroneously—that Hauerwas' phrase "faithfulness to this man as a guide," which he correctly says is "morally central to Christian ethics," means that others simply cannot share *any* of the insights and judgments such faithfulness generates. Otherwise, why the overstated contrast between narrative and "universalizing" tendencies and the attack on the latter? Similarly, when Yoder sees a focus on generalizability as forgetting that "we confess as Lord and Christ the man Jesus," he is giving this confession a practical ethical content unavailable to those outside the confession.

Whatever the case, this exclusive dichotomizing is not the Catholic reading and living of the story; and Yoder's suspicions about dichotomies should have made him suspicious here. Roger Shinn makes this point very well.[53] He notes that the ethical awareness given to Christians in Christ "meets some similar intimations or signs of confirmation in wider human experience." Christians believe, Shinn writes, that the Logos made flesh in Christ is the identical Logos through which the world was created. He concludes: "They [Christians] do not expect the Christian faith and insight to be confirmed by unanimous agreement of all people, even all decent and idealistic people. But they do expect the fundamental

[52] Perhaps this is responsible for Alasdair MacIntyre's mistaken perception that Roman Catholic theologians seem only "mildly interested in God or the world; what they are passionately interested in are other Roman Catholic theologians" ("Theology, Ethics and the Ethics of Health Care," *Journal of Medicine and Philosophy* 4 [1979] 440). I say "mistaken" because these theologians are interested in the positions and arguments of other theologians precisely because they become a part of the ongoing story of God's will for individuals and the community.

[53] Roger L. Shinn, "Homosexuality: Christian Conviction and Inquiry," in Ralph W. Weltge, ed., *The Same Sex* (Philadelphia: Pilgrim, 169) 43–54.

Christian motifs to have some persuasiveness in general experience." It is this "some persuasiveness in general experience" that can found confidence in the possibility of public moral discourse, a possibility Yoder distrusts.

Let me put it this way. For some years there has been discussion framed in terms of how Athens relates to Jerusalem. Jerusalem, it is argued, simplistically I am sure, tells stories but has no theology properly so called. Athens analyzes and rationalizes, without need of a story or in a claimed lofty independence of all stories. Thus, in stark contrast, if you belong to Jerusalem, you have no need of reason; if you are of Athens, you have no need of a story.

The Catholic tradition refuses to accept the desperate exclusivity of these alternatives. Briefly, it reasons about its story. In the process it hopes to and claims to disclose surprising and delightful insights about the human condition as such. These insights are not, therefore, eccentric refractions limited in application to a particular historical community— as if it were wrong to abort Catholic babies but perfectly all right to do so with Muslim, Protestant, or Jewish babies. Quite the contrary. Reasoning about the Christian story makes a bolder claim. It claims at times to reveal the deeper dimensions of the universally human. That is a bold claim, of course, and even an arrogant one unless it is clearly remembered that Christian communities have, more than it is comforting to recall, botched the job.[54]

And that brings us to the third point, Hauerwas' notion of the Church. It is quite rarified. Bennett believes that Hauerwas expects too much of it as a conveyor of ethics. One cannot but be impressed by the fact that the Church has at key times been corrected by secular society, for example, with regard to religious liberty and racism, and now sexism. At present the Catholic Church can learn a good deal from the tradition of civil liberties in the United States.

In a warm and properly appreciative review of Hauerwas' powerful writing, Richard John Neuhaus notes this aspect of Hauerwas' work and correctly says that in Catholic ears it will sound integralist and "Feeney-like."[55] The prophetic-minority notion of the Church Neuhaus regards as "a serious flaw in Hauerwas' argument" and a "romantic indulgence . . . of false consciousness."

I address these three points as questions to Hauerwas and Yoder in the hope, first, that we can grow in understanding of the matter, but secondly because a too exclusivist reading of the Christian story will render their imposing contributions muted in the political lives of Chris-

[54] Cf. Richard A. McCormick, S.J., "Theological Dimensions of Bioethics," *Logos* 3 (1982) 25–45 and forthcoming in *Eglise et théologie*.

[55] Richard John Neuhaus, "The Hauerwas Enterprise," *Commonweal* 109 (1982) 269–72.

tians. That would be both regrettable and unnecessary. One can agree with so much of the Yoder-Hauerwas critique of both moral theology and society that it would be unfortunate if this critique proved to be the vehicle of their marginalization. In this sense I cannot agree with Yoder's pessimism about the communality of language in public discourse. He states that the use of justice language commonly available to all "hardly helped" debates on abortion funding, multinational corporations, and arms limitation. There are many reasons other than justice language for this "hardly helped": for instance, ingrained interests and ideology, the complexity of the matter, differing metaethical suppositions, etc. But that brings us to nuclear deterrence and nuclear war.

NUCLEAR DETERRENCE AND NUCLEAR WAR

On Sept. 24, 1982 an international group of scientists, almost one fourth of them from Soviet-bloc countries, presented Pope John Paul II a document ("Declaration on the Prevention of Nuclear War") on nuclear warfare.[56] The group had met under the auspices of the Vatican's Pontifical Academy of Sciences. The document had its origins a year earlier in an initiative of Theodore Hesburgh and Cardinal Franz König (Vienna). It referred to the arms race as "the greatest moral issue that humanity has ever faced, and there is no time to be lost." It stated that science can offer no real defense against the consequences of war and that "it is the duty of scientists to help prevent the perversion of their achievements." It concluded that the arms race "must be stopped, the development of new more destructive weapons must be curbed, and nuclear forces must be reduced, with the ultimate goal of complete nuclear disarmament."

In a remarkable parallel development, Yevgeny I. Chazov, a member of the Soviet Academy of Medical Sciences and late President Leonid I. Brezhnev's personal physician, addressed a message to the people of the United States.[57] The message concluded as follows:

Nuclear weapons can lead to a nuclear war simply because they exist. That is why all people of the globe, irrespective of nationality, religion or political views, should raise their voices against the nuclear arms race, against plans for the use of nuclear weapons and against the very thought of nuclear war. Nuclear weapons should be outlawed, their production stopped and their stockpiles destroyed.

These statements are not only important in themselves; they are symbols that the vigorous activity within the Catholic community reported in these "Notes" last year is shared by many other groups. Nor has the episcopal concern itself diminished. Three incidents stand out.

[56] *Catholic Review*, Oct. 8, 1982, 1.
[57] *New York Times*, Oct. 16, 1982, A27.

One is the excellent pastoral letter of Roger Mahony (Stockton).[58] Mahony states that the current arms-race policy of both superpowers "has long since exceeded the bounds of justice and moral legitimacy." He condemns as "always morally wrong" the use or intention to use nuclear weapons. As for possession for deterrence, Mahony argues that the legitimacy of such possession depends on three related moral judgments. (1) The primary moral imperative is to prevent any use of nuclear weapons. (2) Possession of such weapons is always an evil that can only be tolerated, but only if deterrent strategy is used to make progress on arms limitation and reduction. (3) The ultimate goal of an interim deterrence policy is elimination of nuclear weapons. Mahony judges that the U.S. and Soviet policies do not meet any of these standards.

Another incident of note was the "Call to Peacemaking" day held Sept. 18, 1982 by the Archdiocese of Washington under the leadership of James A. Hickey. The day was described by Hickey in his pastoral letter[59] as a "program of prayer, reflection, study, and discussion" on nuclear armaments.

The third event of interest was the annual meeting of Pax Christi held at Rochester (Minn.) in early October 1982. Carroll T. Dozier (Memphis, retired) in his keynote address underscored the "emptiness of just-war theories." "The just-war theory," he argued, "must be filed away in that drawer which conceals the flat-earth theory."[60] He expressed disappointment with the first version of the U.S. bishops' pastoral on peace.

In all this episcopal fervor the Catholic Theological Society of America should not be overlooked. The plenary session of the New York meeting (June 1982) passed a motion stating that "the use of nuclear weapons, under any circumstances, is contrary to the will of God." The reason: inability to place traditional constraints on nuclear war. Therefore it endorsed an immediate world-wide freeze, a staged reduction in present arsenals, and eventual total abolition.[61]

The recent activity of the American episcopate is reported by Francis

---

[58] Roger Mahony, "The Catholic Conscience and Nuclear War," *Commonweal* 109 (1982) 137–43. Cf. also *Origins* 11 (1981–82) 504–11.

[59] *Catholic Standard*, June 3, 1982, special supplement.

[60] *Catholic Review*, Oct. 15, 1982, 1. John J. O'Connor, vicar general of the Military Ordinariate, stated at a conference sponsored by the American Catholic Committee: "Far from feeling that we have reached the point that just war tradition is no longer applicable, we have ... reached the point where it is infinitely more important than it ever was" (*Catholic Review*, Oct. 22, 1982, 1). William V. O'Brien had criticized some episcopal statements in "The Peace Debate and American Catholics," *Washington Quarterly* 5 (1982) 219–22. Responses by Monika Hellwig, John Langan, S.J., James Schall, S.J., and Francis Winters, S.J., are found in "From the University: American Catholics and the Peace Debate," *Washington Quarterly* 5 (1982) 120–42.

[61] Council on the Study of Religion, *Bulletin* 13 (Oct. 1982) 103.

X. Winters, S.J.[62] In another extremely interesting study Winters turns his attention to the episcopal stances within the larger Atlantic community.[63] The English hierarchy as a group has been reluctant to do more than state the key questions. Basil Cardinal Hume, however, after condemning total war or its threat, states his personal reluctance to condemn "outright the possession of nuclear arms." But there are two conditions emphasized. First, we must be able in practice to delineate between civilian and noncivilian. Second, use of strategic weapons must not escalate. If these conditions are not fulfilled, even deterrent weapons cannot be justified.

The Scottish hierarchy condemns all use of nuclear weapons as too dangerously escalatory and it rejects the willingness of citizens to leave these crucial decisions to governments. The French hierarchy is notably silent on the whole issue. The German hierarchy is still developing a common response, but Joseph Cardinal Höffner (Cologne, and president of the German Episcopal Conference) has already defended nuclear weapons as a deterrent.

Winters discovers a notable difference in views and drifts between the Continental hierarchies and those in the English-speaking world, these latter being much more outspoken about nuclear deterrence. Proximity to the poised forces of the Warsaw Pact might be a partial explanation. Flexibility of maneuver available to the English-speaking groups might be another. Some will see this as cacophony within the magisterium. Winters, however, sees it as a healthy collegiality, as "the promise of a universal magisterium more supple and responsive to the accelerating urgency of moral challenges."

Without any question, the most discussed event of the past year has been the first version of the American bishops' pastoral on nuclear war and deterrence entitled "God's Hope in a Time of Fear."[64] It may be useful to recall here some of the principles and the reasoning used in the first version. It lists six such immediate principles applying to nuclear war and deterrence.

First, there is no possible justification for the use of nuclear or other weapons "for the purpose of destroying population centers or other

---

[62] Francis X. Winters, S.J., "U.S. Bishops and the Arms Race," *Month* 244 (1982) 260–65. Cf. also Dona Palmer, Jacqueline Haessly, and Daniel Di Donizio, "U.S. Catholic Response to the Arms Race," *Ecumenist* 20 (1982) 17–22; René Coste, "La course aux armements en procès," *Esprit et vie* 92 (1982) 430–32; Karl Weber, "U.S. Bischöfe gegen nukleare Bewaffung," *Orientierung* 46 (1982) 27–30.

[63] Francis X. Winters, S.J., "Nuclear Deterrence Morality: Atlantic Community Bishops in Tension," *TS* 43 (1982) 428–46.

[64] I work with a manuscript version. The document was never published but was widely reported in the Catholic press.

predominantly civilian targets." Furthermore, it is virtually impossible to justify nuclear attacks on military targets "as proportional to any conceivable rational objective" where the targets lie so close to population centers that these centers would be destroyed.

Second, even "deliberate initiation of nuclear warfare, on however a restricted scale" is morally wrong. Thus no first use is justifiable. The pastoral mentioned "very substantial doubt" about the possibility of control, and in the face of such doubt it stated an obligation to "the safest possible moral course."

Third, even the threat to use nuclear weapons against populations and to initiate nuclear war is morally wrong. Such a threat cannot be justified even if it "is not intended to be carried out." Such threats produce degradation between conflicting sides and carry the danger of loss of control.

Fourth, the pastoral notes that "Christians and others of good will may differ as to whether nuclear weapons may be employed under any circumstances." The draft found it difficult to see how what might be justified in theory could be justified in practice. Any use would have to be defensive and then only in an extremely limited and discriminating manner. The bishops confessed that "in all candor we have no confidence whatever that retaliatory and restrictive usage can be kept limited."

Fifth, the committee warns against "rapid, abrupt" abandonment of nuclear weapons on the ground that it would itself lead to instabilities and possible catastrophe. But "temporary toleration of some aspects of nuclear deterrence must not be confused with approval of such deterrence."

Finally, the committee notes that it has outlined "a marginally justifiable deterrence policy." Faced with a deterrent that is in place and that they cannot approve, they appeal to the principle of "toleration of moral evil."

This draft was widely circulated in order to get the broadest possible range of reactions, a process followed throughout the consultations that led to the draft. The reactions came, many hundreds of pages of them. The document was castigated for confusion and accused of everything from political naiveté to moral cowardice. It was said to be based on the "consequentialism" of Fuchs and Curran, both of whom testified before the episcopal committee. The most hotly controverted passage was that dealing with the principle of toleration of moral evil. The reactions were so voluminous that the committee felt compelled to delay the process. As I write (November 1982), the episcopal committee has completed a second version that attempts to listen to the various publics who have responded to the first draft. That will be interesting. The following chronicle will attempt to report some of the reactions and some of the voices to which the final version will have to listen.

Amongst the first the NCCB committee will listen to is the Pope himself. At the present time it is probably inconceivable that the American bishops will take a position incompatible with the Pope's. So what has the Pope said? Two concrete statements can be distilled from his many excellent statements on war and peace. The first constitutes the context of our reflections. At Coventry (May 30, 1982) John Paul II insisted that "today the scale and the horror of modern warfare, whether nuclear or not, makes it totally unacceptable as a means of settling differences between nations. War should belong to the tragic past, to history; it should find no place on humanity's agenda for the future."[65]

The second occurred in his presentation to the special session on disarmament of the U.N. General Assembly. It was read to the Assembly June 11 by Agostino Cardinal Casaroli, Vatican Secretary of State. In that statement John Paul II asserted: "Under present conditions, deterrence based on balance—certainly not as an end in itself, but as a stage on the way to progressive disarmament—can still be judged to be morally acceptable."[66]

It seems clear, therefore, that the Pope regards the present deterrence policy of the superpowers as "morally acceptable"—not desirable, but tolerable. I say "seems clear." The Pope does not say "is morally acceptable"; he says "can still be judged to be." That wording raises a host of questions. (1) "Can" legitimately? (2) "Be judged"—by whom? Objectively? Notwithstanding such questions, it strikes me as inconceivable that the Pope would make such a statement if he judged the present deterrence policies to be clearly immoral.[67]

This point was not missed by Secretary of Defense Caspar Weinberger in his letter to Archbishop Joseph Bernardin.[68] He noted that he was "heartened" by the papal statement and went on to argue that our deterrence policy has maintained peace for thirty-seven years and that

[65] John Paul II, "The Work of Peace," *Origins* 12 (1982) 55.

[66] John Paul II, "The Necessary Strategy for Peace," *Origins* 12 (1982) 81–87, at 85.

[67] Of the Pope's statement Germain Grisez writes: "Even if Pope John Paul had unqualifiedly affirmed the morality of the deterrent, it is not clear that he intended to speak as supreme teacher in the church and to propose teaching to be accepted by the faithful as certain. Hence there would be no difficulty in supposing him to have erred in this statement" ("If the Present United States Nuclear Deterrent Is Evil, Its Maintenance Pending Mutual Disarmament Cannot Be Justified," *Center Journal*, Winter 1982, forthcoming as I write). Here Grisez implies that a pope cannot err when he speaks as "supreme teacher" about something "to be accepted as certain." This is a theologically false expansion of the charism of infallibility. Cf. *Acta synodalia sacrosancti Concilii Vaticani II*, Vol. 2, Pars 8, p. 85..

[68] *Origins* 12 (1982) 292–94.

the first draft of the bishops' pastoral represents a "dangerous departure from the policies which have kept the peace." Weinberger's letter is extremely interesting for its statement of our government's policy. It is, he says, one of "flexible response." That refers to a "credible continuum" of response that would make clear to the Soviet Union that it "would have no incentive to initiate an attack," That "no incentive" phrase is intriguing. The government says that its policy is *not* to target civilians; yet the "no incentive" usage is broad and loose enough to include them.

Other reactions to the first draft are interesting. I shall force the subsequent literature into the mold of a commentary on it. Francis X. Meehan saw it as "fiddling" while the world threatens to burn.[69] Bishop Walter Sullivan (Richmond) stated: "I would like to save the bishops lots of time." This letter should say "no to nuclear weapons, no to their use, no to their manufacture, no to their deployment, no to their existence."[70] Arthur Jones bluntly argued that if they "in any way permit the manufacture and possession of nuclear weapons, the U.S. Catholic bishops may as well resign and move into the anonymous crowd."[71]

Commonweal presented a very interesting symposium of nine responses to the pastoral.[72] John Langan, S.J., saw the pastoral as "incomplete, inconsistent and therefore very useful." I like that attitude. One of the major problems is that there are three realms of discourse involved (moral-religious, technical-strategic, political) that begin with different assumptions, utilize different concepts, and are employed by different experts.

William V. Shannon agrees with the prudence of the episcopal committee in leaving open the question of whether nuclear arms may ever be used. He urges immediate expansion of conventional forces to rein in the "nuclear horses." Joan Chittester regards the pastoral as morally schizophrenic, stepping tentatively between prophetism and nationalism. The document calls upon us to think of war in "an entirely new way" and then fails to do so itself. Philip Odeen dislikes the heavy emphasis on pacifism and argues that the pastoral "incorrectly portrays the main thrust of our strategic policy over the past twenty years." That is, it supposes that our deterrent policy is built around the threat to attack cities and civilians, which Odeen says is not true.

James Finn highlights and praises the dialogical process that went into

[69] *National Catholic Reporter*, July 2, 1982, 6.

[70] Ibid. On the other hand, John Cardinol Krol, in an address at Penn State University, stated that "in light of the decade of Soviet aggression and expansionism, no reasonable person can insist on unilateral disarmament" (*Catholic Chronicle*, Oct. 8, 1982, 4). I am impishly tempted to suggest that the bishops are "confusing the theologians."

[71] *National Catholic Reporter*, July 16, 1982.

[72] "The Bishops and the Bomb: Nine Responses," *Commonweal* 109 (1982) 419–39.

the composition of the document. He faults it for failure to develop a statement about what a properly ordered international community ought to be and for the murky character of its arguments justifying a deterrent policy. Gordon Zahn sees in the document "troubled ambivalence and a yearning for a compromise on essentially irreconcilable issues." He believes that Christians can no longer tolerate dependence on nuclear deterrence. William J. Nagle is convinced that much more hard cross-disciplinary work is called for before any draft can hope to be adequate.

Finally, Charles E. Curran emphasizes that the notion of toleration of a deterrent is novel and problematic because it involves "tolerating one's *own* intention to do evil." However, it might be possible to understand deterrence and hence toleration differently: as referring simply to the existence of nuclear weapons with no declared intent to use them. He concludes by urging that the pastoral be viewed as a contribution to the ongoing teaching-learning function of the Church.

Curran's last point is very important. There is so much uncritical "magisteriolatry" around these days that it can operate as an undue and unfair pressure on a national episcopate. What the American bishops will end up saying on nuclear arms will, of course, be important. However, it would be a mistake for us or them to view it as *their* last word or *the* last word. We still must learn the humbling reality that our grasp of complex and delicate problems is likely to be partial.

In the remainder of this section I should like to concentrate on some longer studies that have been composed as aids in the teaching-learning process of the Church. But before doing so, I should advert to the excellent issue-overview provided by Michael Mahon, S.J.[73] It is an absolutely first-rate summary of the moral issues we confront. Mahon concentrates on three major issues: (1) the pure form of deterrence (mutually assured destruction and the problem of intentionality); (2) proposals for limited nuclear war; (3) discussion of first-strike scenarios. On this last point, for example, Mahon clearly and accurately reviews the exchange between Theodore Draper and the authors (McGeorge Bundy, George Kennan, Robert McNamara, Gerard Smith) of a highly publicized *Foreign Affairs* article urging a no-first-use policy.[74] Throughout Mahon expertly reviews the analyses of well-known authors in these discussions (e.g., Michael Walzer, Francis Winters, Francis Meehan, Michael Novak, Paul Ramsey, John Cardinal Krol, Roger Mahony, William O'Brien, and others).

Mahon's purpose is to lay out the issues, not to adjudicate them; so he exercises admirable restraint. But his personal reflection at the conclusion of the review is well worth the many months he must have labored

[73] Michael Mahon, S.J., "Nuclear Morality: A Primer for the Perplexed," *National Jesuit News*, Nov. 1982, special supplement.

[74] "Nuclear Weapons and the Atlantic Alliance," *Foreign Affairs* 60 (1982) 753–68.

to construct this overview. Mahon suggests that the nuclear discussion has centered on the principles of proportionality, noncombatant immunity, and last resort. He further suggests that "the principle of right authority is due for a comeback." He means, of course, that the unimpeachable authority for nuclear policy should reside with the prospective victims. It is too serious a matter to be left to governments. The mass movements in Europe and the United States clearly indicate that the victims want to delegitimate the use of nuclear weapons by nation-states. Mahon's concern is shared by others, as will become clear below. If one has time for but a single article, Mahon's is the one to read.

Germain Grisez's evaluation of the present nuclear deterrent unfolds like a syllogism.[75] It is always morally wrong to intend, even reluctantly and conditionally, to kill the innocent. But present deterrent policy involves this murderous intent. *Ergo.* The minor is established by reference to the *United States Military Statement,* which refers to a focus on "Soviet values." But even if the targeting was not aimed at cities, Grisez believes the deaths of millions of innocents is essential to the deterrent and therefore direct (intended). To the objection that it is possible to deter with mere possession—and with no intent to use—he responds that this "might have been helpful had it been offered before the present deterrent policy was adopted."

It had been argued by John Cardinal Krol (September 1979) before the U.S. Senate Committee on Foreign Relations that the deterrent could be tolerated provided the deterrent is used to make progress on arms limitation, reduction, and eventual abolition. Grisez rejects this because it perverts the traditional notion of toleration into a justification for one's own immoral activity. Nor can one argue that choosing to kill innocents is the lesser evil; for "this position requires that one be able to weigh (supposedly 'nonmoral') evils" against one another. This we are unable to do rationally. Rather, this "proportionalist" position calls for a choice before judgment. What we choose to do becomes right.

Two points. During the course of his study Grisez mentions the "theologians Charles E. Curran led in dissent from *Humanae vitae.*" They held that spouses may sometimes decide in conscience that contraception is morally acceptable. Of this Grisez states: "Generalized, the position is: Christians may responsibly decide according to their conscience that any sort of act ... in some circumstances is permissible." Generalized, it means nothing of the kind. They did not say, nor can their statement be forced to say, that "any sort of act" could be permissible in some circumstances. They said that contraception was not always a morally evil act. That leads to no generalization whatsoever about "any sort of act." It is painful to have to remind others that disputes are not

[75] Cf. n. 67 above.

clarified by misrepresentation.

Second, in his continuing battle with "proportionalists," Grisez does not seem to realize that his arguments bite back. For instance, if the "proportionalist" must choose before judgment, how is this any different from the "nonproportionalist" who argues legitimate national self-defense against an aggressor? Does such a person not have to weigh political freedom against the loss of human life in defending it and *decide* that it is reasonable to suffer this evil for that good? If values are incommensurable for the "proportionalist," how are they any less so for the person applying the fourth condition of the double effect (proportionate reason)? In this study Grisez answers as follows: "They may not do to an enemy's population (even as a side effect) what they would not have the other nation's leaders do to them and their people. In such cases, proportionality reduces to the Golden Rule."

But that is not an adequate answer. The question—which requires a rational answer if Grisez's critiques against "proportionalists" as arbitrary deciders are to carry any weight—is: *Why* would they not want it done to themselves? Why would a war become "unduly burdensome"?[76] Is it not because the overall evils do not stand in a proportionate relationship to the values to be protected or achieved? Does that not demand the very weighing and balancing Grisez says is rationally impossible? Was it proportionate or disproportionate for the Russians to lose twenty million lives defending the fatherland? Every episcopal and theological document that I have consulted in this summary involves the type of weighing and balancing Grisez excludes in principle. To say that proportion is a matter of political prudence and sometimes imprecise is not to say that it is irrational or arbitrary.[77]

---

[76] That little phrase hides a weighing and balancing that we all make but that Grisez cannot admit *in principle* because, he claims, it involves incommensurables. "Unduly burdensome"? With regard to what? Concretely, if a war can become "*unduly* burdensome," it can become so only because the cost (in life, economic sacrifice, etc.) is not judged proportionate to the good being protected (e.g., political self-determination). But how does one measure such incommensurables? Grisez says that we cannot. Yet he does so. Otherwise there is no distinction between what is *unduly* burdensome and what is *appropriately* burdensome. Burdens are acceptable or not depending on what is gained or lost if the burden is not borne. David Hollenbach states this well when he notes: "According to this view [traditional double effect] one is still bound . . . to weigh the evil consequences which indirectly accompany the attack against the good effects which flow from it" ("Nuclear Weapons and Nuclear War: The Shape of the Catholic Debate," *TS* 43 [1982] 577–605, at 594). Hollenbach correctly states that these are prudential judgments "not subject to logically certain demonstration." That is not to say that they are not rational.

[77] In his new book *The Nuclear Delusion* (New York: Pantheon, 1982) George Kennan states: "There is no issue at stake in our political relations with the Soviet Union—no hope, no fear, nothing to which we aspire, nothing we would like to avoid—which could conceivably be worth a nuclear war" (cf. *New York Times Book Review*, Nov. 7, 1982, 38). Surely there is a weighing going on here.

John Langan, S.J., reviews what he calls the absolutist position.[78] Langan admits that this position has power and clarity; but does it work? Its basic claim, Langan asserts, is "that every use of nuclear weapons is morally wrong." That is precisely the weakness of the absolutist position. One can conceive of cases where nuclear weapons meet the controlling criteria of the just-war theory. While these may seem antiseptic and abstract (a kind of "two-battleships-at-sea scenario"), Langan regards them as "crucial for understanding the limits of the absolutist argument." If *some* use of nuclear weapons is in principle justifiable, "then possession and production of nuclear weapons must be allowable in principle," and the absolutist case collapses. Unattractive as this may seem, Langan sees it as freeing us to "understanding the balancing of values which is required in shaping strategic policy."

Langan prefers a contextualist approach to deterrence, one in which the serious danger of a catastrophic exchange plays a central role, but not one that justifies an exceptionless moral rule. Dangers can be greater or less, and where policy is concerned one must get involved in the weighing and balancing of risks: for instance, the likelihood of enslavement of free political communities without a deterrent against the likelihood of nuclear catastrophe with one. We are faced with the danger of doing terrible things and the danger of suffering terrible things. Langan lists three things that no policy may do or threaten to do, and whose risk must be minimized: the destruction of humanity, the destruction of an entire society, direct attacks on noncombatants. If a policy involves doing or committing us to do these things, it is immoral. But it need not so involve us, because there is the possibility in principle of a moral use of nuclear weapons. Langan concludes by insisting that the American bishops should not ban the bomb "but should adopt a stance which affirms the limitations of violence that are central to the just-war tradition and which at the same time points to the dangers of using nuclear weapons and of allowing the arms race to continue."

Langan's study is carefully crafted and sensitive to the distinction between moral and political judgments. Grisez would doubtless regard him as a "proportionalist," since Langan sees the need to weigh values and disvalues of very different kinds, as I believe anyone applying just-war criteria must.

I would raise a single point with Langan's essay. He is clarifying his position against something like a straw man. That is, there is probably no one who holds the absolutist position that *theoretically* any use of a nuclear weapon is clearly morally wrong. That would be a difficult, indeed impossible, position to defend once one had accepted the moral legitimacy

[78] John Langan, S.J., "The American Hierarchy and Nuclear Weapons," *TS* 43 (1982) 447–67.

of national self-defense. What many would hold is a universal moral prohibition (Langan's "exceptionless rule") against use of nuclear weapons because of the almost unavoidable danger of escalation. The single question to be put to Langan, then, is this: Does the *abstract* possibility of a morally justified use of a nuclear weapon really justify the *concrete* retention of an arsenal that has no relationship to the abstract scenario? In other words, what is morally allowable in fact must be related to what is likely to occur in fact. As the second draft of the bishops' pastoral states, "The issue at stake is the *real* as opposed to the *theoretical* possibility of a 'limited nuclear exchange.'"[79]

What Langan's argument does, then, is destroy a so-called pure absolutist position that asserts that any conceivable use of a nuclear weapon is morally wrong. It does not have the same effect on a universal prohibition based on real escalatory dangers. And if a universal moral prohibition of use can still be powerfully argued from escalatory risk, then what is to be said of production and possession of nuclear weapons?

Some of the points just mentioned are made in a challenging study by David Hollenbach, S.J., in this journal.[80] Hollenbach concludes that any use of strategic counterforce weapons cannot be morally justified. Such strategy violates the *in bello* criteria of discrimination and proportionality and the *ad bellum* criterion of reasonable hope of success (because of probability of escalation to mass slaughter). He then turns to tactical nuclear weapons and draws the very same conclusion.

Next he turns to hypothetical cases such as those raised by Langan and states that "such hypotheses have little or nothing to do with the real international situation." Hollenbach's conclusion: "the use of nuclear weapons can never be morally justified." I agree with this conclusion, even though I could imagine with Langan antiseptic cases where the use would be controlled.

But what about possession and the threat to use nuclear weapons as a deterrent? Hollenbach refers to the pastoral letter of the American bishops (1976) in which they condemned attacks on civilian populations and threats to do so. John Cardinal Krol repeated this in 1979 but distinguished between threatening and mere possession, justifying toleration of the latter as the lesser of two evils, providing that meaningful negotiations were taking place toward reduction and elimination of nuclear weapons. The Krol testimony, Hollenbach notes, sees in the *threat* to use such weapons the *intention* to do so; but it also assumes that possession is compatible with an intention not to use them.

Hollenbach wrestles with this testimony on two grounds. First, we

[79] *Origins* 12 (1982) 315.
[80] Cf. 76 above.

must distinguish the intention to use nuclear weapons and the intention to deter their use. To pursue policies that make war less likely, even though they involve threats, "is to *intend* the avoidance of war." Making war less likely is what is to be judged where specific policies are concerned, not deterrence in the abstract. Second, with regard to toleration, Hollenbach feels that Krol's notion is essentially correct but that it could be formulated more helpfully. He means that the conditions of toleration should be: (1) any policy must make war less likely; (2) any policy must increase the possibility of arms reduction, not decrease it. These twin conditions acknowledge that the moral judgment about deterrence is one about *the direction in which we are moving.*

Hollenbach's study has the great virtue of locating the discussion within the strong overall presumption against violence central to the Christian tradition. The key to his conclusion (carefully conditioned toleration of possession) is the distinction between intent to use nuclear weapons (never permitted) and intent to avoid war. Will it stand up? Specifically, a wary critic might point out that there is a means-end relationship between the two, that the intent to avoid war is indeed the *ultimate* intent but that it is served and achieved by the intent to use necessarily involved in any serious threat. In other words, the instrumental intention is not swallowed up in or obliterated by the good of the consummatory intention. Is it not there and still problematic?[81]

Hollenbach's study thrusts intention back to center stage. At this point of the discussion enter John R. Connery, S.J.[82] Connery asks whether the threat of use as a deterrent is morally legitimate. The deterrent comes from mere possession and "would not call for any express intention on the part of the country possessing it." Connery narrows the question by excluding any indiscriminate strikes (nuclear or other) and any first strike of an aggressive kind. The sole remaining question is that of a controlled, defensive response. He argues that nuclear response with tactical nuclear weapons can be controlled and discriminate. To make it so is our moral challenge.

For the assessment of the morality of practical policy, Connery has eliminated the problem of intention. How? In two ways. First, since no express intention is required by mere possession, that possession does

[81] Robert L. Spaeth distinguishes between "the intention to launch nuclear missles" and "a policy decision to launch them if attacked by nuclear weapons." This latter, he says, "shows a supremely moral aspect of deterrence." That is, it has a "moral goal." I fail to see Spaeth's distinction. For "a policy decision to launch if . . ." contains a conditioned intention. Can a "moral goal" eliminate this? ("Disarmament and the Catholic Bishops," *This World*, no. 2, Summer 1982, 5–17).

[82] John R. Connery, S.J., "The Morality of Nuclear Warpower," *America* 147 (1982) 25–28.

not create an insuperable problem. Indeed, Connery states that it is hard to see how strategic weapons "could legitimately serve any other but deterrent purposes"—which presumably he would countenance. Second, where tactical weapons are concerned, there is no intention problem because their use is justifiable when discriminate. All we need do, in our possession of nuclear weapons, is have the intention to use them discriminately.

Connery's article did not go without response. In a letter to the editor, Dan DiLuzio referred to it as a "remarkable rationalization." The use of any weapon could be judged sufficiently controllable, but only in "some idealized construct of the world."[83] Similarly, Walter Sullivan protested that the article did "not seem to be touched by the nuclear reality" that arsenals are located near population centers, that limited exchange carries enormous risk of escalation.[84] Furthermore, he rejects the distinction between merely having the bomb and intending to use it. The bomb exists for one reason: to be used if necessary.

From what has been said above, it is clear that I would agree with Hollenbach against Connery that no use of nuclear weapons can be justified in the present circumstances because of the unjustifiable risk of escalation. Second, can mere possession be divorced from some intent to use, as Connery asserts along with Winters (below)? That is a key question in the moral analysis. Langan, Sullivan, and others believe that such divorce is not possible. Langan states that "a firm and settled intention not to use nuclear weapons in all foreseeable circumstances makes the possession of such weapons literally useless as well as irrational and needlessly provocative."[85] In other words, he argues that *some* intention is there. The problem of intention just will not go away.

Now enter Michael Novak and Joseph O'Hare, S.J.[86] Novak insists that the question is not Vatican II's "an entirely new attitude" toward war, but whether Catholic teaching is "moral, realistic, and prudent." After that little rhetorical salvo—involving, as rhetoric usually does, false alternatives—he states the two purposes of deterrence: to deter military use of nuclear weapons, and secondarily to deter nuclear blackmail. To achieve these objectives, mere possession of nuclear weapons is not enough. "It must be intentional." Novak notes that intentionality when applied to political systems is only analogous to intention in individual subjects. It is like ("but not exactly like") the intentionality embedded in acts themselves: for example, in sexual intercourse as "objectively

[83] *America* 147 (1982) 101.

[84] Ibid. 61.

[85] Langan, "American Hierarchy and Nuclear Weapons" 452.

[86] Michael Novak, "Nuclear Morality," *America* 147 (1982) 5–8; Joseph A. O'Hare, S.J., "One Man's Primer on Nuclear Morality," ibid. 9–12.

ordered to procreation" regardless of subjective intentions of individual agents.

Thus the objective intentionality of a nuclear deterrent is "readiness for use." It is this readiness that threatens and deters. The system is *designed* to convey a sense of readiness for use. But, he asks, is it moral to maintain a system whose very existence threatens use if it is immoral ever to use it? His answer: that depends on the purpose of the system. If it is to deter use of nuclear weapons, the threat aims at a high moral purpose (a good) and "does so in a morally sound way." Thus he justifies the nuclear deterrent but disagrees with Cardinal Krol on the condition. Krol had stipulated that possession is tolerable only if efforts are being made toward nuclear disarmament. Thus Krol's criterion would seem to apply only if other nuclear powers were willing to engage seriously in disarmament negotiations.

What move has Novak made? He has, if I understand him, attempted to finesse the classic problem of intention by shifting the "intention" from the agent to the system itself. But there are problems in doing that. Let me put it as follows. If one constructs a system that has inbuilt intentionality ("readiness to use"), does not the intention of the maintainer have to conform to this inbuilt intentionality? What sense does it make to construct a whole system whose very sense is "readiness to use" if the constructor is absolutely unready to use it? And if the constructor is ready to use it, is that not exactly what Novak would condemn?

Another way in on my problem with Novak's analysis is his discussion of "the purpose of the system." May we, he asks, maintain such a system? "That," he says, "depends on the purpose of the system." If it is deterrence, then we may; if it is other than deterrence, no. But who decides this purpose other than the agent? And if it is clearly the agent (political authorities) who intend to deter, what else must they intend to achieve this? Must the agent not intend conditionally to use the system if the deterrence is to be credible? Here we are back to the question I put to Hollenbach. The intention to deter is obviously noble, but can it obliterate the instrumental intention to use? If not, we are back to the problem of the agent's intention, which Novak rather cavalierly dismissed at the outset as "rather traditional stuff."

Francis X. Meehan is very close to Novak's understanding of intention.[87] He believes that distinguishing mere possession from intention to use confuses individual with social morality. In individuals possession may be distinguished from threat or intention to use. Not so in social morality. At this level there are mechanisms beyond individual control (e.g., chains of command, planned operating procedures, computers), all

[87] Francis X. Meehan, "The Moral Dimensions of Disarmament," *New Catholic World* 226 (1982) 68–70.

of which carry an "inbuilt objective intention." To view the matter otherwise is Platonic. Meehan further suggests that the Church may well be at an exciting "kairotic" moment. That is, we are literally pulled by historical circumstances to rediscover the early Christian witness and transform ourselves from within.

What does this dynamic mean with regard to arms possession? Meehan distinguishes the Church's address *ad intra* and *ad extra* (policymakers, the world at large). He understands the appeals of the "peace bishops" for unilateral disarmament to be addressed *ad intra* and to be altogether appropriate. When, however, the Church addresses a larger public (*ad extra*), she cannot realistically call for unilateral disarmament. But by addressing a clear moral message to her own adherents, the Church can create a kind of "third force" that will bring pressure on governments of both superpowers. The only and obvious problem with Meehan's scenario is that there is virtually no effective public opinion in the Soviet Union.

Joseph O'Hare, editor of *America* magazine, has Novak in his sights in his companion article. He protests Novak's dismissal of Vatican II's call for "an entirely new attitude" by noting that war waged with nuclear weapons "would almost certainly be total." O'Hare believes that the preoccupation of Catholic debate with the purity of moral intention distracts us "from the actual moral choices available to us." He rejects unilateral disarmament as morally irresponsible, defends the present deterrent as "the least dangerous of the choices available to us," but insists on unilateral initiatives toward arms reduction by the United States.

The key to O'Hare's analysis is the phrase "least dangerous." On the one hand, there are the dangers associated with unilateral disarmament— dangers that something would happen to us and the Western world. On the other hand, the danger involved in keeping a deterrent is that we would do something to others with it. The first seems to be a risk of enormous nonmoral evil; the second is the risk of doing moral evil. I can fairly hear Grisez shouting "consequentialist" at O'Hare's essay.

Francis Winters, S.J., also engages Novak's dispute with the bishops.[88] He believes that Novak is especially rankled by the "power of the bishops to articulate binding moral imperatives." Winters is startled at the first version of the proposed episcopal pastoral because it allows some retaliatory use of nuclear weapons when it can be reasonably expected that it will escape human control, as "the professional consensus believes." This

---

[88] Francis X. Winters, S.J., "Catholic Debate and Division on Deterrence," *America* 147 (1982) 127–31.

more permissive attitude, which one finds also in Connery's study, fails to deal with the condition that war be waged by competent authority. In a nuclear war competent authority will be *hors de combat* very quickly and the control will slip to the unco-ordinated command of multiple subordinates—in a word, the control will be gone.

Winters argues that as between an immoral military strategy and subjugation to godless communism, there still remains a third option: retention of the nuclear arsenal without any intent to use it. The arsenal *in itself* is "the necessary and sufficient condition of strategic deterrence." Novak had dismissed this by postulating that weapons do not deter apart from the public consensus to use them, because they have an inbuilt intentionality ("ready for use"). Winters believes this is a postulate without proof. Equivalently, then, Winters is reiterating the Krol distinction between threat/intention/use and mere possession. The latter need not involve the former.

This is the way the recent discussion has gone. It is a rich and lively literature. It represents a believing community trying agonizingly to discover God's will in a very complex and dangerous world. A few remarks might not be out of place here.

First, as noted, it would be unrealistic to see the American episcopal document as the final word on the subject. The bishops, like anyone else, discover the Christian truth on these questions through an arduous groping process. If anything is clear from the literature I have reviewed, it is that there is little theological unanimity to aid and inform this process. For this reason I would qualify Winters' assertion that the teaching "will be binding in conscience on American Catholics." No, bishops ought not shrink into harmless statements about "moral ambiguity" when matters are clear and certain. But not all matters are.

Second, given the different views within the Catholic community and the strong feelings that accompany those views, the bishops are in something of a no-win situation. Some, perhaps many, Catholics are bound to be disappointed. We will almost certainly hear further accusations either of "accommodationist" or of "political naiveté." But given the state of the discussion, that should not surprise us or lead to genuine divisions, even schism within the community, as some have suggested. Rather, it should make us aware of the fact that bishops, as a group, deliberate and speak from a certain "social location" both within the broader community and the Church and are probably unavoidably sensitive to jostling and pressures from all sides, not excluding Rome, other national hierarchies, the United States government, etc., sides where they would wish to retain credibility and effectiveness. That is one reason for viewing their ultimate pastoral document as a transitional contribution to a still developing public opinion in the Church.[89] It is also a reason for individual bishops—and all of us—to continue to explore and speak out on this most serious of all contemporary moral problems. Whatever they do, the American bishops should not be viewed as closing the debate, as the always insightful George Higgins notes.[90]

Third, there is a growing conviction (popular, strategic, moral-theological) that any use of nuclear weapons is morally irresponsible. The issue most hotly debated is that of possession for deterrence and the conditioned intention apparently involved in it.[91] The possession question, as a moral question, raises and rests on three issues. (1) Does mere possession with no intention to use factually deter, as Winters and Connery would argue against Novak, Langan, and others? (2) Is it possible to possess weapons which do deter without intending (conditionally) to use them, as Winters, Krol, and others would maintain against Langan, Meehan, William O'Brien, Matthiesen,[92] and others? (3) Is it possible to threaten (something that seems essential to deterrence) the use of nuclear weapons without the intention to use them? In other words, is the notion of threat different from conditioned intention? It will be recalled that Dubarle proposed years ago that a threat does not necessarily involve such an intent.[93]

Fourth, it has become increasingly clear that the one instrumentality capable of influencing the bureaucratic paralysis that leads to superpower deadlock on nuclear weapons is public opinion.[94] There were 400,000

[89] It is interesting to note here the pastoral letter of Francis T. Hurley (Anchorage), Robert L. Whelan, S.J. (Fairbanks), and Michael H. Kenny (Juneau). It concerns Proposition 6 and the withdrawal of public funding for abortion in Alaska. The bishops invite their diocesans to reflect and pray about this matter and "come to a decision." They are careful not to dictate the decision ("On Christian Life and Christian Responsibility," *Inside Passage* 13 [Oct. 8, 1982] 4–5). John Reedy, C.S.C., has properly called attention to the distinction between the religious and moral values involved in contemporary issues and specific political choices (e.g., a nuclear freeze, the Hatch Amendment). On these latter the bishops have no particular competence. When this distinction is not observed, there is a "degradation of teaching authority" ("Bishops and Public Issues," *Catholic Telegraph*, June 25, 1982, 4). For an interesting article in support of a nuclear freeze, cf. James L. Hart, S.J., "The Case for a Freeze on Nuclear Arms," *America* 147 (1982) 226–28.

[90] George Higgins, "Nuclear Debate: A Caution," *Catholic Standard*, Nov. 4, 1982, 9.

[91] It is interesting to note that the English bishops cite lack of clarity about a government's intention as a reason for their perplexity ("Désarmement et paix," *Documentation catholique* 64 [1982] 818).

[92] Leroy Matthiesen states: "The possession of nuclear weapons is the same thing as a threat to use them" (*Time* 120 [Nov. 8, 1982] 18).

[93] D. Dubarle, "La stratégie de la menace nucléaire devant la morale internationale," *Revue de l'action populaire*, 1964, 645–60.

[94] Two episcopal documents call attention to the importance of public opinion in this matter. Cf. "Le désarmement," *Documentation catholique* 64 (1982) 682, and "Le désarmement: Point de vue d'église de France," ibid. 787–88. When Robert S. McNamara was asked

demonstrators in Amsterdam, 200,000 in Bonn, 200,000 in Rome, 150,000 in London, 200,000 in Brussels, 200,000 in Paris, 200,000 in Athens, 300,000 in Bucharest, and many more in the United States. These protests do have an effect. I believe that we need our prophets, politically naive and theologically imprecise as they may at times seem. They provoke public opinion out of its sense of powerlessness, a sense undoubtedly nourished by the "principalities and powers" because it ends in apathy. They provoke us to visualize in faith a different future and to challenge the endless wrangling of strategic experts mired in the mathematics of destruction.[95] George F. Kennan, former ambassador to the Soviet Union, proposed (Washington, D.C., 1981) that the President suggest to the Soviet government an immediate across-the-board 50% reduction of the superpowers' nuclear arsenals. We need that type of bold and sweeping gesture, just as we need the prodding of the Hunthausens, the Gumbletons, the Matthiesens, the Sullivans of the episcopate.[96]

Whatever the case, this roundup has summarized and critiqued the work of others, especially as they went about informing the bishops. It is only fair to expose to the favor of criticism my own response to the first draft. The response suggested the following episcopal wording on two matters touching nuclear weapons.[97]

1. *Retaliatory defensive use.* Some of our military and political consultants believe that the use of tactical nuclear weapons can be isolated and limited, and therefore that such use cannot be morally excluded. Much as this might be true in an abstract scenario, the lessons of history, both past and more recent, lead us to believe that any use of nuclear weapons is inseparable from the *danger* of escalation and totalized warfare. We can identify no human or political purpose that will purge this risk of irresponsibility.

2. *Possession for deterrence.* For us the very possession of nuclear weapons has been the most difficult of all problems. We are aware that many people of good

---

by Robert Scheer how the tremendous nuclear buildup occurred, he answered: "Because the potential victims have not been brought into the debate yet, and it's about time we brought them in" (Cf. Kermit D. Johnson, "The Nuclear Reality: Beyond Niebuhr and the Just War," *Christian Century* 99 [1982] 1014–17). Johnson concludes his fine article by noting that if our politicians cannot exercise moral leadership on this matter, "then it is time for the leaders to be led." Similarly, Roger Ruston, O.P., in his study *Nuclear Deterrence: Right or Wrong* (published under the auspices of the Commission for International Justice and Peace of the Bishops' Conference of England and Wales) puts great emphasis on public opinion (cf. *Tablet* 236 [1982] 862 and 631).

[95] For an excellent study of faith and visualization, cf. Walter Wink, "Faith and Nuclear Paralysis," *Christian Century* 99 (1982) 234–37.

[96] For other valuable suggestions, cf. Alan Geyer, "Disarmament Time at the U.N.: It's Never Enough to Say No," *Christianity and Crisis* 42 (1982) 127–30. Geyer is one of our best-informed and most influential Christian ethicists in the area of disarmament.

[97] Personal communication to Bryan Hehir, July 12, 1982.

will believe that possession of nuclear weapons has served as a deterrent for many years. Furthermore, they believe that unilateral disarmament would be destabilizing and would heighten the possibility of the use of weapons of mass destruction by an irresponsible and adventuresome political adversary. Others believe that since there can be no morally legitimate use of nuclear weapons, and no morally justifiable threat to use them—a belief we share—then even possession of nuclear weapons is morally unjustified. We believe that both sides of this discussion make valid points. That is the very meaning of a "sinful situation." It is a situation we should not be in in the first place. There is no choice without some regrettable and destructive aspect. We cannot justify any use of or any serious threat to use nuclear weapons. On the other hand, we cannot entertain the greater possibility of such use that would seem to be associated with the imbalance created by unilateral disarmament. This is a paradoxical situation. The very evil that must be avoided at all costs can only be avoided *for the present* by maintaining its own possibility. There are risks in retention of nuclear weapons. There are risks in their unilateral abandonment under present conditions. And the risk is the same—that nuclear weapons might ever be used. Perception and judgment of this risk differ amongst people of good will, people with hearts and minds firmly set on the maintenance of peace. In such a situation of difference of factual perception, moral clarity is agonizingly difficult to achieve.

We have been able to arrive at only the following clarities. (1) The possession of nuclear weapons is at the very best morally ambiguous, and therefore at best only tolerable. It may not even be that. (2) Such possession is tolerable only for the present and under certain conditions. (3) These conditions are: a firm resolve never to use nuclear weapons and a firm resolve to work immediately to assure their abolition, in law and in fact. (4) While unilateral disarmament may not be a clear moral mandate, unilateral steps toward multilateral disarmament certainly are.

We realize that some, perhaps many people will view this matter somewhat differently. We are aware that even some American bishops have taken a different individual stand. We encourage such forthrightness and courage. In a matter so morally problematic and ambiguous, this is understandable. There is room, even need for a variety of approaches lest apathy freeze the *status quo*. Warfare of any kind represents the collapse of rational political discourse and in this sense it is always irrational. It is at the very fringe of the justifiable. Nuclear war is beyond that fringe. That being the case, it is understandable that there can be many people who believe that even possession of nuclear weapons is morally intolerable. We share that conviction, but as a goal to be achieved without increasing the threat that such weapons will be used as we move toward the goal. If our government does not take unilateral steps toward multilateral nuclear disarmament, the only morally acceptable option may soon become unilateral disarmament.[98]

[98] A Church of England report stated that Britain should renounce its independent nuclear deterrent. "The evils caused by this method of making war are greater than any conceivable evil which the war is intended to prevent." It also noted: "You may either decide for a nuclear component in deterrence and risk nuclear war, or decide against it and

It is to be noted that these suggestions state about possession of nuclear weapons that it is "at best only tolerable. It may not even be that." Serious scholars disagree on the three questions raised concerning possession, threat, and intention. The proposed wording is a *rebus sic stantibus* matter meant to reflect this unclarity and leave the question open.

Just as these "Notes" are being completed, the second draft of the pastoral has been made public.[99] A full analysis would expand this chronicle beyond tolerable limits. Therefore only a few points related to the previous literature will be highlighted, always with the reminder that we are still dealing with a draft subject to further discussion and modification by the bishops.

Within an overall theology of peace, the document does the following: (1) It condemns all targeting of civilians. (2) It rejects attacking targets whose destruction would devastate nearby populations. ("The relevant moral principle in this case is the disproportionate damage which would be done to human life.") (3) It rejects any initiation of nuclear war, however limited. ("Nonnuclear attacks by another state must be resisted by other than nuclear means.... We find the moral responsibility of beginning nuclear war not justified by rational policies.") (4) It expresses scepticism about the realism of so-called "limited nuclear war," a tenet of some weapons technicians. (5) It refers to nuclear deterrence as a "sinful situation" composed of five negative dimensions. (6) It tolerates in a strictly conditioned way (as long as there is hope of reducing and totally abolishing nuclear weapons by negotiation) the possession of nuclear weapons as the lesser of two evils. However, "If that hope were to disappear, the moral attitude of the Catholic Church would certainly have to shift to one of uncompromising condemnation of both use and possession of such weapons." In sum, then, the second draft states: "Our arguments in this pastoral must be detailed and nuanced; but our 'no' to nuclear war must, in the end, be definitive and decisive."

We shall have to watch the reaction to this second version and summarize it next year. My own reaction is that the conclusions are

---

risk the political and human consequences and defeat by someone with fewer moral inhibitions." For a Christian the second risk is preferable, for "the issue is not whether we will die for our beliefs but whether we will kill for them." The committee included a Catholic moral theologian (Brendan Soane). Its report was expected to be hotly debated in the February 1983 general synod (*Catholic Review*, Oct. 22, 1982, A2). Robert F. Rizzo argues that the momentum of just-war reasoning is carrying the American Catholic bishops toward pacifism, "which will reject the technological weapons of modern warfare, whether conventional or nuclear" ("Nuclear War: The Moral Dilemma," *Cross Currents* 32 [1982] 71–84).

[99] *Origins* 28 (1982) 306–28.

correct, a not surprising response in light of the submissions cited above. But one thing is absolutely clear: the U.S. bishops are eyeball to eyeball with the deterrence policies of the government. They were not content to state principles. They cite the *U.S. Military Posture Statement for FY 1983*, which calls for the "manifest will to inflict damage on the Soviet Union disproportionate to any goals that rational Soviet leaders might hope to achieve." Simply and straighforwardly they reject as clearly immoral such a deterrence policy aimed at "targets of value."

There remains a problem, however, in the wording of the document. On the basis of the 1976 pastoral (*To Live in Christ Jesus*) it accepts the idea that one may not threaten to do what it is immoral to do . However, it seems to say that the evil intention can be overcome by the good of deterrence. My own suggestion for modification to avoid this contradiction would be that the document acknowledge the unclarities involved in the possession/threat/intention discussion and conclude that an absolutely clear moral proscription of possession for deterrence cannot be drawn in the face of such unclarities.

WOMEN, NEWBORNS, AND THE CONCEIVED

These subjects are grouped together merely for convenience, the convenience being a report of some important literature without expanding into more sections. In no way is this grouping intended as reinforcement of the notion that anatomy is destiny. There is, however, a thread of unity in this section. That thread is violence.

For the past two years the U.S. bishops' Committee on Women in Society and in the Church has been dialoguing with representatives of the Women's Ordination Conference. The content and results of this important dialogue were published recently.[100] The goal of the dialogue was "to discover, understand, and promote the full potential of woman as person in the life of the Church." In summarizing their experience of the dialogue ("a unique event in U.S. Catholicism"), the NCCB representatives acknowledged sexist attitudes as pervasive among members of the Church and its leadership. They noted the discrepancy about the Church's teaching on women as applied in civil society and within the Church itself. They conceded that the notion of "complementarity" in church documents often practically implies subordination of women to men. Finally, they admitted that patriarchy had "deeply and adversely influenced the Church in its attitude toward women as reflected in its laws, theology, and ministry."

The Women's Ordination Conference, for its part, is strongly committed to the conviction that only when the ministries of priest and bishop

[100] "The Future of Women in the Church," *Origins* 12 (1982) 1–9.

are open to women will there be genuine equality. They adverted to the tension between the personal beliefs and inclinations of the bishops and the institutional roles to which they are committed, as well as to the "ponderous weight of the institutional structures we hope to see transformed." They left the dialogue more deeply persuaded "that our cause is a matter of justice that is intrinsic to the gospel message." If one wants to catch up on the state of the question, this would be the document to read first.

There are three interesting statements emanating from dioceses. The first is that issued over the signature of John S. Cummins (Oakland).[101] It notes that this decade has produced singular discernment of the place of women in the Church and that these are but the initial stages of an "obviously new and continuing development." The statement, drawn up by a committee of the priests' senate, made several concrete recommendations. For instance, those in charge of formation and continuing education should see to it that their programs are sensitive to and supportive of women's ministry. Other recommendations included greater financial support for women's ministerial education and a clearinghouse for women seeking ministerial placement.

The second statement is a pastoral letter issued jointly by Victor Balke (Crookston) and Raymond Lucker (New Ulm).[102] The letter was written in "the hope that it will raise to a new level of awareness the issue of Christian feminism and the sin of sexism." It includes excellent and very detailed questions for an examination of conscience for members of the Church regarding attitudes and pastoral practices involving women. Rectifying sexist attitudes and practices is a matter of justice deserving "high priority."

The third document is that of Matthew Clark (Rochester).[103] Clark stated: "Women of every state of life and nation, every financial stratum, every culture and religious tradition are asking for what is rightfully theirs." In an excellent, even if somewhat wordy, pastoral, Clark notes that some women view their life in the church as "painfully confusing." This has led them to perceive the Church as "generating and reinforcing circumstances oppressive to them." He urges diocesan agencies to make participation of women a priority. Clark acknowledges that current norms on women's ministry "are a source of suffering." But he asks all to face these questions in an "open and communal manner." Finally, Bishop

[101] "Oakland Statement on Women in Ministry," ibid. 331–33.

[102] Victor Balke and Raymond Lucker, "Male and Female God Created Them," *Origins* 11 (1982–82) 333–38.

[103] Matthew Clark, "American Catholic Women: Persistent Questions, Faithful Witness," *Origins* 12 (1982) 273–86.

Clark proposes sixteen "courses of action." For instance, he makes it a priority for the Rochester diocese to bring women into the various agencies of the diocese. Women should be on all study commissions and advisory boards. All educational programs should include the role of women in their curricula. Women's participation in liturgical functions should be encouraged "in those roles now open to them."

These are just three recent initiatives by American Catholic bishops. Others have preceded them.[104] What are we to make of them? It would be easy to dismiss these moves as episcopal fads. But that would be a mistake, and for two reasons. First, the feminist movement has been heard in these quarters and the hearers have done their homework. Second, the very practical and concrete policy moves mandated show a profound moral seriousness. In summary, I believe we are witnessing an inchoate change in consciousness in the Church. The very first step leading to this change is, of course, the realization of the extent and depth of sexism in the Church—in its policies, leaders, structures, symbols, liturgy. All three pastorals cited acknowledge such sexism.

A change of consciousness does not happen overnight and without preparation. There have been theologians working for years, often thanklessly, on this problem. One thinks of Anne Carr, Rosemary Ruether, Elisabeth Schüssler Fiorenza, Margaret A. Farley, Carol P. Christ, Judith Plaskow, Anne E. Patrick, and Phyllis Trible, to mention but a few. On the narrower problem of women and the priesthood, Bernhard A. Asen brings together an excellent bibliography.[105]

There are two comments one frequently hears vis-à-vis this literature and movement. First, it is asked: How can we get interested in feminist theology when the world is plagued with the problems of hunger, war and peace, racism, political oppression? This theology is middle-class and peripheral. Second, it is argued that the contemporary theological literature on women stems from a vociferous and alienated minority hardly representative of most women in the Church.

The appropriate response to the first comment is to show the interrelationship of these problems as Schüssler Fiorenza has done.[106] The answer to the second statement is properly a *retorqueo* in this form: that may be factually correct, but it simply underlines the extent and depth of patriarchy in contemporary society and the Church.

An excellent begining for one interested in pursuing this matter theo-

---

[104] Cf. *Origins* 12 (1982) 286.

[105] Bernhard A. Asen, "Women and the Ministerial Priesthood: An Annotated Bibliography," *Theology Digest* 29 (1981) 329–42.

[106] Elisabeth Schüssler Fiorenza, "Sexism and Conversion," *Network* 9, no. 3 (May–June 1981) 15–22.

logically would be Anne Carr's essay in this journal.[107] Carr notes that the major work of feminist theologians thus far has been negation, the unmasking of cultural and religious ideology that denies women's full humanity. Many Christian symbols are one-sidedly patriarchal and have been interpreted in a way that legitimates subordination of women. Carr shows convincingly that this need not be the case, that symbols can be purified and brought to bear on society and religion in a transformative way.

Daniel Maguire, in his presidential address to the Society of Christian Ethics, argues that the exclusion of women from most of the centers of power in most civilizations has impoverished the species.[108] The experience of women gives them certain advantages in moral perceptivity (e.g., at-homeness with bodily existence, integration of affect in moral judgment, association with children). By contrast, the experience of macho-masculine culture has in varying ways impeded male sensitivity (e.g., via proneness to violent modes of power, anticommunitarian tendencies, disabling abstractionism, a consequentialist bias, hatred of women). Maguire is not proposing the triumph of femininity over masculinity, but an emerging humanity that banishes stunted femininity and macho-masculinity. The study is particularly helpful in suggesting the debilitating effects of macho-masculinity on the discipline of Christian ethics.

Some feminists, recognizing that androcentric language and patriarchal traditions have stamped the Bible, argue that biblical religion is not retrievable. It merely legitimates prevailing sexism. Not so Elisabeth Schüssler Fiorenza.[109] She refuses to abandon the Bible to the Right. In a fascinating study, she uses the *Haustafeln* texts to exemplify "the political function of biblical remembrance." This function can be seen in the interpretative trajectory of those texts down through the history of the Christian Church. These texts, with their patriarchal themes of submission, have blunted the earlier NT ethic of coequal discipleship. She then moves to establish a "feminist hermeneutics of the Bible." By this she means a combination of the critical analytic methods of historical biblical scholarship and the theological goals of liberation theology. She would make the biblical texts and their interpretation the object of scrutiny in order to break the tyranny of the submissive patriarchal

[107] Anne Carr, B.V.M., "Is a Christian Feminist Theology Possible?" *TS* 43 (1982) 279-97.

[108] Daniel C. Maguire, "The Feminization of God and Ethics," *The Annual* (Society of Christian Ethics) 1982, 1-24. A modified version is found in *Christianity and Crisis* 42 (1982) 59-67.

[109] Elisabeth Schüssler Fiorenza, "Discipleship and Patriarchy: Early Christian Ethos and Christian Ethics in a Feminist Theological Perspective," *The Annual*, 1982, 131-72.

ethics present there. We must bring to such texts a bias against oppressive patriarchal structures.[110]

The studies of Carr, Maguire, and Schüssler Fiorenza—all acknowledged scholars—are presented as examples, from different points of view, of a growing awareness that in sexism we face one of the great moral problems and challenges of our time. I will say no more about it here lest these "Notes" bloat the literature on women written by men. But two things are clear. First, feminist theology is locked into some of the most neurological issues of the historical Christian faith (symbols and practices such as celibacy, ministry of women, sexual ethics, theological language, hierarchy, and patriarchy). Second, it deserves to be taken very seriously, and it is, if my reading of the burgeoning episcopal pastorals is correct.

Subordination of women, or anyone, wherever it occurs, is a form of violence. A more radical and final form of subordination is homicide. That brings us to the problem of newborns. On April 15, 1982 "Infant Doe," a week-old Down's syndrome baby, died in Bloomington, Indiana. The parents had obtained a court order barring doctors from feeding or treating him. The infant suffered from tacheoesophageal fistula, a condition that, unless surgically corrected, prevents ingestion of food. This case received widespread publicity and aroused a great deal of public concern about the protection of newborn infants. Indeed, Richard S. Schweiker, Secretary of the Department of Health and Human Services, stated on May 18, 1982 that "the President has instructed me to make absolutely clear to health care providers in this nation that federal law does not allow medical discrimination against handicapped infants."[111] At the same time Betty Lou Dotson, Director of HHS's Office for Civil Rights, sent a letter to the nation's nearly 7000 hospitals reminding them of the applicability of section 504 of the Rehabilitation Act (1973) to these cases. That section stipulates: "No otherwise qualified handicapped individual . . . shall, solely by reason of his handicap, be excluded from the participation in, be denied the benefits of, or be subjected to discrimination under any program or activity receiving federal financial assistance."[112]

Dotson's letter to the hospitals stated: "Under section 504 it is unlawful for a recipient of federal financial assistance to withhold from a handicapped infant nutritional sustenance or medical or surgical treatment required to correct a life-threatening condition, if: (1) the withholding is based on the fact that the infant is handicapped; and (2) the handicap

[110] Cf. the suggestive responses to Fiorenza's study by Bruce C. Birch and Thomas W. Ogletree, *The Annual*, 1982, 173–89.

[111] *Washington Post*, May 19, 1982, A21.

[112] *Hastings Report* 12 (Aug. 1982) 6.

does not render the treatment or nutritional sustenance medically contraindicated."[113]

This directive has been commented on by two authors well known in bioethics. Norman Fost, M.D. (University of Wisconsin School of Medicine) lauds the intent of the directive but faults it—correctly, I believe—on almost every other score.[114] First, the language ("handicap") is imprecise. After all, the reason we do not bring lifesaving treatment to patients is precisely that their handicap is so severe (e.g., metastatic carcinoma) that prolongation is no longer in their best interest. Clearly, then, "handicap . . . is a morally valid reason for withholding treatment *in some cases.*" Second, the directive refers to treatments that are "medically contraindicated." Fost rightly insists that judgments to withhold or withdraw life-prolonging treatments are ethical judgments, not medical (scientific) ones. He concludes that the fundamental flaw of the directive is "its failure to distinguish between handicaps that justify nontreatment and those which do not."

John R. Connery, S.J., takes a different point of view.[115] The regulation "coincides with traditional moral norms which allow one to forgo a means the patient judges too burdensome or useless to prolong life." He believes that the directive "can only improve the lot of handicapped infants." In the course of his essay Connery explains that the patient's best interest is the criterion to be used. If means are judged to be excessively burdensome or if they offer no hope of preserving life in any significant way, they are no longer in the patient's best interest. "Whether the patient is handicapped makes no difference. A substandard quality of life would not justify forgoing means to preserve life. . . ."

As between these two approaches, I prefer Fost's. The traditional burden-benefit distinction cannot be separated out from the condition of (handicap of) the patient as cleanly as Connery suggests. As Fost puts it, "The reason we let patients die and withhold lifesaving or life-prolonging treatment is that they are so handicapped (by pain, or mental incapacity, or disability) as to make further life, and therefore further treatment, not in their interest." In other words, if the handicap "makes no difference," Connery would be forced to demand a kidney transplant for a child totally and permanently devoid of consciousness or of mental capacity if this treatment is given to other nonhandicapped babies. That, in my judgment, is not in the best interest of the patient.

---

[113] Ibid.

[114] Norman Fost, M.D., "Putting Hospitals on Notice," ibid. 5–8.

[115] John R. Connery, S.J., "An Analysis of the HHS Notice on Treating the Handicapped," *Hospital Progress* 63 (1982) 18–20.

Robert Veatch brings this point out well.[116] After adverting to the useless-burdensome criteria, Veatch rightly notes that these are value judgments. In some cases the judgment that the treatment is useless is directly related to the handicap. As he puts it, "in some cases the handicap becomes the factor that leads us to decide whether a treatment is fitting or not." Veatch gives the example of an infant with Lesch-Nyhan syndrome, a genetic disease afflicting males characterized by severe mental and physical retardation and bizarre aggressive behavior including self-mutilation that leads literally to chewing away lips and fingers. It is sometimes accompanied by kidney failure, difficulty in eating, and repeated vomiting. Death almost always occurs under five years of age. Such children are subject to pneumonia. Veatch suggests that penicillin may be withheld from such a child "because of uselessness or grave burden *even though these are causally linked to the presence of a handicap.*"

Veatch concludes by noting that some of these calls are close and that parents should be given limited discretionary freedom "to choose among reasonable, morally responsible courses of action."

Allen Verhey, in an excellent article, states bluntly that the "Infant Doe" decision was morally wrong, a verdict shared by every commentator I have encountered.[117] Verhey is especially good in pointing up why this could happen. First, there is growing confusion about the physician's role. Medicine, practiced as a neutral skill separated from a value tradition, is "being conscripted to serve consumer wants and desires, hired to do the autonomous bidding of the one who pays." Similarly, there is growing confusion about the parental role. Contemporary attitudes are fostering a notion of parenting that reduces our options to the perfect child or the dead child.

Compassion exercised outside of a moral tradition of parenting is quite capable of seeing its task as killing. Verhey correctly sees the minimalistic concepts of autonomy and privacy as reducing role relations (e.g., parental) to contractual ones. The Christian community is an inclusive one that welcomes society's outcasts. It is such a storied tradition that provides our best chance of returning to health the roles of physician and parent. What is interesting and appealing about Verhey's analysis is the bridge it builds between character-virtue considerations and right-wrong perspectives.

Fost had suggested the need to distinguish between handicaps that justify nontreatment and those that do not. Veatch is equivalently saying

[116] Robert Veatch, "Should We Let Handicapped Children Die?" *Newsday,* Aug. 8, 1982, 1, 8–9.

[117] Allen Verhey, "The Death of Infant Doe," *Reformed Journal* 32 (June 1982) 10–15.

the same thing. What we seem to need is criteria that will aid us in making this distinction and therefore in fostering the best interest of these tiny patients. I have tried to provide some help by offering four guidelines.[118] They are as follows.

1) Lifesaving interventions ought not to be omitted for institutional or managerial reasons. Included in this specification is the ability of *this particular family* to cope with a badly disabled baby. This is likely to be a controversial guideline, because there are many who believe that the child is the ultimate victim when parents unsuited to the challenge of a disadvantaged baby must undertake the task. However, it remains an unacceptable erosion of our respect for life to make the gift of life once given depend on the emotions or financial capacities of the parents alone. At this point society has some responsibilities.[119]

2) Lifesaving interventions may not be omitted simply because the baby is retarded. There may be further complications that justify withholding life-sustaining treatment. But retardation alone is not an indication. To say that it is constitutes fundamentally unequal treatment of equals.

3) Life-sustaining interventions may be omitted or withdrawn when there is excessive hardship, especially when this combines with poor prognosis (e.g., repeated cardiac surgery, increasingly traumatic oxygenization for low-birthweight babies, low-prognosis transplants).

4) Life-sustaining interventions may be omitted or withdrawn at some point when it becomes clear that expected life can be had only for a relatively brief time and only with the continued use of artificial feeding (e.g., some cases of necrotizing enterocolitis).

Obviously, such rules as these do not solve all problems. But they do provide *some* guidance for *many* instances. And I would emphasize the word "some." Concrete rules cannot make decisions. They do not replace prudence. Rather, they are simply attempts to provide some outlines of the areas in which prudence should operate. Unless we attempt to concretize further the altogether valid burden-benefit categories, I fear that we may have more "Infant Doe" cases, that is, cases of compassionate and well-meaning homicide.[120]

---

[118] Richard A. McCormick, S.J., "Les soins intensifs aux nouveau-nés handicapés," *Etudes*, Nov. 1982, 493–502.

[119] It is sad and even inconsistent that the very administration that insists that handicapped infants be treated is the one drastically reducing the funds to make this care possible.

[120] Readers should be alerted to a forthcoming report on treatment of handicapped newborns by the President's Commission for the Study of Ethical Problems in Medicine and Biomedical and Behavioral Research. It is very well done.

Finally, this section and these "Notes" will conclude with a few references to nascent life. As is well known, the Hatch Amendment, backed by the American bishops, failed in this congressional session. But the issue will not go away. A thorough review of the issues involved both in the Helms initiative and the Hatch Amendment is provided by Mary Seegers.[121]

The next lively discussion in bioethics may well be the experimental use of embryos. Recently Pope John Paul II stated to a distinguished group of scientists meeting in Rome: "I condemn, in the most explicit and formal way, experimental manipulations of the human embryo, since the human being, from conception to death, cannot be exploited for any purpose whatsoever."[122] I say "lively" because it is well known that some theologians (e.g., Karl Rahner) have come to a different conclusion where the preimplanted embryo is concerned.[123] However, further discussion of this and other matters will have to await another edition of these "Notes."

[121] Mary Seegers, "Can Congress Settle the Abortion Issue?" *Hastings Report* 12 (1982) 20-28.

[122] *Catholic Standard*, Oct. 28, 1982, 6.

[123] For further recent literature and techniques involving the moral status of the fetus, cf. LeRoy Walters, "Biomedical Ethics," *Journal of the American Medical Association* 247 (1982) 2942-44. Cf. also Clifford Grobstein, "The Moral Use of 'Spare' Embryos," *Hastings Report* 12 (1982) 5-6, as well as O. de Dinechin, S.J., "A propos de la recherche scientifique sur embryons humains," *Cahiers de l'actualité religieuse et sociale*, no. 243 (1982) 203-6.

CURRENT THEOLOGY

NOTES ON MORAL THEOLOGY: 1983

RICHARD A. McCORMICK, S.J.

Kennedy Institute of Ethics and Woodstock Theological Center, D.C.

These "Notes" will focus on four areas of contemporary concern: (1) conversations in fundamental moral theology, (2) doctrinal development, (3) pastoral problems, (4) the episcopal pastoral *The Challenge of Peace*.

CONVERSATIONS IN FUNDAMENTAL MORAL THEOLOGY

I have entitled this section "conversations" rather than "disputes" in order to underline the open and communicative character that should pervade scholarly exchanges. Furthermore, the term allows reportage of literature that would not fit easily under a single rubric.

In an important article, Joseph Fuchs, S.J., discusses the tensions between bshops and theologians.[1] Fuchs first adverts to the mission of bishops. One aspect of that mission is the unity of the faithful. However, there is the danger that bishops can confuse unity in faith with uniformity about moral teaching. "If Vatican II noted that believing Christians of upright conscience could at times come to different solutions in important human questions (therefore ethical questions), then that indicates that the unifying function of the bishops in moral questions, even on the basis of the one faith, is not unlimited."[2] Unity in the faith is much more important than unity in moral questions. "Church history shows repeatedly that functional unity in moral questions does not mean the truth of the moral formulations implied in this unity." Therefore episcopal service should aim not above all at functional conformity, but at unity in the truth. Many regrettable events could have been avoided if this had been remembered through centuries of church history (Fuchs mentions religious freedom, sexual-ethical formulations, and the defense of the unjust use of force). Subjective certainty in moral questions has sometimes taken precedence over the truth.

In the years prior to Vatican II, Neo-Scholastic theological tendencies, both in theology and in hierarchical statements, were more in the service of certainty than of truth. This led to a regrettable "positivism" of the Christian moral message. One of the strongest critics of such positivism

---

[1] Joseph Fuchs, S.J., "Bischöfe und Moraltheologen: Eine innerkirchliche Spannung," *Stimmen der Zeit* 201 (1983) 601–19.

[2] Ibid. 603.

was Josef Ratzinger, who referred to the "transformation of the Christian ethos into an abstract natural-law system" and added that "even graver is the ever more pronounced positivism of magisterial thinking that embraces and regulates this ethical system." Fuchs insists that in conceiving their unity-task bishops remember that it is unity *in truth* that we are after and that this is rarely well served by discussion-ending edicts.

Fuchs next turns to the mission of the theologian. The past century has witnessed the growth of a strong juridical understanding of the magisterium. This culminated in *Humani generis* (1950) but was attenuated by Vatican II's insistence on the presence of the Spirit to the entire People of God. In the present situation Fuchs sees four dangers. First, there is the danger of magisterial positivism that functions as a real obstacle to the discovery of truth. Moreover, such positivism often involves a one-sided privileging of a single school of theology. Next there is the danger that we give support to the notion that concrete directives are a matter of God's revealed will. The third danger is a certain narrowing of the field of moral-theological reflection. Finally, the situation is calculated to deepen a sense of ethical immaturity in the discovery of moral truth.

The work of moral theologians is often said to be the source of "dangerous confusion." In most instances Fuchs reads this as fear of the loss of peaceful ecclesiastical functioning, which is basically fear of more responsible and arduous dialogue. Still, Fuchs insists that mere repetition of past formulations is an inadequate description of theology's task. Human beings, including Christians, never cease to reflect on their lives. But they do so in the circumstances of different times and cultures. This means that in moral theology there will always be new insights, understanding, values, and judgments. It also means, Fuchs argues, that bishops who are not moral theologians will often be unfamiliar with the new problems of moral theology.

Fuchs then lists three acute problem areas that intensify the difficulties of bishops in carrying out their service of promoting "unity in truth." The first concerns the possibility of distinguishing good and evil. It is asserted that moral theologians are making it more difficult for the Church to distinguish the two. Fuchs rightly notes that this accusation builds on an inadequate distinction between the pairs good-evil and right-wrong. The notions of good and evil concern the person. It is the person who is good or evil. Right-wrong refers to one's conduct. The living-out of one's Christian faith is primarily a matter of personal goodness, only secondarily of rightness-wrongness of conduct. And where personal goodness is concerned, there are no uncertainties and differences of view in contemporary moral theology.

It is universally acknowledged that a person must not act against a responsibly formed conscience; that a person must in his/her decisions always be morally good, never evil; that one must always regard and treat every human being as a person; that one must, as far as possible, avoid evil in the development of the world; that one must pursue the development of innerworldly reality with justice, mercy, magnanimity, chastity etc. . . ; that one must never use a means known as morally wrong to achieve a good end.[3]

Once one realizes that the determination of the rightfulness and wrongfulness of our actions, important as it is, is of secondary importance, one is better positioned to tolerate peacefully a certain pluralism of method and response where rightfulness and wrongfulness are concerned.

To one who is confused by contemporary theological work and maintains reservations about it, Fuchs suggests consideration of several basic points. For instance, in the past theological reflection did not always arrive at identical moral judgments in certain areas such as sexuality. Thus, for centuries sexual intimacy with any other motive than procreation was seen as sinful, while during the first five centuries masturbation received practically no moral consideration. Or again, failure to provide convincing reasons for certain norms can be reason for doubting their accuracy. Fuchs gives as examples the *propositiones* of the 1980 Synod of Bishops on contraception and reception of the Eucharist by the divorced-remarried person.

The second problem area is the relation of faith to morality. Some people erroneously believe that concrete norms of rightness and wrongness are exhaustively grounded in the Christian faith. Catholic tradition, by contrast, says they are grounded in *recta ratio*. While faith in Jesus Christ can illumine reason, it does not replace it.

Finally, there is the distinction between authority and competence. If one is to pass judgment on the rightfulness and wrongfulness of concrete human conduct, clearly one must have the competence to understand and judge the many factual dimensions involved in such problems. If this judgment is to be issued to the Christian community, one must have authority. As for competence, it is the same for bishops, moral theologians, and others. For instance, anyone wishing to determine the rights and wrongs of genetic interventions must be competent in the field. Where authority is concerned, Fuchs concedes that bishops have authority by reason of their mission. But it is not identical with competence. Furthermore, he cautions about an overexpansive interpretation of *de fide et moribus*. Neither Vatican I nor Vatican II meant this to include in an unqualified way all moral problems however concrete.

The study ends by reflecting on the pastorals of the American and

[3] Ibid. 611.

German hierarchies on war and peace. One of the great lessons to come from the American experience is that clarity on complex moral questions is not easy, requires time, and must draw on a variety of competences. Another lesson is that not everything the magisterium teaches has equal authority.

The most important emphasis in Fuchs's study is that episcopal concern for unity must be unity *in the truth*, not mere conformity. Furthermore, there is a hierarchy of truths.[4] Those pertaining to personal goodness or evilness (in contrast to rightness and wrongness) are primary and should be those that basically forge the unity bishops are missioned to achieve and protect. Where rightness and wrongness of conduct is concerned, insistence on a similar unity would be untrue to history, insensitive to the complexity of some moral problems, unresponsive to the historical and cultural changes we live with, and finally damaging to the credibility of the magisterium.

Yet it is unity on such right-wrong questions that seems to preoccupy too many authorities and some theologians. For instance, there are still bishops who exclude from their dioceses theologians who dissent on relatively marginal points of the moral life, especially in the area of sexuality. Unless and until bishops refrain from such jurisdictional overkills, uniformity will be confused with unity in the faith and unity in truth.

Furthermore, the tension noted by Fuchs is only heightened, and the achievement of truth impeded, by Roman interventions that are not dialogical but are straightforwardly an exercise of ecclesiastical muscle (cf. below under "Pastoral Problems"). Though the pope has no divisions, he does have his congregations. Their potential for good is great, but by the same token their potential for damage is incalculable. On Nov. 8, 1963, Cardinal Frings adverted to this when he confronted Cardinal Ottaviani in the most dramatic moment of Vatican II. He referred to the Holy Office, "whose methods and behavior do not conform to the modern era and are a source of scandal to the world."[5] Whenever concrete moral conclusions are imposed through intimidation—and that is being done in our time—those responsible for it must bear the heavy burden of Frings's indictment.

Those who treasure the magisterium should realize that the greatest threats to it may well be largely from within. Three stand out. First, there are some of the archconservative personnel of the Roman congre-

---

[4] Charles Curran has treated these matters well as they touch the pastoral minister. He emphasizes and develops two points that may be of aid to pastoral ministers: dissent and the difference between moral theology and pastoral counseling. Cf. "Discipleship: The Pastoral Minister and the Conscience of the Individual," *Clergy Review* 68 (1983) 271-81.

[5] *Catholic Review*, March 4, 1983, 1.

gations. They consistently confuse and identify the truth with conformism to Roman formulations, many of which are no more than the "school theology" of a minority group who happen to be consultors and advisors. Second, there are growing numbers of reactionary theologians who support this type of thing with insistence on a verbal conformity that is utterly incredible to the modern—and, I would add, open—mind. Third, there are the reactionary reporters and letter writers (to Rome) mentioned by Archbishop John Roach in his opening speech (Oct. 14, 1983) to the N.C.C.B.[6] and by the distinguished historian John Tracy Ellis.[7] It is clear that these three "threats" are quite capable of crippling the magisterium in the contemporary world. For reasons such as these Fuchs's article is extremely timely.

Fuchs notes that faith can illumine reason when it deals with concrete moral problems, but not replace it. That opens on another interesting question. In recent years there has been discussion about the relationship of morality to Christian faith. Specifically, what does Christian faith add at the level of concrete norms? The discussion, especially in Germany, developed into a lively debate. Jean-Marie Aubert summarizes the debate and proposes a synthesis.[8]

Vatican II emphasized the need of dialogue with the contemporary world. Many moral theologians saw this as a mandate to highlight the communicable dimensions of the Christian heritage. They built on two foundations: secularization (the independent value of earthly realities) and the Thomistic tradition of reason. A. Auer's *Autonome Moral und christlicher Glaube* was one of the opening shots in the debate. Auer argued for an autonomous morality at the level of concrete norms, but an autonomy enriched by the horizon of understanding (*horizon de compréhension*) provided by faith. In virtue of this horizon, the Christian, enlightened by faith, gives a different and deeper meaning to his inner-worldly activity. Furthermore, such a Christian will discern values underesteemed by the world and thus through faith exercise a critical role in the world.

Aubert notes that the autonomy thesis was adopted by "the majority of contemporary moralists" with nuances unique to each proponent. He mentioned Bruno Schüller, S.J., Dietmar Mieth, Joseph Fuchs, S.J.,

[6] *New York Times*, Nov. 15, 1983, A18.

[7] "I have the impression that certain curia officials are listening too much to one side—and that side is usually the far right" (*Catholic Review*, Nov. 18, 1983, A6). This "far right" was identified by both *Time* (Nov. 28, 1983, 96) and *Newsweek* (Nov. 28, 1983, 115) as the truculent tabloid out of St. Paul, the *Wanderer*. The "listening officials" are identified by *Newsweek* as Cardinal Angelo Rossi, Archbishop Augustin Mayer, and Cardinal Silvio Oddi.

[8] Jean-Marie Aubert, "Débats autour de la morale fondamentale," *Studia moralia* 20 (1982) 195–222.

Franz Böckle, B. Frailing, F. Furger, W. Korff, R. Hofmann—to mention but a few—as well as Edward Schillebeeckx and Hans Küng.

The reaction to this current of thought was quite polemical, "mingling unjust accusations with abusive simplifications." Aubert sees in it a kind of "ecclesiastical politics" determined to repair the split between the hierarchy and others (theologians and the faithful in general); for if concrete morality is autonomous, "the authority of the hierarchy in ethical matters is correspondingly diminished."[9] Thus, G. Ermecke argued that a morality founded on reason "risks losing its unconditional character and tumbling into subjective utilitarianism." According to him, faith will manifest itself at the level of concrete norms.

But the chief champion of this "ethic of faith" is B. Stöckle. He denounces the idea of restricting the influence of faith to motivations and horizons. Reason is unable to perform the function (discovery of right and wrong) that autonomists assign it. Two traits characterize the thought of this minority school: ethical pessimism (loss of confidence in reason) and depreciation of the human. Besides Ermecke and Stöckle, Aubert lists as adherents K. Hilpert, A. Laun, J. Scheffczyk, A. Voegtle, H. Oberheim, and Hans Urs von Balthasar. This last has a notion of nature that is profoundly pessimistic and is closer to Barth than to St. Thomas. Thus the need to have recourse to Scripture to discover concrete norms.

Aubert believes a resolution of this problem is possible, but only if we recognize the deficiencies of both schools of thought. Both schools suffer from what he calls the "modern Kantian context" of the debate. In such a context morality is viewed above all as the proposal of duties and norms. For the autonomists, reason is too easily closed in on itself, whereas an "ethic of faith" too easily becomes fideism and sectarianism. To integrate the concerns of both schools, the casuistic character of the debate must be abandoned. Aubert suggests a return to the Thomistic perspective, which is more global but nicely integrates theological claims with the claims of reason. In the Thomistic synthesis it is the whole person who is transformed by grace and the theological virtues, not just the intentionality. But against the "ethic of faith," Aubert insists with Thomas that reason is the rule of the entire moral life.[10]

Aubert comes close to pulling off a neat trick. He wants to reconcile opposing tendencies by creating a moral global synthesis, a kind of third alternative. He does so by actually siding with one side on the substantial issue. He denies biblical foundations for concrete norms and along with St. Thomas asserts the role of reason in their discovery. And that is what

[9] Ibid. 205.

[10] 1-2, q. 108, ad 2: "Ad opera virtutum dirigimur per rationem naturalem quae est regula quaedam operationis humanae."

the debate was largely about in the first place. It was not about whether the entire person and his/her acts are penetrated and transformed by grace. Clearly they are. It was not about whether the theological virtues are central to the Christian moral life. Of course they are.

In an interesting article rather closely related to the discussion reported by Aubert, James Gaffney dialogues with Bruno Schüller, S.J., and this author on the distinction between parenesis and normative ethics.[11] He uses Stanley Hauerwas' approach to abortion as the vehicle for his reflections. Hauerwas, it will be recalled, thinks of a Christian as one who is trying to become a particular sort of person and presents abortion as profoundly at odds with that ideal. "It is this basis of opposition to abortion that, in Hauerwas' opinion, Christians should be telling people about and he thinks that telling about it is much more like telling a story than it is like building a case."[12]

My analysis of this, Gaffney correctly notes, was that it does not determine or state the rightness or wrongness of any particular abortion (as Hauerwas would admit) and therefore pertains to the category of parenesis. The story-approach does not have the "normative equivalency" or validity of a more analytic or argumentative approach. Gaffney accurately reports that I believe Hauerwas may have been confusing parenesis and justification, much as Schüller had rejected final ethical appeals to biblical revelation as embodying such a confusion. Gaffney has reservations about this contention because he has a "strong suspicion that parenesis is a less clear and distinct phenomenon than Schüller and McCormick seem to think." Furthermore, he has a strong sympathy with Hauerwas' approach.[13]

What suggestion does Gaffney make? As I understand his essay, he believes that the dichotomy between the parenetic and the normative is not as sharp as Schüller and I seem to think. Why? Because every ethical norm is parenetic (e.g., the statement "it is wrong directly to kill an innocent person" contains implicitly the exhortation "do not do so"). This leads Gaffney to suggest that the type of narrative Hauerwas employs may be more normative than we think and more useful than a too-sharply-drawn distinction between parenesis and normative discourse would suggest.

I am prepared to admit that every concrete norm is implicitly parenetic.

[11] James Gaffney, "On Parenesis and Fundamental Moral Theology," *Journal of Religious Ethics* 11 (1983) 23–34.

[12] Ibid. 27.

[13] For Hauerwas' most recent summary of his approach, cf. his "Casuistry as a Narrative Act," *Interpretation* 37 (1983) 377–88.

But I do not believe that this blurs the distinction between parenesis and normative discourse to the extent of allowing the former to do the work of the latter. In other words, normative discourse may contain implicit parenesis, but this does not convert into the statement that parenesis and normative discourse are insufficiently distinct. At least I do not believe it does.

This may seem a very technical point at the margins of the ethical enterprise. Quite the opposite is the case. It touches on the types of justification we give for some very concrete sorts of actions, for judging such actions morally right or wrong. If appeals that are broadly parenetic in character are considered to be justifications for some very concrete moral prescriptions or proscriptions, we are vulnerably exposed to some rather frightful isms: fundamentalism, positivism, and authoritarianism in morals.

Let a recent study by Bruno Schüller, S.J., exemplify this.[14] Schüller cites Hans Urs von Balthasar's defense of *Humanae vitae*. It reads in part as follows:

> Is it indeed a sign that mankind has entered into the final phase of its history? Through fear of overpopulating the planet, it regulates procreation by tearing asunder the unity of human love. A mutual love that excludes from its expression the chance or danger of offspring is no longer unreserved love.... We simply ask: Can married love between Christians that builds into itself such decisive reservations be love modeled after the following of Christ? We appeal now not to the natural law, but rather we prefer to recall the well-known pericope from Ephesians (5/21–23) where Paul places the living-out of marriage under the prototypical love of Christ and the Church.[15]

Schüller sees the phrases "tearing asunder the unity of human love" and "builds into married love decisive reservations" as "persuasive descriptions" ("persuasive Kennzeichnung") that contain their own evaluation. They purport to be mere descriptions but are so colored that the action is *ex definitione* morally wrong. This is the logical error of subreption—an inference obtained through fraudulent concealment. When Balthasar comes to the difference between natural family planning and contraception, he states that "the difference is great for those who think in a Christian way." Equivalently, then, Schüller argues, Balthasar says: be a Christian, think as a Christian, decide for love without reservations, and the truth of *Humanae vitae* will no longer be doubtful. Schüller

[14] Bruno Schüller, S.J., "Zur Begründung sittlicher Normen," in *Der Mensch und sein sittlicher Auftrag*, ed. Heinz Altaus (Freiburg: Herder, 1983) 73–95.

[15] Ibid. 90.

rightly sees this as parenesis that leaves the normative question untouched—or rather it supposes the answer to the normative question.[16]

This example shows, I believe, that it remains important to continue to distinguish parenesis from moral argument, a point I think Gaffney would concede. The only point of difference between us that I can detect is the extent to which a rather exclusively narrative approach to normative questions endangers the distinction.

Nothing said above should be understood as diminishing the importance of parenesis in the moral life. The New Testament is sufficient witness to such importance. Indeed, I would argue that to diminish the importance of parenesis is, by implication, to reduce the moral life to "quandary ethics." In summary, I want to agree with Gaffney's suggestion that parenesis and normative ethics are complementary. Neglect of either, or confusion of the two, is a threat to both.

A discussion similar in some respects to that about parenesis and normative ethics is that about the foundation of moral norms themselves. In a previous edition of these "Notes" I had dialogued with my friend and colleague John R. Connery, S.J., and made some criticisms of his critiques of so-called "proportionalism."[17] One of his major criticisms was that Catholic tradition has taught that certain actions are morally evil *ex objecto*. He further contended that "proportionalists" cannot say this. I responded by saying that this misses the point of what this school of thought is saying. "When contemporary theologians say that certain disvalues in our actions can be justified by a proportionate reason, they are not saying that *morally wrong* actions (*ex objecto*) can be justified by the end. They are saying that an action cannot be qualified morally simply by looking at its *materia circa quam*, or at its object in a very narrow and restricted sense. This is precisely what tradition has done in the categories exempted from teleological assessment (e.g., contraception, sterilization). It does this in no other area."[18] I further argued that the

---

[16] It is interesting to compare Balthasar's statements with those of John Paul II (Sept. 17, 1983). Repeating his rejection of contraception, he stated: "To think or to say anything to the contrary is tantamount to saying that in human life there can be situations where it is legitimate not to recognize God as God." He added: "The contraceptive act introduces a substantial limitation from within of this reciprocal donation and expresses an objective refusal to give to the other all the good of femininity or masculinity" (*St. Louis Review*, Sept. 23, 1983, 8).

[17] For discussions of this matter in some recent books, cf. David Hollenbach, S.J., *Nuclear Ethics* (Ramsey: Paulist, 1983); Neil Brown, *The Worth of Persons* (Sydney: Catholic Institute of Sydney, 1983). Cf. also Felix Podimattam, "Conflict Morality: An Interpretation," *Jeevadhara* 12 (1982) 409–54; George Lobo, "Moral Absolutes: Toward a Solution," ibid. 455–69. These latter two articles are in substantial agreement with the perspectives adopted in these "Notes" over the years.

[18] *TS* 43 (1982) 85.

term "object" was so inconsistently used (sometimes including circumstances, sometimes not) that it might be better to abandon the object-end-circumstances in favor of *materia circa quam* plus morally relevant circumstances.

Connery has graciously replied to these suggestions and made several points.[19] Since his rejoinder appeared in this journal, I will synthesize the points quite briefly, but I hope his major concerns will be clear. He does not believe that this new terminology clarifies anything. Indeed, he argues that "proportionalists" collapse into *materia circa quam* whatever they do not wish to consider a value term ("e.g., masturbation, contraception, contraceptive sterilization, killing an innocent person, and even adultery"). Rather, some of these are morally definable "merely by consideration of the object of the act, e.g., in solitary sexual acts." Or again, "one can make a moral judgment of sterilization when one knows that it is contraceptive," and therefore "apart from the kind of calculus the proportionalists would demand."He further argues that the chief reason for the vulnerability of "proportionalism" is "the reduction to *materia circa quam* or premoral evil of acts that had previously been considered immoral." Connery believes that one must not "weigh all the good and evil in the act, including all the consequences," for that would make our decisions "more difficult." Moreover, tradition used *ratio proportionata* only for affirmative obligations and positive legislation, not for negative obligations, "e.g., killing an innocent person."

I cannot respond in detail to many of the peripheral statements in Connery's article. For instance, whether "proportionalists" consider adultery or killing an innocent person value terms (actually I do so consider them) is of secondary importance. What is of greater importance is that those who oppose this *Denkform* do consider such terms value terms and then go about saying that "proportionalists" justify what has already been defned to be morally wrong. No "proportionalist" does that.

Again, Connery argues that *ratio proportionata* traditionally did not apply to negative obligations such as direct killing of the innocent. What he fails to observe is that this restrictive interpretation ("direct," "innocent") of killing could only have been made by a teleological procedure. In other words, we gradually arrived at a *moral* definition of certain actions ("*direct* killing of the *innocent*") by weighing all the good and evil in certain actions and then concluding that, all things considered, they could never be morally acceptable. Whenever a moral norm is inadequately formulated, this process of restrictive interpretation must occur. But that is not to make exceptions to accepted moral formulations.

[19] John R. Connery, S.J., "The Teleology of Proportionate Reason," *TS* 44 (1983) 489–96.

It is to critique the adequacy of the formulations themselves. If we get to a *moral* definition of an act (as morally wrong) by a teleological procedure, then clearly the act so defined is subject to teleological inspection if we are to be consistent.[20]

But there are several points in Connery's response that I want to lift out for further dialogue.

1) *The term "materia circa quam."* I am surprised that Connery sees my usage as "new." It is adapted from St. Thomas, and indeed in this very area. For instance, Thomas writes: "The objects as related to the exterior acts are the *materia circa quam*, but as related to the interior act of the will they are ends, and it is from their being ends that they give the species to the action, but as *materia circa quam* of the exterior action they are also termini by which the movements are specified."[21] I had suggested some such usage because the term "object" is used so inconsistently. Sometimes it includes morally relevant circumstances (theft = "taking another's property against his reasonable will"), sometimes it does not (masturbation). For this reason the term "ex objecto" becomes ambiguous, and not terribly useful, because it is not clear whether the moral wrongness roots in the object or the circumstances, as Karl Hörmann has recently noted.[22]

There are two ways to avoid this problem. The first is to cease speaking of the object and to speak of *materia circa quam* with all morally relevant circumstances. The second is to continue to use the term "object" but to include in it all morally relevant circumstances, as Thomas did.[23] For all practical purposes the two are the same.

2) *The proportionalist calculus.* Closely connected with the above point is Connery's insistence that there are actions that are morally definable "apart from the kind of calculus the proportionalist would demand." I am not sure what that means. It looks very much like a misconception. It makes me wonder what Connery is thinking of when he says "proportionalists" would demand a calculus beyond an already morally defined act. If an act is *morally* defined, obviously no further calculus is needed. And every "proportionalist" would say that. But a calculus is often called for before the act can be so defined.

At several points Connery refers to and rejects "weighing all the good

---

[20] Cf. John F. Dedek, "Intrinsically Evil Acts: The Emergence of a Doctrine," *Recherches de théologie ancienne et médiévale* 50 (1983) 191–226.

[21] 1–2, q. 72, ad 2; cf. also 1–2, q. 18, ad 2, 3.

[22] Karl Hörmann, "Die Unveränderlichkeit sittlicher Normen im Anschluss an Thomas von Aquin," in *Sittliche Normen*, ed. Walter Kerber (Düsseldorf: Patmos, 1982) 33–45, at 42.

[23] 1–2, q. 18, a. 10c: "principalis conditio objecti"; ad 2: "Circumstantia . . . in quantum mutatur in principalem conditionem objecti, secundum hoc dat speciem."

and evil in the act, including the consequences." Perhaps this is the "calculus" to which he refers. He says that this is unnecessary and only complicating because certain actions are morally definable without it. I would turn that around and say that certain actions are *morally* definable precisely because and only insofar as "all the morally relevant good and evil in the act" has been weighed. Sometimes that is very easy, as when Thomas says that *occisio innocentis* is always wrong. Sometimes it is not. But it can never be bypassed; otherwise we have given the act its moral character independently of morally relevant circumstances.[24]

That is exactly what tradition has done in some instances. Take Connery's example of the "solitary sex act." He says that a moral judgment can be made "merely by a consideration of the object of the act." That is, it is always wrong regardless of the circumstances. This is precisely the type of physicalism many theologians reject (I say "physicalism" because the entire moral meaning of the act is gathered in precision from morally relevant circumstances and based on its physical structure). Thus we find theologians like L. Janssens, M. Vidal, F. Scholz, B. Häring, E. Chiavacci, L. Rossi, A. Valsecchi, and many others rejecting such an analysis and approving masturbation in the procreative circumstances of artificial insemination by husband. They distinguish "moral" from "biological" masturbation, or masturbation from "ipsation." The terminology is irrelevant. Connery is defending a tradition many, perhaps even most, theologians reject. If one sticks with that tradition, then one must buy its methodological implications, which many theologians think indefensible.

At this point it would be helpful to introduce some remarks of Louis Janssens. In a recent study[25] he notes that Thomas gave four classifications for the objects of external action as they relate to reason. (1) External actions whose object is indifferent, e.g., to pick up a blade of straw from the soil. Such actions get their morality from the end. (2) Actions which because of their object are good *secundum se*, e.g., to give

---

[24] Sebastian MacDonald, C.P., sees this discussion in terms of a shift away from scholastic syllogistic reasoning to an argument from fittingness, "a resolution based on a harmonious relation of goods that evidences signs of fittingness and appropriateness." He concludes: "Catholic moral theology is on the verge of a new era in methods and procedures. It will gradually emerge from a transition period of wide diversity in methods, as it has done in the past, and move toward consensus, though of a different kind. It will depend on a newly gained ability to discover and weigh the goods and the values (and the evils and disvalues) associated with proposed courses of action, to the point where arguments, guidelines, principles and laws gain public warrant and legitimacy because of this fittingness and appropriateness in helping people to live out their Christian lives well in this complex world" ("Can Moral Theology Be Appropriate?" *Thomist* 47 [1983] 543–49, at 549).

[25] Louis Janssens, "St. Thomas and the Question of Proportionality," *Louvain Studies* 9 (1982) 26–46.

an alms. These can become evil by reason of an evil end. (3) Exterior actions that by reason of their object "involve an inseparable moral evil," e.g., adultery, fornication, perjury, killing of the innocent. Of these we may say *mox nominati sunt mali*; or, in Janssens' words, "Certain words are used to name an action not merely under its material aspect, *but precisely insofar as it is a morally evil act.*" Such actions are given value descriptions, and insofar as they are, no further calculus is needed to pronounce them immoral, even though some calculus may be needed to decide what should count as fitting those categories. (4) Actions which, when abstractly considered, contain some important deformity or disorder but are made morally right by circumstances, e.g., in Thomas' words, "The killing and beating of a man involve some deformity in their object. But if it is added to this that an evildoer is killed for the sake of justice or that a delinquent is beaten for punishment, then the action is not a sin; rather it is virtuous."[26]

At this point Janssens makes several important points. First, the deformity or disorder Thomas refers to in category 4 is not *moral* deformity. "Were he speaking of moral disorder or deformity, then it could never be counterbalanced." In other words, no calculus need be made if the action is already g'ven a moral definition. Therefore the deformity is ontic or premoral.[27] Second, while we have the duty to prevent such deformities to the best of our abilities, still, "as the examples given by Thomas show, there are situations in which ontic evil may even be caused—killing or beating a man—and is made morally good by outweighing circumstances."[28] The service of justice and the reasonableness of punishment "can be proportionate reasons to justify the causation of ontic evil." That is utterly clear in Thomas' example, an example that shows how traditional is the notion of "proportionalism."

Reflection on these last two classes of objects leads to the conclusion that a balancing or calculus is called for in the analytic process only when elements of an action are considered abstractly, before giving them a moral definition. For example, if no calculus were required, every killing would be a murder. None would ever be justified. Or, as Janssens notes, "To understand the meaning of the term 'murder,' we have to know the proportionate reasons why some killing is not murder."[29] We have to

---

[26] *Quaestiones quodlibetales* 9, q. 7, a. 15.

[27] I do not understand G. E. M. Anscombe's problem with such terminology; cf. her "Medalist's Address: Action, Intention and 'Double Effect,'" *Proceedings of the American Catholic Philosophical Association* 56 (1982) 12–25. The concept behind the terminology is quite traditional; cf. *Quaestiones quodlibetales* 9, q. 7, a. 15; also Franz Scholz, "Sittliche Normen in teleologischer Sicht," *Stimmen der Zeit* 201 (1983) 700–710, at 705.

[28] "St. Thomas and the Question of Proportionality" 40.

[29] Ibid. 40.

know what Janssens calls the "outweighing circumstances." And this is precisely what official and traditional teaching has not done in certain cases (contraception, sterilization, masturbation). As Thomas noted, some circumstances become "the principal condition of the object."[30] Now if this is true of the abstractly considered act of killing, why is it not true of an abstractly considered act like masturbation? The only reason I can think of is that the biological reality has been allowed to exhaust the notion of the *objectum actus*, as it does for Connery.

So it is not morally defined acts that are susceptible of a weighing and balancing—as Connery and others often assert or imply—but the goods and evils in the single action prior to giving a moral description. To say anything else is to exclude morally relevant circumstances from the assessment of the act. That would be very untraditional.

3) *Permissiveness and proportionalism.* Connery continues to assert that "proportionalism" is vulnerable to abuse and "must bear part of the blame" for the permissiveness experienced in recent years. Furthermore, he claims that there is evidence that this *Denkform* "has given rise to relaxation in attitudes toward moral norms." So many documented factors have been noted for this cultural phenomenon that to attribute it in any significant way to an academic discussion in moral theology is unreal.

But the occasion of Connery's remarks stimulates me to two glosses on this matter. First, if—*dato non concesso*—the discussion of "proportionalism" has indeed influenced an abusive laxness in conduct, then one might more accurately place the blame at the desks of those who misrepresent what many contemporary theologians are saying. I have read repeatedly over the past ten years assertions that many theologians are proposing that a good end justifies a morally evil means. That is, of course, totally false.[31] I have read repeatedly other misrepresentations.[32]

---

[30] 1-2, q. 18, a. 10.

[31] Bruno Schüller, S.J., calls attention to this and suggests that the eighth commandment still does make demands. Those who neglect or forget this seem not to realize that by inaccurately attributing to others the axiom "the end justifies (any) means," they themselves act objectively according to that axiom. Cf. "Die Reductio ad absurdum in philosophischer und theologischer Ethik: Zur Moral wissenschaftlicher Kontroversen über Moral," in *Die Wahrheit tun*, ed. B. Fraling and R. Hasenstab (Würzburg, 1983) 217–40, at 237.

[32] The most recent is that of Ronald D. Lawler ("Critical Reflections on Current Bioethical Thinking," in *Perspectives in Bioethics* [New Britain, Conn.: Mariel, 1983] 9–27, at 21). He caricatures teleological tendencies in the understanding of moral norms as "one does a deed that is in itself simply a doing of evil . . . in the hope that something good may come of it." Or again: "It is a view that producing good effects, having fine things *happen* in the world, is better and more important than *doing* actions which are free deeds honoring God by their goodness." I know of no contemporary theologian who would tolerate such totally misleading statements as a fair presentation of contemporary discussions. Similarly, Paul Quay, S.J., a physicist, has stated with vigor, and certainty in inverse

When priests hear such misrepresentations associated with the names of our outstanding theologians (Häring, Fuchs, Böckle, Schüller, Auer, Janssens, Vidal, Furger, Scholz, Weber, Curran, and a host of others), perhaps it is understandable that they are bewildered. But it must be remembered that we are dealing with a misrepresentation. Let blame fall where it is due, on the misrepresentation.

Second and more importantly, there is solidly based evidence that Catholics have adopted certain permissive attitudes because (among many other cultural factors) of the Church's apparent intransigence and unwillingness to dialogue in any meaningful way on sexual matters. The *Humanae vitae* phenomenon revealed this. The phenomenon was repeated in *Persona humana*, as the literature reported in these "Notes" testifies.[33] Many people with whom I have spoken over the years are convinced that Roman theology, and to that extent the official Church, is incapable of dealing with sexuality honestly and openly. *For this reason* people begin to develop their own approach to things. This is also documentable.[34] But once again, let blame fall where it is due.

---

proportion (if I may) to his grasp of the issues, that "proportionalists" propose that "the alternatives proposed in moral deliberation are, with only a few rare exceptions, nonmoral." He regards this as a "serious error," sufficient "of itself to vitiate the revisionists' entire approach to morality" ("The Unity and Structure of the Human Act," *Listening* 18 [1983] 245–59). He attributes this position to Knauer, Schüller, Fuchs, Janssens, Curran, and this author. "Proportionalists," of course, say nothing of the kind. Obviously, every choice is of an action with a *moral* character. What "proportionalists" do say is that, before assigning or determining that moral character, one must evaluate relevant circumstances. St. Thomas obviously held this; otherwise he would never have been able to approve (as he did) an action that involved the killing of a human being. Janssens makes this very clear in the article cited above. Quay's wild assertions are a reminder that we have a duty to understand the terms of a discussion or exercise self-restraint in entering it. Quay, I am sorry to say, has done neither.—For an accurate representation of the views in question, cf. Walter Kerber, S.J., ed., *Sittliche Normen* (Düsseldorf: Patmos, 1982). Of this book Bernard Häring writes: "Very seldom have I read a collection with such full agreement as I have this rich book, to which proven and well-known moral theologians and the esteemed exegete Heinz Schürmann have contributed." Häring concludes his review as follows: "If all those with magisterial authority, if theologians and pastors of souls would study this little book carefully and discuss it with each other, many misunderstandings would be dissipated and the pastoral peace of the Church would be well served.... It would be a pity were this world-wide consensus of established authors not sufficiently noted" (*Theologie der Gegenwart* 26 [1983] 66–67). Cf. also Franz Scholz as in n. 27 above.

[33] It was no less than Joseph Ratzinger who wrote in 1971: "I should like to emphasize once more that I fully agree with Küng's distinction between Roman [school] theology and [Catholic] faith. I am convinced that Catholicism's survival depends on our ability to break out of the prison of the Roman-school type" ("Widersprüche im Buch von Hans Küng," in K. Rahner, ed., *Zum Problem Unfehlbarkeit* [Freiburg, 1971] 97–116, at 105).

[34] For instance cf. the interesting replies to a questionnaire on "Secular Ethics and Nonbelief" circulated by the Secretariat for Nonbelievers (*Atheism and Dialogue* 18 [1983] 4–34). Bjørn Halvorsen, O.P. (Norway), compares the different reception accorded social

Another interesting conversation concerns theological "notes" or the status of teaching in the Church. It will be recalled that John C. Ford, S.J., and Germain Grisez argued in these pages that the traditional Catholic teaching on birth regulation is infallibly taught.[35] Ford and Grisez had stated their premise as follows:

> We do not assert that the norm is divinely revealed. This question is one from which we have prescinded. Our position rather is this: if the norm is not contained in revelation, it is at least connected with it as a truth required to guard the deposit as inviolable and to expound it with fidelity. . . . Admittedly, it does not seem there is any way to establish *conclusively* that this teaching either pertains to revelation or is connected with it apart from the fact that the ordinary magisterium has proposed the teaching in the manner in which it has, and the faithful as a whole until recently have accepted the norm as binding. But a similar state of affairs has been used as a basis for solemnly defining at least one dogma: that of the Assumption of the Blessed Virgin Mary.[36]

In the process of a very thorough study of the ordinary magisterium, Francis A. Sullivan, S.J. (Gregorian University), deals with this premise.[37] I say "premise" because the paragraph deals with the proper object of infallible teaching, a condition of infallible teaching. Sullivan interprets the paragraph as follows: "If I understand this correctly, what it means is that we can know for certain that this is a proper object for infallible teaching from the fact that the magisterium has taught it infallibly."

---

and sexual teachings. "On the other hand, however, the Church's teaching in the field of sexual ethics generally meets with negative reactions, even with ridicule." He believes that the values the Church is upholding would be better achieved "by a more positive presentation of them than what is generally the case." Patrick Masterson notes the same thing in Ireland: "Since *Humanae vitae* there has been somewhat of a qualitative change in the way in which Catholic moral theology is *received*." Reporting from India, Aelred Pereira, S.J., notes: "Catholics reject the Church's teaching on sexual ethics without having a substitute position—they find it inconvenient and impracticable." The Episcopal Conference of Belgium notes: "Even though there is not question here of a capital point in Christian ethics, still we must not misunderstand the fact that it is especially the presentation of the Christian principles concerning sexual life that provoked the greatest resistance since the appearance of *Humanae vitae*."

[35] John C. Ford, S.J., and Germain Grisez, "Contraception and Infallibility," *TS* 39 (1978) 258–312. This article was published as a brochure in Germany (*Das unfehlbare ordentliche Lehramt der Kirche zur Empfängnisregelung*, Siegburg, 1980). It occasioned several exchanges: cf. *Theologisches* 139 (1981) 4341–42; 144 (1982) 4583–85; *Theologie und Glaube* 72 (1982) 14–39; *Theologisches* 149 (1982) 4819–27. These references were provided to me through the kindness of Joachim Piegsa, professor of moral theology, Augsburg.

[36] "Contraception" 286–87.

[37] Francis A. Sullivan, S.J., *Magisterium: Teaching Authority in the Catholic Church* (Dublin: Gill and Macmillan, 1983). I cite from the proofs and therefore no accurate pagination is available at this writing.

Sullivan rejects this on several grounds. First, the analogy with the Assumption breaks down. The Assumption was accepted for centuries as a matter of Christian *faith*. The same is not the case with the prohibition of contraception. Sullivan thinks it more likely that it was accepted "as a binding law of the Church."

Next, Sullivan rejects the supposition of the Ford-Grisez argument: that is, if the magisterium speaks in a definitive way about something, it must necessarily be the case that what they speak about is a proper object of infallibility. This would eliminate independent criteria for determining whether something is a proper object of infallibility. Against this view, Sullivan urges that there would be no point in the insistence of Vatican I and Vatican II that the magisterium can speak infallibly only on faith and morals. "It would have been necessary to say only this: whenever the magisterium speaks in a definitive way, it must be speaking infallibly, because the very fact that it speaks in a definitive way would guarantee that what it speaks about would be a proper matter for infallible teaching." Sullivan sees this as an open door to absolutism. He finds no evidence to show that the teaching is so necessarily connected with revelation that the magisterium could not safeguard and expound revelation if it could not teach it infallibly. In other words, it is not a proper object of infallible teaching.

Finally, Ford-Grisez base their case for infallibility on the contention that for many centuries the doctrine was taught by the universal episcopate as a norm *to be held definitively*. Sullivan, along with Rahner and others, insists that "to be held definitively" means to give an irrevocable assent. There is no evidence that this is what the centuries-old teaching meant to do. As Sullivan words it, "In other words, it is one thing to teach that something involves a serious moral obligation; it is quite another to claim that this teaching is now absolutely definitive, and demands irrevocable assent." If the Ford-Grisez thesis were correct, "it would mean that the Church could not declare any mode of conduct gravely wrong unless it were prepared to make an irreversible judgment on the matter. This would practically rule out any ordinary, noninfallible exercise of the Church's teaching authority on moral questions." I find Sullivan's arguments and his concluding synthetic overview of the Church's teaching authority in these matters persuasive.

DOCTRINAL DEVELOPMENT

When doctrinal development occurs in the Church, it is usually not without a kind of last-gasp neurological twitch that reveals the pain of the transition. In moving to a new level of understanding, something is left behind, and that abandonment is not in all respects different from a kind of dying. We saw this in the struggle that culminated in *Dignitatis humanae* (on religious liberty). To accept the doctrine on religious liberty of Vatican II, the Church had to admit, at least implicitly, that Gregory XVI and Pius IX were wrong.[38] In doing so, she had to concede that subsequent popes were and are no less vulnerable. Still, for a Church with an enormous recent investment in the notion of papal authority, that admission was slow and traumatic, even though it should shock no one with a knowledge of history. The authority problem explained much of the vigorous and at times almost bitter resistance to change on religious liberty. John Courtney Murray, S.J., recognized and acknowledged this privately on numerous occasions.

In a pilgrim Church that exists in diverse cultures and rapidly changing times—to say nothing of existing "between the times"—such doctrinal development should be expected. Archbishop John Quinn adverted to this in his intervention during the 1980 Synod of Bishops. However, if such developmental shifts are to occur pacifically in the Church, it might be useful to attempt to highlight their broad structural outlines. The contemporary literature on artificial insemination and *in vitro* fertilization may serve as a vehicle here. As I write, some 300 babies have been born by this latter procedure.[39]

The Government Committee of Inquiry into Human Fertilisation and Embryology (the "Warnock Committee," so called because it is chaired by Oxford philosopher Mary Warnock) was established in England to review the problems associated with *in vitro* fertilization. Three Catholic groups made submissions to the Warnock Committee: the Bishops' Joint Committee on Bioethical Issues, the Bishops' Social Welfare Commission, the Catholic Union and Guild of Catholic Doctors.[40] All are opposed to the involvement of third parties (donor sperm or ova, womb-leasing) and to experimentation on fertilized embryos.

However, they differ markedly on *in vitro* fertilization to aid infertile couples. The Catholic Union and Guild of Catholic Doctors favors the procedure. The Social Welfare Commission repeats the statement of welcome which it issued in 1978 when Louise Brown was born: "Some married couples have a deep desire for children as the supreme joy of their marriage, but are physically unable to conceive children in the normal way. In these cases science can support the loving and natural ambition of the couple to produce new life."[41]

---

[38] The reconciliation of *Dignitatis humanae* with *Mirari vos* and the *Syllabus of Errors* is not an easy undertaking, to say the least. What is more interesting than the obviously strained attempts at reconciliation (*Faith and Reason* 9 [1983] 182–248) is the felt need—the implication being that the earlier popes could not have been inaccurate in their rejection of religious liberty. An expansive and unwarranted understanding of the ordinary magisterium has created an unnecessary problem.

[39] Personal communication from Dr. Gary Hodgen, National Institutes of Health.

[40] *Tablet*, June 4, 1983, 523.

[41] Ibid.

The Bishops' Joint Committee, however, argues that *in vitro* fertilization, as well as artificial insemination by husband, severs procreation from sexual intercourse in such a way that the child comes into existence "in the manner of a product." This involves for the child a status "of radical inequality" in contrast to the equality enjoyed by the child of natural sexual union. The committee believes that "the great evils of destructive experimentation, observation and selection" are symptoms of this flaw. They refer to the long-run evils inseparable from procreation severed from the marital act:

Undesirable and scarcely reversible changes in the way parents regard their children; in the way partners in marriage regard each other; and in the way men and women regard their bodily life and the most intimately involving personal interaction within that life. Each of these changes, bad in themselves, would also make more difficult, in principle and in practice, resistance to the general trivialising of sexual intercourse; commercialisation and/or state control of reproductive activity; selection of children on eugenic grounds; the moulding of children's most basic characteristics by parents, technicians and other interested persons, groups and governments; and even more extensive resort to that awesome instrument of compassion become ruthless and inhumane, the embryo bank.[42]

What is one to make of this? I would agree with the committee's rejection of experimentation that endangers the embryo, of selective destruction of embryos, embryo storage without the prospect of transfer to the proper mother, of third-party involvement. But what about the "undesirable changes" in attitude (toward the child, each other, and their bodily life) associated with severing procreation from sexual intercourse? It is such changes that led most of the committee to reject on moral grounds *in vitro* fertilization as well as artificial insemination by husband. The weakness of the argument is its lack of evidence. Even the committee's wording unwittingly acknowledges this. It refers to long-run evils that "*may be involved* in arranging procreation severed from the central marital act." Without evidence that such evils will very likely occur, the committee's analysis remains more a caution than an argument. The same thing can be said of the committee's assertion that the IVF child may be likened to a "product."

Lorenzo Leuzzi, a physician and moral theologian, presents a useful summary of theological thought in Italy on artificial insemination.[43] G. Pesce, Carlo Caffarro, D. Tettamanzi, and G. Perico are opposed to

---

[42] The citation is from the original manuscript kindly provided to me by LeRoy Walters, Kennedy Institute of Ethics.

[43] Lorenzo Leuzzi, "Il dibattito sull'inseminazione artificiale nella riflessione medico-morale in Italia nell'ultimo decennio," *Medicina e morale* 22 (1982) 343–71.

artificial insemination by husband and a fortiori to *in vitro* fertilization. For instance, Pesce adverts explicitly to the inseparability of the unitive and procreative dimensions of sexual intimacy underlined in *Humanae vitae*. This excludes both contraception and artificial insemination. Tettamanzi insists that the unity of these dimensions cannot be restricted to the intention.

Leuzzi summarizes: "The most frequent and urgent critique made by theologians who express a more favorable judgment of A.I.H. is that this [condemnatory] judgment stems from a biological and physiological notion of human nature."[44] Thus Enrico Chiavacci wonders whether the separation of biologically generative activity from personal intimacy is a *malum in se* independently of the accompanying intention. When the procreative intention is so strong that it is required by the overall good of the couple, then the two dimensions (unitive and procreative) are "united by intention" since "the separation is only at the biological level." Chiavacci concludes: "My judgment is positive providing we limit the procedure to husband insemination in cases where procreation is otherwise impossible."

A. Delepierre studies the texts of Pius XII and rejects Pius' condemnation of husband insemination because it is the result of an identification of biology with the natural law. Leuzzi also cites Häring's approval: "When the sperm comes from the husband and the whole marriage is lived in a climate of love, then not only is he biologically the father but there is not that total severance between the unitive and the procreative meaning of marriage."[45]

Marciano Vidal, the outstanding moral theologian in Spain, associates himself with the position of Chiavacci and M. Di Ianni, as does L. Rossi. As for obtaining semen by masturbation, Di Ianni, Vidal, Häring, Valsecchi, Delepierre, and Rossi find little problem, since we must distinguish this biological phenomenon from egoistic self-petting.

[44] Ibid. 357.

[45] Bernard Häring, *Medical Ethics* (Notre Dame: Fides, 1973) 92. Häring's most recent judgment is that "fertilization *in vitro* . . . can be evaluated on the same principle as artificial insemination with the husband's sperm" (*Free and Faithful in Christ* 3 [New York: Crossroad, 1981] 25). On artificial insemination he cites George Lobo ("In the present state of the discussion . . . a couple . . . would not be doing wrong by having recourse to A.I.H.") and remarks that "Lobo can be sure of finding vast assent." Janet Dickey McDowell comes to a conclusion similar to Häring's. She believes that "love (as expressed in sexual activity) is preconditional to reproduction, and in that sense the two purposes [unitive, procreative] remain linked. . . . The fact that conception does not take place as the *direct* result of love made concrete through intercourse is less significant; provided that both love and the desire to procreate are elements of the couple's total relationship, IVF would not be problematic" ("Ethical Implications of In vitro Fertilisation," *Christian Century* 100 [1983] 936–38).

Leuzzi concludes his report with a synthetic overview. Two key points stand out: (1) There should be no procreation without conjugal love. (2) Procreation should not be reduced to a technological thing ("fatto technico"), because that would open the door to a consumer mentality toward procreation. A very useful overview.

Two articles represent totally opposing points of view on *in vitro* fertilization. The first is that of Francesco Giunchedi, S.J.[46] He adverts to the studies of P. Verspieren and W. Molinski, both of whom approve the procedure.[47] The former sees *in vitro* fertilization as a prolongation of the sexual life of the sterile couple. Giunchedi sees it rather as a substitution, one that completely separates the exercise of sexuality and the transmission of life in a way that does not allow procreation to achieve its full dignity. By contrast, Henri Wattiaux agrees with Verspieren that *in vitro* fertilization may be viewed as a prolongation of sexual intimacy.[48] Since this is the case, there is not the radical severing of the unitive and procreative.

Hermann Hepp, after attending to the possible misuses that could be associated with *in vitro* procedures, concludes that *abusus non tollit usum*.[49] "I believe that, in an overall view of human persons, here of the loving couple whose love can reach completion only through artificial impregnation, husband *in vitro* fertilization must be approved as a last resort." Hepp is aware that this runs counter to the thesis of the inseparability of the unitive and procreative dimensions proposed by Paul VI and John Paul II. But he sees it as in the service of life, and agrees with J. Gründel that not everything that is artificial is unnatural in the moral sense.

Josef G. Ziegler approaches the problem through two basic principles: (1) the inviolable worth of the human being; (2) the threefold relation of our conduct to God, the neighbor (society), the self.[50] "Conduct in marriage qualifies as 'good' when it corresponds to the principle of the integration of the three stated basic elements." The first principle is violated when embryos are treated like things, experimental objects. The second may be violated in a number of ways. For instance, he argues that

[46] Francesco Giunchedi, S.J., "La fecondazione 'in vitro,'" *Rassegna di teologia* 24 (1983) 289–307.

[47] P. Verspieren, S.J., "L'Aventure de la fécondation in vitro," *Etudes*, Nov. 1982, 479–92; W. Molinski, "Sittliche Aspekte der extracorporalen Befruchtung," *Arzt und Christ* 28 (1982) 141–47.

[48] Henri Wattiaux, "Insémination artificielle, fécondation 'in vitro' et transplantation embryonnaire," *Esprit et vie* 92 (1983) 353–64.

[49] Hermann Hepp, "Die In-vitro-Befruchtung: Perspektiven und Gefahren," *Stimmen der Zeit* 201 (1983) 291–304.

[50] Josef G. Ziegler, "Zeugung ausserhalb des Mutterleibes," *Theologisch-praktische Quartalschrift* 131 (1983) 231–41.

donor insemination offends against all the components in principle 2: "against the relationship to God, who established the unbreakable oneness of marriage; against the relationship to oneself, the self who achieves fulfilment within the marital partnership; against the relationship to society, which has a right to know where children come from."[51]

Ziegler is particularly concerned about the severing of the life-giving from the love-making element in *in vitro* procedures. "Is not the function of the wife as life-bearer featured in an isolated way and thereby her personal worth undermined?" In response to this he emphasizes that sexual intimacy, to be worthy of persons, depends on "the intentional or moral unity of partnering and parenting." It is precisely in uniting toward a common goal or responsibility that a married couple achieve true unity. In this case the goal is the fulfilment of their deep desire to have a child.

The study concludes by refusing to give an unconditioned yes or no to *in vitro* fertilization. Each case must be considered on its own. But it is clear that Ziegler would approve some instances as last resorts. And if I read him correctly, he must refuse to give an absolute, determinative value to the physical inseparability of the unitive-procreative as this is proposed in official Church analyses.

William May (Catholic University) believes that the official formulations (Pius XII) against artificial insemination and *in vitro* fertilization "can be shown to be true."[52] He offers the following syllogism:

Any act of generating human life that is nonmarital is irresponsible and violates the reverence due to human life in its generation. But *in vitro* fertilisation and other forms of laboratory generation of human life, including artificial insemination whether by vendor or husband, are nonmarital. Therefore these modes of generating human life are irresponsible and violate the reverence due to human life in its generation.

May argues that the minor does not require "extensive discussion." When the sperm or ova are from outside the marriage (donors, vendors), the insemination is "evidently nonmarital." It comes from outside the marriage. So far, clear. But he then says that even when sperm and ovum come from husband and wife, the procedure is "nonmarital in nature." Why? "Because they are *in principle* procedures that may be effected by persons who are not spouses." May then adds: "In addition and more significantly, the spousal character of the man and woman participating in the procedures is not intrinsic to the procedures even though they may happen to be husband and wife. What makes husband and wife

[51] Ibid. 241.
[52] William E. May, "'Begotten, Not Made': Reflections on the Laboratory Generation of Human Life," in *Perspectives in Bioethics* (New Britain, Conn.: Muriel, 1983) 31-60.

capable of participating in such activities is not their spousal union but the simple fact that they are beings who produce gametic cells."[53]

With all due respect, May's minor does require far more "extensive discussion" than he has given it. It is the term "nonmarital" that is the problem. It is the nub (middle term) of his argument. But I fail to see what the term means. In fact, I find his use of it impenetrable. In his own definition, it refers to an action of which a couple is "capable" only by being spouses. But what is such an action? Surely not sexual union. For we could reword May as follows: "What makes husband and wife capable of participating in such activities is not their spousal union but the simple fact that they are beings who have sexual organs." Perhaps "nonmarital" means an action in which spouses *ought not* participate. But then May's syllogism involves a straightforward *petitio principii*. Until he explains far more clearly than he has the meaning of the term "nonmarital," the argument remains as strong as its weakest link.

Donald McCarthy, in comparing the new procedure of low tubal ovum transfer (LTOT), where the ovum is transferred to the uterus to be fertilized by natural intercourse, with *in vitro* fertilization, contends that it "differs radically and essentially" from the latter.[54] In IVF there is "no personal involvement of the parents with each other." They simply supply their gametes. Secondly, in IVF there is no expression of the marriage covenant and the child is produced by technology. Thus he approves LTOT but rejects IVF.

I think we must grant these differences. But what is their ethical significance? To accept one technology (LTOT) and reject the other (IVF), the meaning of McCarthy's descriptive differences must be: (1) The parents must be personally involved through sexual union in the procreation of new life. (2) In the conception of new life the marriage covenant must be expressed through sexual union. But these assertions are, of course, the very things to be established if IVF is to be totally rejected. *Why* must the parents be personally involved in all, even exceptional and last-resort, cases of generation of new life? Merely to describe differences and then give them ethical mileage is what Schüller referred to as "persuasive description." It nearly always contains a *petitio principii*.

This, then, is some of the recent literature on artificial reproductive technologies. It is clear that many theologians (cf. Häring's "vast assent") have moved beyond the formulations of Pius XII. It is also clear that in doing so they must, in some way or another, modify the understanding of the inseparability of the unitive-procreative dimensions of sexual

---

[53] Ibid. 49.
[54] *Medical-Moral Newsletter* 20 (Oct. 1983) 30–31.

expression asserted in *Humanae vitae* and *Familiaris consortio*. That raises the interesting question of the development of doctrine in moral theology. That such development has occurred in the past is unquestionable. For instance, Walter J. Burghardt, S.J., states the conviction of many when he asserts that "I am convinced that Vatican II's affirmation of religious freedom ... is discontinuous with certain explicit elements within the Catholic tradition."[55] That such development can occur in the present ought to be unquestionable. But the matter is extremely sensitive, as John Courtney Murray, S.J., recognized when he stated of *Dignitatis humanae* that it was the most controversial document of Vatican II "because it raised with sharp emphasis the issue that lay continually below the surface of all the conciliar debates—the issue of the development of doctrine."[56]

I do not wish for the moment to argue that growing theological acceptance of artificial procreative techniques *is* an example of doctrinal development or *ought to be accepted as such*. The wish is too easily father of the thought. That may or may not be the case. If it is the case, then like *Dignitatis humanae* it will involve certain discontinuities with the past. What is important to highlight is that *if* such a development occurred, it would probably have a recognizable structure, something we could look for in other developing areas. Using the emergence of *Dignitatis humanae* as a vehicle, I would tentatively suggest attending to a three-step process: (1) the earlier formulation and the reasons and circumstances that explain it, (2) a change in the circumstances and reasons that supported the earlier formulations, (3) experience and reflection leading to an altered formulation.

Concretely, there were cultural and historical circumstances that led to Gregory XVI's *Mirari vos* and made it quite intelligible in those circumstances. But the circumstances had gradually changed by 1965 and "the American experience" had been reflected upon sufficiently to generate efforts at a new formulation of the Church's concerns.[57]

---

[55] Cf. *Religious Freedom, 1965 and 1975* (Ramsey: Paulist, 1977) 72.

[56] *The Documents of Vatican II*, ed. Walter M. Abbott, S.J. (New York: America, 1966) 673.

[57] In his doctoral dissertation Robert E. Lampert argues that "reading the signs of the times" was the methodology operative in the development of *Dignitatis humanae* (*An Investigation of Reading the Signs of the Times* [Ann Arbor: University Microfilms, 1980] ,302–42). Indeed, John Courtney Murray stated this explicitly: "The link between religious freedom and limited constitutional government, and the link between the freedom of the Church and the freedom of the people—these were not nineteenth-century theological-political insights. They became available only within twentieth-century perspectives created by 'the signs of the times.' The two links were not forged by abstract deductive logic, but by history, by the historical advance of totalitarian government, and by the corresponding new application of man's dignity in society" (*The Problem of Religious Freedom* [Westminster, Md.: Newman, 1965] 100).

This is only to admit that the Church's formulations of her moral convictions are historically conditioned. This should surprise no one, for even dogmas are historically conditioned. The Congregation for the Doctrine of the Faith (*Mysterium ecclesiae*, 1973) acknowledged a four-fold historical conditioning. Statements of the faith are affected by the presuppositions, the concerns ("the intention of solving certain questions"), the thought categories ("the changeable conceptions of a given epoch"), and the available vocabulary of the times.[58]

Could an evaluation similar to the one that led to *Dignitatis humanae* be occurring with regard to procreative technologies? One who defends that thesis could point to rather clearly identifiable circumstances that led Pius XII to reject all A.I.H. Specifically, there was the influence of F. Hurth, S.J. Hurth was largely responsible for the major writings of Pius XII on sexual and medical questions. Hurth regarded procreativity as the exclusive primary finality of human sexuality. For him, this was "the intention of nature inscribed in the organs and their functions." Thus artificial insemination by husband was to be excluded as against nature. At one point in his analysis of the marriage act Hurth states:

Our whole argument proves not only that nature has determined the means for man by which he is capable of serving the species, but also that he may only serve it by this means, i.e., the natural marriage act. It would be absurd that nature determined the means for men in every respect (anatomical, physiological, psychological) to place himself at the service of the species and that it indicated the manner of acting to the smallest detail with an almost unbelievable efficiency in order to thus allow man the right to choose his manner of acting as he pleases or to substitute another means for it which he had found himself. Nature contains no such inner contradiction. Let me conclude: This analysis of the psychosomatic sexual apparatus demands that we say that man's right to use the sexual organism, and especially the germ cells, is limited to the execution of the natural marriage act with all that prepares for, accompanies and follows from it in a natural way.[59]

It is clear, then, that for Hurth the moral law and the biological law coincide. Indeed, Hurth states exactly that: "Man only has disposal of the use of his organs and his faculties with respect to the end which the Creator, in his formation of them, has intended. This end for man then is both the biological law and the moral law, such that the latter obliges him to live according to the biological law."[60]

In the nearly forty years since those lines were written, there has been

[58] Cf. *Catholic Mind* 71 (Oct. 1973) 58–60.

[59] F. Hurth, S.J., "La fécondation artificielle: Sa valeur morale et juridique," *Nouvelle revue théologique* 68 (1946) 402–26. I take the translation of this and the following citation from L. Janssens, "Artificial Insemination: Ethical Considerations," *Louvain Studies* 8 (1980) 3–29.

[60] Cf. n. 59 above.

a change in the circumstances surrounding the discussion. The principal change is the criterion to be used in judging the rightfulness or wrongfulness of human conduct. Vatican II proposed as the criterion not "the intention of nature inscribed in the organs and their functions" but "the person integrally and adequately considered." To discover what is promotive or destructive of the person is not a deductive procedure. As Louis Janssens has noted, "History itself testifies to so many mistakes which man later had to admit or ignore because he had too quickly condemned what was new without allowing for the experience, the time or the opportunity to work out whether or not something was worthy of man."[61]

This is not to blame Pius XII in any way. His achievement was magnificent. He was, after all and as it should be, dependent on his theologians. Similarly today, the pope must depend on theological advisors who, like all of us, are pilgrims and see only darkly. There are two points to emphasize in saying this. First, when teaching on doctrinal questions, the pope must be careful to prevent his circle of advisors narrowing so as to exclude legitimate currents of theological thought, as Rahner has repeatedly noted. Second, even with the broadest and best consultation, authoritative teaching will unavoidably be time- and culture-conditioned. A certain form of ecclesiastical fundamentalism tends to forget this.

Is an evolution occurring with regard to the understanding of the unitive and procreative dimensions of sexuality? Much of the literature brought under review would have to answer in the affirmative. If a development of doctrine is occurring, the thread that yields both continuity and change is the notion of the inseparability of the unitive-procreative dimensions of sexuality. The continuity: the general validity of the insight. The change: a broadened understanding away from an act analysis of this inseparability. Whatever the case, the aforementioned inseparability-principle must promote the person "integrally and adequately considered." When it becomes an obstacle to that promotion, it loses its (generally operative) normative force; for it is subject to and judged by the broader criterion.

Should there be doctrinal development in the Church's teaching on abortion? Daniel Maguire thinks so.[62] He contrasts the attitudes of the United States Catholic bishops on peace and abortion. With regard to peace, they caution in their recent pastoral against "a simple answer to complex questions," whereas on abortion there is "only a simple answer to complex questions." Maguire indicts the silence or indifference of

---

[61] Janssens, as in note 59 above, at 11.

[62] Daniel C. Maguire, "Abortion: A Question of Catholic Honesty," *Christian Century* 100 (1983) 803–7.

"many Catholic theologians who recognize the morality of certain abortions but will not address the subject publicly." It is his view that a sizable number of theologians disagree with some aspects of official teaching; and for this reason he believes probabilism is applicable, making it possible to act on "the liberal dissenting view." As he words it:

There are far more than five or six Catholic theologians today who approve abortions under a range of circumstances, and there are many spiritual and good people who find "cogent," nonfrivolous reasons to disagree with the hierarchy's absolutism on this issue. This makes their disagreement a "solidly probable" and thoroughly respectable Catholic viewpoint.[63]

Maguire then proceeds to list the factors that generated the present official stand on abortion and argues that they were deficient or have changed in our time. (I would note that this is the very structure I suggested above.) Among the factors: heavily juridical arguments; an external-judge approach; excessively physical arguments; abstract and rationalistic arguments; lack of an ecumenically sensitive theology; inaccurate biological knowledge; lack of dialogue with the laity; pervasive sexist attitudes. In combination, these produced a one-sided absolutism.

Maguire concludes by arguing that abortion deserves respectable debate because there are "good reasons and reliable authorities" standing behind the opposition to the absolutism of official Catholic teaching. This is all the more reason why there should be freedom and not coercion at the public-policy level.

What is one to make of this? Reactions, I would guess, will be quite predictable, as they so often are in discussions about abortion. Maguire will be accused of verbal sophistry, of one-sided feminism, of antihierarchyism, and a host of almost printable things. He will also be praised for honesty and courage. Such rhetorical flourishes are not very enlightening.

This reviewer has two reactions. First, I believe Maguire has overstated the case in several ways. He refers to "far more than five or six Catholic theologians today who approve abortions under a range of circumstances." Who are these theologians? And above all, what does "a range of circumstances" include? Specificity is required here. I know of theologians who have problems with certain marginal cases. But I know of precious few who would extend this over an unspecified "range of circumstances." But Maguire expands this into the "solid probability" of a dissent against "the hierarchy's absolutism on this issue." That is just too vague. What is actual theological opinion on this matter? Franz Böckle (in his *Handbuch der christlichen Ethik*) presents what Bernard Häring calls "the common opinion among Catholic moral theologians."

[63] Ibid. 805.

Böckle allows interruption of pregnancy only where otherwise the mother cannot be saved. "Beyond this case I do not see any plausible reasons that could morally justify an interruption of pregnancy."[64]

Then there is the matter of "solid probability." Maguire asserts that "there are many spiritual and good people who find 'cogent,' nonfrivolous reasons to disagree with the hierarchy's absolutism on this issue. This makes their disagreement a 'solidly probable' and thoroughly respectable Catholic viewpoint." Once again we encounter vagueness. "Disagreement with absolutism" is one thing. A single exception in a marginal instance (e.g., anencephaly) would warrant such a statement. But Maguire carries the matter far beyond that to a vaguely asserted "liberal dissenting view" and asserts its probability. Nothing that I know in Catholic tradition would justify such a loose expansion of "solid probability." It is opinions about *specific cases* that may be said to be probable or not. And when Maguire addresses specific cases, a further ambiguity enters the picture. Citing a 1982 Yankelovich poll, he adduces the following instances: rape, risk to health, genetically damaged fetus, physically handicapped woman, teen-age pregnancy, welfare mother who cannot work, a married woman who already has a large family.

Maguire cites these as instances where a majority of Catholic women would judge abortion morally justified. But what are we to make of that? Does he propose these as justifiable cases? I know of no reputable Catholic theologian who would justify abortion in such a litany of cases. The fact that many Catholic women do raises more questions than answers. It is, of course, notoriously true that under permissive abortion laws many more women see abortion as a solution to their problem than would otherwise be the case. Daniel Callahan has noted that a change to permissive abortion laws "appears—from *all data* and in *every country*— to bring forward a whole class of women who would otherwise not have wanted an abortion or felt the need for one."[65] This means, of course, that the very culture or atmosphere has conditioned their judgment. Or, to use Maguire's probabilistic language, many more will judge their reasons for abortion "cogent" in such circumstances. That leaves relatively unexamined the moral question of whether they *are* cogent—unless one reduces the moral question to a question of the individual women's judgment.

That brings me to my second and major problem with Maguire's essay. Put quite simply, he has attempted to move the problem from a life issue to an exclusively women's (choice) issue. He opposes "absolutism." Fair enough; I suppose many of us do. But in doing so he is—as I read him—

[64] Bernard Häring, *Free and Faithful in Christ* 3 (New York: Crossroad, 1981) 33.

[65] Daniel Callahan, "Abortion: Thinking and Experiencing," *Christianity and Crisis* 32 (1973) 296.

proposing just two *moral* options: the absolutism of the tradition or the prochoice option. (I emphasize the word "moral" because the legal level is a different matter.) I say the prochoice option because the broad range of instances he cites is equivalent to that. That seems to me to trivialize the morality of abortion. Whatever one's moral position may be, I believe it is off course if it is not seen as centrally—even if not exclusively—a life problem. Certain abortions may be morally justifiable (I do not argue the matter here). But if they are, it is because it is at times justifiable to take nascent human life. *That* is the matter that must be discussed and that is the conclusion that must be justified; for on any realistic account of things that is what is happening in abortion. Major Protestant theologians like James Gustafson, James Childress, Arthur Dyck, Paul Ramsey, William May—whatever their moral conclusions might be—conceive the issue in this way. A "prochoice" moral position abandons this structure and the arduous wrestling involved in determining if and when it is tragically justifiable to end fetal life. In doing so, it trivializes the moral problem.

In summary, whatever development Catholic moral teaching may undergo in this area, it would be a mistake were it to abandon its concern with the problem as a life problem.[66]

In this section I have been interested above all in doctrinal development in moral theology, what to look for and what to avoid, so to speak. What kind of development one will look for, hope for, recoil from, tolerate, etc., will be influenced very much by one's methodological frameworks. Some frameworks will accommodate development, some will resist it. David F.

---

[66] Those with a yen for nourishing suspicions, discovering causal influences, tinkering with etiologies, and other forms of putting two and two together could have a field day comparing Maguire's study with that of Marjorie R. Maguire ("Personhood, Covenant and Abortion," *Annual of the Society of Christian Ethics*, 1983, 117–45). The latter Maguire argues that fetal personhood comes into being if and when the mother consents to the pregnancy. This total relativizing of personhood and of the morality of abortion is a recrudescence of the proposals made some years ago in *Etudes* by Bruno Ribes. Ribes' analysis proved unpersuasive to virtually all commentators. I see no reason for a different verdict about Marjorie Maguire's thesis. Indeed, in a sense, it is itself a strong refutation of her operating hypothesis that the notion of person is essential to discussions of abortion. That is a hypothesis still searching for support. Any notion of personhood (and therefore of "being treasured by God") that allows for the idea that two women at the identical gestational age and with perfectly healthy babies could differ in that one was carrying a person, the other a nonperson, is a not so subtle form of dualism that is effectively discriminatory. This point is brought out very well by Mary Seegers in her review of Beverly Harrison's *Our Right to Choose* (Boston: Beacon, 1983). She notes: "Some feminists worry that if you deny equal value (or personhood) to one member of the human species, you compromise every other contemporary egalitarian movement, whether for sexual or for racial equality" (*Christianity and Crisis* 43 [1983] 412). Precisely.

Kelly (Duquesne University) brings this out very well in his discussion of the development of medical ethics within Catholicism.[67]

The Catholic medical ethics of the first half of the twentieth century had two methodological frameworks "within which other principles were applied and to which they were subordinated: physicalism and ecclesiastical positivism." By "physicalism" Kelly means "a normative ethical approach which emphasizes the physical and biological properties, motions and goals of the action." Physicalist criteria are used to determine the *finis operis*, with other aspects (social, relational, psychological, and spiritual) neglected. Above, Hurth was cited as an example. "Ecclesiastical positivism" is that approach which overemphasizes a single source for the discovery of God's will, "the authoritative pronouncements and interpretations of the Roman Catholic magisterium." Joseph Ratzinger, as we saw, scored such positivism years ago.[68]

In combination, these frameworks led to a kind of "normative absolutism" which allowed moral theologians to arrive at "precisely specified conclusions" backed by or drawn from authoritative pronouncements. One of the many shortcomings of this approach, according to Kelly, is that it failed to allow genuinely theological themes to nourish our reflection and to exercise their influence on our ever-deepening and fresh understanding of our creaturehood but also our coagency with God, our need to suffer but also to fight suffering. While such themes will not solve ethical dilemmas, they will help us wrestle with them in a way that prevents what Kelly calls "ethical short-cuts." He obviously regards physicalism and ecclesiastical positivism as short-cuts.

I would add but a single reflection to Kelly's detailed and perceptive

---

[67] David F. Kelly, "Roman Catholic Medical Ethics and the Ethos of Modern Medicine," *Ephemerides theologicae Lovanienses* 49 (1983) 46–67.

[68] John Noonan notes that "many legislators—Justinian, the Emperors of China, the Council of Trent—have thought to terminate all controversies by forbidding interpretation of their decrees. Legal texts and moral rules are by their very nature open to being interpreted. *Humanae vitae*, to use a modern instance, cries out for it. Such interpretation is within the province of the moral philosopher. Those who block interpretation by repeating the letter of the text engage in a fundamentalism no more likely to be successful than Justinian's" ("The Role and Responsibility of the Moral Philosopher," *Proceedings of the American Catholic Philosophical Association* 56 [1982] 1–10, at 5.)—I would hesitate to call a recent study by Patrick R. Hughes an interpretation. Hughes proposes the good of the species as the overall criterion of marital sexual conduct. It can be violated by overpopulation as well as underpopulation. In this light he proposes a distinction between birth *control* and birth *prevention* (total closedness to life). On this basis he sees no moral difference between so-called "natural" means and artificial ones ("Artificial Birth Control Revisited," *Euntes docete* 35 [1982] 319–26). For a contrary view, cf. M. Zalba, S.J., "Innovatum tentamen aequiparandi usum continentiae periodicae et recursum ad media artificialia pro regulanda natalitate," *Periodica* 72 (1983) 141–80.

remarks. It is precisely an ongoing and deepening appropriation of these theological themes in changing circumstances that will provide both the possibility of and guidance for doctrinal development.

PASTORAL PROBLEMS

1) *The Sisters of Mercy of the Union and Sterilization.* Margaret Farley, R.S.M., reveals an extremely interesting and in many senses troubling episode in recent American Church history.[69] Some of the more significant events could be detailed with the following chronology.

In 1978 the Sisters of Mercy of the Union, sponsors of the largest group of nonprofit hospitals in the country, began a study of the theological and ethical aspects of tubal ligation. The study resulted in a recommendation to the General Administration of the Sisters of Mercy that tubal ligations be allowed when they are determined by patient and physician to be essential to the overall good of the patient. The General Administrative Team accepted this recommendation in principle. In a Nov. 12, 1980, letter to their hospital administrators the General Administrative Team reported the results of the study and indicated a desire to draw concerned persons into dialogue on the issue. They did not, as was inaccurately reported to the bishops of this country, mandate a policy.

Copies of the original study, the position statement of the General Administrative Team, and the letter to the hospitals somehow fell into the hands of officials in Rome and of the Committee on Doctrine of the N.C.C.B. One thing led to another until finally a dialogue was initiated between a committee of five bishops (headed by James Malone of Youngstown) and six Sisters of Mercy, both groups with their theological consultants. Two meetings were held (Sept. and Dec. 1981). These were largely exploratory, get-acquainted-with-the-problem meetings. At the December meeting it was decided that the next meeting (March 1982) would enter the substance of the problem. The sisters were to present a single-page position paper stating why they thought that not all tubal ligations were morally wrong. The episcopal committee was to do the same, showing why they were.

Early in 1982 the sisters were informed that the dialogue was off and that a Committee of Verification had been appointed by Rome. The purpose of this committee (composed of three bishops, again headed by Bishop Malone) was to verify the Administrative Team's answer to two questions: (1) Does it accept the teaching of the magisterium on tubal ligation? (2) Will it withdraw its circular letter (Nov. 12) to its hospitals? On May 11, 1982, the Administrative Team addressed their response

---

[69] Margaret Farley, R.S.M., "Power and Powerlessness: A Case in Point," *Proceedings of the Catholic Theological Society of America* 37 (1982) 116–19. Cf. also *National Catholic Reporter*, Nov. 11, 1983, 1.

to Pope John Paul II. The pertinent answers read as follows:

1. We receive the teaching of the Church on tubal ligation with respectful fidelity in accord with *Lumen gentium* 25 (*obsequium religiosum*). We have personal disagreements as do others in the Church, including pastors and respectable theologians, with the formulation of the magisterium's teaching on sterilization. However, in light of present circumstances, we will not take an official public position contrary to this formulation.

2. We withdraw our letter of Nov. 12, 1980 and will notify the recipients of the letter of such withdrawal.[70]

The letter concluded by urging "continued study and consultation within the Church on this issue."

The Committee of Verification seemed quite pleased with the response. The Apostolic Delegate informed the Administrative Team that their response had been accepted. The matter seemed quietly put to rest. However, the sisters received a letter dated Aug. 30, 1982, from E. Cardinal Pironio (Prefect of the Congregation for Religious and Secular Institutes). In part it stated: "In light of all the sentiments expressed in your letter of May 11, as well as your letter of withdrawal, dated May 17, 1982, your reply is not considered fully satisfactory and, indeed, your interpretation of the *obsequium religiosum* is judged incomplete." The sisters were told by Cardinal Pironio that a "subsequent response" would be coming from the congregation.

This subsequent response was a letter from Cardinal Pironio to Sister M. Theresa Kane dated Nov. 21. The letter insisted that the religious submission of mind and will (*obsequium religiosum*) "calls for the Catholic not only not to take a public position contrary to the teaching of the Church but also to direct his or her efforts, by an act of the will, to a more profound personal study of the question which would ideally lead to a deeper understanding and eventually an intellectual acceptance of the teaching in question." The letter also requested the sisters to write another letter to their hospitals "clearly prohibiting the performing of tubal ligations in all the hospitals owned and/or operated by the Sisters of Mercy of the Union."

A letter dated July 6, 1983, was drafted by Sister Theresa Kane to the chief executive officers of the Mercy Sisters' hospitals and forwarded to Cardinal Pironio. It read as follows:

On November 21, 1982, the Sacred Congregation for Religious and Secular Institutes (SCRIS) requested that we write you stating our reevaluation of tubal ligation and clearly prohibiting the performance of tubal ligations in Mercy hospitals owned and/or operated by the Sisters of Mercy of the Union.

[70] These and subsequent citations are taken from documents kindly provided by the Sister of Mercy of the Union.

As requested by SCRIS to reevaluate, we, the Mercy Administrative Team, have spent additional time in study and consultation on tubal ligation. In obedience to the magisterium we will take no public position on this matter contrary to Church teaching. As you face pastoral problems regarding tubal ligation, we ask that you continue to work in close collaboration with your local ordinary in implementing Church teaching.

The Congregation for Religious responded to this draft in a letter to Bishop James Malone dated Aug. 22. The congregation insisted that the second and third sentences of paragraph 2 be changed to read as follows: "In obedience to the magisterium we will continue to study and reflect on Church teaching with a view to accepting it. We, therefore, direct that the performance of tubal ligations be prohibited in all hospitals owned and/or operated by the Sisters of Mercy of the Union." If any sister does not accept this, she is to specify the dissent in writing and with signature. Furthermore, Bishop Malone stated that "upon enquiry I have learned that the letter from the congregation is indeed a 'formal precept' to you." That was specified to mean that "no further compromises or word changes . . . will be entertained by the congregation."

This happening is heavy with theological implications that invite explication. Margaret Farley's brief paper highlighted the powerlessness of women in the Church. Here three other points will be noted.

First, in the exchanges over a two-year period, the substantive issue was never discussed. Indeed, at the very point (March 1982) in the dialogue where the substantive issue (Is direct sterilization intrinsically evil?) was to be discussed, Rome (SCRIS) intervened to terminate the dialogue and appoint the Committee of Verification on the grounds that "there is nothing to be gained by further dialogue on this issue."

Is there really nothing to be gained by further dialogue? That would be the case only if it were antecedently clear and certain that the magisterial formulation was absolutely and unquestionably accurate. Yet, how can one sustain this in light of the very widespread theological questioning of that clarity and certainty? I have discussed this matter with very many established theologians throughout Europe and the United States and can report as a fact that most would endorse the approach and analysis of Johannes Gründel reviewed several years ago in these "Notes."[71] Surely this fact needs discussion, unless we are to exclude in principle the relevance of theological analysis.

[71] J. Gründel, "Zur Problematik der operativen Sterilisation in katholischen Kranken-haüsern," Stimmen der Zeit 199 (1981) 671-77. Recently Bernard Häring has endorsed a similar concept. He rejects the reduction of the problem to "a simple distinction between direct and indirect sterilization" and argues for the moral acceptability of "therapeutic" sterilization. "For some, sterilization is 'therapeutic' only if it is therapy concerning solely a sick sexual organ. In spite of the reality of psychotherapy as an important asset in today's medical world, these people would confine healing to organs alone. This not only leads to

The second theologically pertinent issue is the notion of *obsequium religiosum*. The Mercy Administrative Team had responded that "we receive the teaching of the Church on tubal ligation with respectful fidelity in accord with *Lumen gentium* 25 (*obsequium religiosum*)." The Congregation of Religious responded to this by saying that it was incomplete because a Catholic must also "direct his or her efforts ... to a more profound personal study of the question which would ideally lead to a deeper understanding and eventually an intellectual acceptance of the teaching in question."

This raises a host of interesting issues. First, the assumption seems to be that the members of the Administrative Team have not so "directed their efforts." But what is the evidence for that? Surely it is not the simple fact of dissent. That would rule out dissent in principle and elevate the teaching to irreformable status—both theologically untenable. More positively, surely a group that has conducted a three-to-four-year study, consulting opposing theological viewpoints and a variety of competences, has satisfied the demands of *obsequium religiosum*. If not, what more is required? Is this "direct his or her efforts" a duty with no time limit? Does it go on forever with no discernible *terminus*?

Next, the congregation uses the word "ideally" of the outcome of such directed efforts. What if it does not turn out that way? Furthermore, what if a group such as the Administrative Team discovers that many competent and demonstrably loyal theologians throughout the world have had similar problems? Are these simply regrettable but ultimately irrelevant failures? If magisterial inaccuracy or error is possible and if dissent is the vehicle that reveals this, is there not a point at which obligations begin to return to and weigh upon the proponents of the disputed formulation? Specifically, must they not re-examine *their* position if it is truth and not juridical position that is our dominant concern? To say anything else is to discount the significance of personal reflection in the teaching-learning process of the Church. In other words, it is utterly to juridicize the search for truth.

Finally, the "Mercy Affair" seems to have all the characteristics of an "enforcement of morals." Bishop Christopher Butler, O.S.B., distinguishing between the irrevocable and provisional in Church teaching, states of the latter: "To require the same adhesion for doctrines that are indeed taught by officials with authority but to which the Church has not irrevocably committed itself is to abuse authority, and if this requirement is accompanied by threatened sanctions it is also to abuse the power of

---

wrong and narrow-minded solutions in the case of sterilization, but is more dangerous because it betrays a wrong image of man and God. God does not care only for the health of discrete organs; he cares for the healthy person and for healthy relationships" (*Free and Faithful in Christ* 3 [New York: Crossroad, 1981] 20).

constraint."[72] Whether these words fit this case in all respects, one need not judge. But if they do, their true theological importance should not be overlooked. One effect is to relieve bishops of their collegial task. An immediate implication of that relief is the undermining of authority in the Church. Those who treasure the magisterium as a privilege must view such a prospect, because of its generalizable implications, with profound sadness.

At the heart of this matter is the question of the proper response to authoritative noninfallible teaching. Vatican II described the response in the phrase *religiosum voluntatis et intellectus obsequium.* The best and most balanced treatment I have seen of this notion is that of Francis Sullivan, S.J.[73] Sullivan, after noting that free will can influence judgment, states that *obsequium* involves renunciation of attitudes of obstinacy and adoption of attitudes of docility. In sum, "an honest and sustained effort to overcome any contrary opinion I might have, and to achieve a sincere assent of my mind."

Sullivan then spells out two implications of this. First, since assent is an act of judgment, the magisterium must offer clear and convincing reasons for its teaching. "When the norm itself is said to be discoverable by human reasoning, it would be a mistake to rely too heavily on merely formal authority in proposing it for acceptance by thinking people." Why a mistake? Because the magisterium "will not be offering to the faithful the help that many of them will need to rid themselves of their doubts."

Second, if Catholics have made a sincere and sustained attempt to achieve assent but have failed to overcome their strong doubts, "I do not see how one could judge such non-assent, or internal dissent, to involve any lack of obedience to the magisterium. Having done all that they were capable of doing toward achieving assent, they actually fulfilled their obligation of obedience, whether they achieved internal assent or not." Therefore Sullivan regards it as "unjust to treat all dissent from the teaching of the ordinary magisterium as disobedience, or to turn agreement with this noninfallible teaching into a test of loyalty to the Holy See."

Certain aspects of the "Mercy Affair" lead me to believe that these points can easily be overlooked. It must be remembered that *Dignitatis humanae* stated: "In the formation of their consciences, the Christian faithful ought carefully to attend to the sacred and certain doctrine of the Church."[74] An emendation was proposed for "ought carefully to attend to." It read: "ought to form their consciences according to." The Theo-

---

[72] Cf. Charles Curran and Richard McCormick, eds., *Readings in Moral Theology* 3 (Ramsey: Paulist, 1982) 185.

[73] Cf. n. 37 above.

[74] *Documents of Vatican II* 694.

logical Commission rejected the emendation and stated: "The proposed formula seems excessively restrictive. The obligation binding on the faithful is sufficiently expressed in the text as it stands."[75]

2) *The Preservation of Life.* In a recent case (Kaiser Permanente Hospital, Harbor City, Calif., 1981) Clarence Herbert underwent surgery for closure of an ileostomy. Shortly after successful completion of the surgery, Herbert suffered cardio-respiratory arrest. He was revived and immediately placed on life-support equipment. Within the following three days it was determined that Herbert was in a deeply comatose state from which he was very unlikely to recover. Tests performed by several physicians indicated that he had suffered severe brain damage, leaving him in a vegetative state which was likely to be permanent.

At that time Herbert's physicians, Robert Nejdl and Neil Barber, informed Herbert's family of his condition and the extremely poor prognosis. The family then drafted a written request to the hospital personnel stating that they wanted "all machines taken off that are sustaining life." Nejdl and Barber complied and removed Herbert from the respirator. Herbert continued to breathe. After two more days, Nejdl and Barber, after consulting with the family, ordered removal of the intravenous line and nasogastric tube that provided hydration and nourishment. Shortly thereafter Herbert died.

Nejdl and Barber were accused of murder by the Los Angeles District Attorney. Los Angeles Municipal Judge Brian Crahan dismissed the case. It was reopened (May 5, 1983) by Superior Court Judge Robert A. Wenke on the grounds that the dismissal was erroneous. The Herbert case received widespread publicity. The implications of Wenke's decision were stated simply by Barber: "No doctor will take a patient off a respirator now."[76]

Clare Conroy was an 84-year-old terminally-ill woman, mentally incompetent. She was fed by a nasogastric tube. On Feb. 2, Judge Reginald Stanton (State Superior Court, Essex County, N.J.) yielded to the wishes of her only relative (a nephew) and ordered the tube removed. The order was never carried out, since the decision was immediately appealed. Conroy died of natural causes thirteen days later.

These two cases raise interesting questions. Is it permissible to remove intravenous drips and nasogastric feeding tubes from dying, incompetent patients? In the Conroy case, John J. Delaney, Jr., a court-appointed lawyer, and Joseph A. Rodriguez, the New Jersey Public Advocate, argued that removing feeding tubes was quite different from removing a respirator. The latter may or may not cause death; the former certainly will.

John Paris, S.J., testified on behalf of Nejdl and Barber. Of this

---

[75] *Acta synodalia Conc. Vat. II* 4/6, 769.
[76] *Los Angeles Times*, May 6, 1983, 20.

testimony John Popiden (Loyola Marymount University) stated: "My own appraisal of Father Paris' position is that it is not in line with the Church's teaching." He further asserted that the positions of persons like Paris and this author are "much more in line with American liberal thought than with Church teaching on the subject."[77] It is unfortunate that Popiden does not seem to understand his own tradition on these matters. Quite traditional authors such as Edwin Healy, S.J., Gerald Kelly, S.J., and Charles J. McFadden, O.S.A., allow for the cessation of intravenous feeding in circumstances similar to those of Herbert.[78]

Several recent studies take up this problem. Hospice nurse Joyce V. Zerwekh asks whether it is always more merciful to administer I.V. fluids to a dying patient than to let the patient experience dehydration.[79] Her answer is no. There are both beneficial and detrimental effects associated with dehydration and the judgment must be individualized.

Kenneth Micetich, M.D., Patricia Steinecker, M.D., and David Thomasma (all of Stritch School of Medicine, Loyola University, Chicago) agree that I.V. fluids may not be morally required under a threefold condition.[80] (1) The patient must be dying. "Death will be imminent (within two weeks) no matter what intervention we may take." (2) The patient should be comatose. Comatose patients would experience no pain, thirst, etc. (3) The family must request that no further medical procedures be done in the face of impending death.[81]

James Childress and Joanne Lynn, M.D., after acknowledging that provision of adequate nutrition and fluids is a high priority for most patients, ask whether this is true of all patients.[82] Limiting their considerations to the incompetent patient, they first propose a general rule: one should decide as the incompetent person would have if he or she were competent, or decide according to the person's best interest when

[77] National Catholic Register, Aug. 28, 1983, 1 and 8.

[78] Cf. Gerald Kelly, S.J., TS 11 (1950) 219–20; Medico-Moral Problems (St. Louis: Catholic Hospital Association, 1958) 130; Charles J. McFadden, O.S.A., Medical Ethics (Philadelphia: F. A. Davis, 1967) 246–47; Edwin Healy, S.J., Medical Ethics (Chicago: Loyola, 1956) 80.

[79] Joyce V. Zerwekh, "The Dehydration Question," Nursing 83, Jan. 13, 1983, 47–51.

[80] K. Micetich, P. Steinecker, D. Thomasma, "Are Intravenous Fluids Morally Required for a Dying Patient?" Archives of Internal Medicine 143 (1983) 975–78.

[81] Bonnie Steinbeck seems to be in substantial agreement with Micetich, Steinecker, and Thomasma ("The Removal of Mr. Herbert's Feeding Tube," Hastings Center Report 13 [Oct. 1983] 13–16). She distinguishes the Herbert case from that of Clare Conroy and states: "Whether or not we wish to extend the argument to patients in Miss Conroy's condition, it seems clear that removal of life-support apparatus, including feeding tubes, from irreversibly comatose patients is not morally, and should not be construed legally as, murder."

[82] James Childress and Joanne Lynn, "Must Patients Always Be Given Food and Water?" ibid. 17–21.

individual preferences cannot be determined. Is it, then, ever in a patient's best interest to be malnourished and dehydrated? Childress and Lynn believe there are such cases, even if they are relatively few. They give three kinds of situations. First, the procedures that would be required could be so unlikely even to restore nutritional and fluid parameters toward normal that they could be considered futile. Second, the improvement in nutritional and fluid balance, though achievable, could be of no benefit to the patient (e.g., persistent vegetative state, some preterminal comas). "Thus, if the parents of an anencephalic infant or a patient like Karen Quinlan in a persistent vegetative state felt strongly that no medical procedures should be applied to provide nutrition and hydration, and the care givers agree, there should be no barrier in law or public policy to thwart that plan." Finally, there are cases where the burdens to be borne in receiving the treatment may outweigh the benefit. Terminal pulmonary edema, nausea, and mental confusion may be more likely in some patients as a result of artificial hydration and nutrition. The article concludes with some useful reflections on terminology (Childress and Lynn regard the ordinary-extraordinary distinction as misleading) and the difference between withholding and withdrawing (they see no *moral* difference). A well-informed and carefully-reasoned study.

Daniel Callahan agrees that it is morally licit to discontinue feeding in the circumstances noted by Lynn and Childress.[83] Yet he is profoundly uneasy with that conclusion. The feeding of the hungry, whether they be poor or physically unable to feed themselves, is "the most fundamental of all human relationships." It is extremely dangerous to tamper with so central a moral emotion. Even under legitimate circumstances there remains a deep-seated revulsion at the stopping of feeding. Thus Callahan experiences a struggle between head and heart.

Is there a resolution? As I read him, Callahan would respect this revulsion and continue feeding. He sees this as "a tolerable price to pay to preserve—with ample margin to spare—one of the few moral emotions that could just as easily be called a necessary social instinct."

Joanne Lynn was an Assistant Director of the President's Commission for the Study of Ethical Problems in Medicine and Biomedical and Behavioral Research. It is not surprising, then, that the Childress-Lynn study reflects the suggestions earlier made in that commission's excellent *Decisions to Forego Life-Sustaining Treatment.*[84] At a key point the commission notes:

Most patients with permanent unconsciousness cannot be sustained for long without an array of increasingly artificial feeding interventions—nasogastric

---

[83] Daniel Callahan, "On Feeding the Dying," ibid. 22.

[84] Washington: Government Printing Office, 1983.

tubes, gastrostomy tubes, or intravenous nutrition. Since permanently unconscious patients will never be aware of nutrition, the only benefit to the patient of providing such increasingly burdensome interventions is sustaining the body to allow for a remote possibility of recovery. The sensitivities of the family and of care giving professions ought to determine whether such interventions are made.[85]

A footnote to that last sentence notes that it can be anticipated that courts will grant requests to withhold or withdraw further treatment, including I.V. drips, from such patients. And that is, indeed, how the Nejdl-Barber case has turned out. On Oct. 12, 1983, Judge Lynn Compton of the Court of Appeal exonerated Nejdl and Barber of any unlawful conduct.[86] In the course of this opinion the court made several interesting and important points. First, Compton notes that even though life-support devices are self-propelled, still each drop of I.V. fluid is "comparable to a manually administered injection or item of medication." Hence disconnecting such devices is "comparable to withholding the manually administered injection." Second, the court views intravenous nourishment and fluid "as being the same as the use of the respirator." Third, *medical* nutrition and hydration resemble medical procedures rather than typical ways of providing nutrition and hydration. Hence they are to be evaluated in terms of their burdens and benefits. Finally, since the court viewed the physicians' actions as omissions rather than affirmative actions, the resolution of the case depends on whether there was a duty to continue to provide life-sustaining treatment. The court asserts that there is no such duty once the treatment is useless. And it was useless in Herbert's case because it merely sustained biological life with no realistic hope of a return to a cognitive, sapient state. Thus continued use of life-sustainers was "disproportionate."

This carefully-reasoned decision should go a long way toward clearing the atmosphere surrounding the use of *any* life-sustainers for the dying incompetent patient. That atmosphere has been clouded by the use of freighted language, particularly by use of the word "starve." Equivalently Judge Compton is saying—correctly, I believe—that "starving" a patient is not to be identified with any act whereby impending death is hastened by omission of nutrition and/or hydration, but only with omission *where the physician had a duty not to omit medical nutrition or hydration.* He has a duty not to omit when the benefit of such procedures predominates over the burdens. In cases of some dying incompetents (e.g., vegetative state), there is simply no appreciable benefit.

[85] *Decisions* 190.
[86] I work from a xeroxed copy of the original decision kindly forwarded by John Paris, S.J.

The Nejdl-Barber decision makes it clear that "starving" language[87] is out of place in cases like that of Clarence Herbert. Judge Compton followed closely the guidelines established by the President's commission. He could hardly have chosen a better guide.

3) *The Case of Agnes Mary Mansour.* The basic facts of this tragic incident are quite familiar, though there is disagreement on some particulars.[88] Madonna Kolbenschlag, H.M., discusses the theological implications at length.[89] She distinguishes general moral teachings from specific policy decisions, a point not always clear in the minds of many Catholics. The Mansour incident also reveals a confusion about the distinction between clerics and women religious, these latter being treated as "quasi-clerics" in some respects. In matters of power, sacramental and ecclesiastical, women religious are treated as laity. In questions of discipline they are treated as clerics.

But, according to Kolbenschlag, one aspect of the case is not complex. "I refer to the flagrant violation of due process." She refers to the fact that Mansour never had the opportunity to present her views on Medicaid funding of abortion to Roman authorities. Authorities within the Sisters of Mercy were bypassed. Mansour was approached by the Roman delegate without being informed of the nature of the options to be given. She sees Mansour as the "victim of arbitrary and unfounded Church discipline" which threatens "the survival and identity of religious communities of women."

Theologian Thomas E. Clarke, S.J., commenting on an editorial in *America*, insists that the central issue in the Mansour case is not abortion funding but the fidelity to the gospel of certain Church laws and procedures.[90] The laws of the Church do not sufficiently respect the charismatic character of religious life, hence its greater autonomy when compared to the clerical state. But the most central issue is: "How can we develop ecclesiastical processes for dealing with baptized Christians which do not degrade those who participate in them?" Clearly, Clarke, who is profoundly respectful of authority and therefore profoundly sensitive to its abuse, views the Mansour proceedings as degrading.

There is a sharp difference in view about the justice and fairness of

---

[87] Cf. also Bernard Towers, "Irreversible Coma and Withdrawal of Life Support: Is It Murder If the I.V. Line Is Disconnected?" *Journal of Medical Ethics* 8 (1982) 203–5.

[88] Cf. *Origins* 13 (1983) 197–206 for a chronology of events as presented by Bishop Anthony Bevilacqua, Agnes Mary Mansour, and the Provincial Team of the Sisters of Mercy of the Union.

[89] Madonna Kolbenschlag, H.M., "Sister Mansour Is Not Alone," *Commonweal* 110 (1983) 359–64.

[90] *America* 149 (1983) 20.

the proceedings leading to Mansour's dispensation from her vows. The *ad hoc* delegate of the Holy See (Anthony Bevilacqua) summarized the matter as follows: "Justice, the requirements of fair and canonical process, and the protection of rights were scrupulously attended to."[91] He further stated: "The Holy See would not countenance any miscarriage of justice, infringement of rights or violations of required canonical process."

However, the Sisters of Mercy of the Union did not see it this way at all. At their eleventh general chapter (Sept. 1–6, 1983) they issued a statement that reads in part as follows:

We speak because serious harm has been experienced by the Church, by our congregation and by one of our members; we are deeply concerned for all involved. It is our belief that the fullness of justice is not achieved by the law alone. We are particularly distressed:

1. that adequate dialogue between congregational and hierarchical authorities was lacking.
2. that responses to questions and sufficient information regarding the canonical processes to be used were not made available to congregational leadership or to Sister Agnes Mary Mansour.
3. that, at crucial points, legitimate authorities of the congregation were ignored.
4. that prior to final action by Roman authorities the congregation was not officially requested to represent its position, nor Sister Agnes Mary Mansour hers.[92]

Kolbenschlag ended her study by noting that the overall outcome of the Mansour case will depend very much on the response of the American bishops. It was for this reason that a group, most of whom are stationed in Washington and represent a variety of backgrounds, addressed the following letter (reproduced only in part here) to all of the American bishops.[93]

This series of events raises very grave issues in and for the Church.

First, there is the matter of due process. As Catholics we are justly proud of the steps the Church has taken to protect human rights in civil society. We are correspondingly distressed by the absence of respect for such rights within the Church itself. Bishop Anthony Bevilacqua, the Ad Hoc Delegate of the Holy See in this matter, has stated in his report that canonical norms of due process were "scrupulously attended to." This surely raises the question of whether these legal

---

[91] *Origins* 13 (1983) 199.

[92] Document kindly provided by the Sisters of Mercy of the Union.

[93] Signatories were: Mary Burke, James Hug, S.J., Keith Brennan, S.D.S., Mary Collins, O.S.B., James Coriden, Barbara Cullom, Charles Curran, Vincent Cushing, Alfred Hennelly, S.J., David Hollenbach, S.J., Mary Hunt, Madonna Kolbenschlag, H.M., Lora Ann Quinonez, C.D.P., Mary Daniel Turner, S.N.D., Philip Land, S.J., Maria Riley, O.P., and this author.

norms are an adequate guarantee of genuine justice. The basic fact remains that Sister Mansour's only contact with Roman authorities occurred after it had already been decided that a process of dismissal would be initiated against her if she continued to hold her government position. She was never permitted to explain or defend her position with authorities in Rome, even though this was requested. In a matter of such gravity this is a clear violation of the kind of justice we have a right to expect in the Church.

Second, the reason given for these developments is that Sister Mansour's position is "contrary to the magisterium" (Archbishop of Detroit). This is simply inaccurate. While the magisterium does teach that abortion is morally wrong, it does not specify what kind of cooperation with it is tolerable in what circumstances. Such specifications involve further factual assessments, and people of good will can and do disagree about them. Your excellent pastoral letter *The Challenge of Peace* makes it very clear that Christians committed to the protection of human life can legitimately disagree about how to pursue this commitment in public policy.

Third, the way this matter was handled raises all kinds of cognate issues relevant to the good of the Church: the nature of religious vows, the propriety of public office for priests and religious, the place of women and their ministry in the Church, the collegiality of the American episcopate, the manner of the exercise of authority in the Church etc.

The letter ends with a request that the bishops reflect on the incident and make an appropriate pastoral response. If the Mansour decision cannot be changed, "at the very least there would be the consolation that there are still official voices in the Church ready to insist on justice. That would go a long way toward repairing the public damage done by the swift and ill-considered treatment accorded to Sister Mansour"—treatment that the letter describes as an "abuse of authority."

At least one bishop, Thomas Gumbleton, has spoken out. He referred to the Church's treatment of Mansour as a "clear injustice."[94] While I disagree with Mansour's judgment on Medicaid payments for abortion, I agree with the editors of *America* when they write: "To find her position on this issue unacceptable is vastly different from declaring her unfit for office or for religious life or unorthodox in Catholic doctrine."[95] It is this "vast difference" that seems to many to constitute the chasm between justice and injustice, regardless of what procedures were used and what protocols followed.

This incident is mentioned in these "Notes" because its importance

---

[94] *Catholic Chronicle*, July 1, 1983, 1.

[95] *America* 148 (1983) 409. The matter is only further confused by inaccurate statements such as that of James Hitchcock. He asks: "How, then, can a nun stay in a job which requires her going directly contrary to Catholic moral teaching on an extremely serious issue?" (*Catholic Chronicle*, Oct. 7, 1983, 9). The answer: there is no such teaching on Medicaid funding of abortions.

stretches far beyond an individual person or congregation. It looks very much like the working out of an ecclesial vision, one that is in noticeable contrast to some of the perspectives of Vatican II and hierarchical insistence on the foundational character of human rights in society. As such, it will constitute the atmosphere in which theology must perform its modest service.

THE CHALLENGE OF PEACE

On May 3, 1983, the American hierarchy overwhelmingly (238 to 9) approved *The Challenge of Peace: God's Promise and Our Response.*[96] Without delay I want to identify myself with the statement of the remarkable Theodore Hesburgh, C.S.C.: "I believe it is the finest document that the American Catholic hierarchy has ever produced."[97] That is not to say it is without problems. It is not. It is to say that in process, style, and substance it did and will continue to make people think. Surely that is a fine first step. Hesburgh gives four reasons for his judgment. First, the bishops had the courage to address "the greatest moral problem that has ever faced humanity," knowing that they would face serious criticism no matter what they said. Second, there were precious few theological precedents to structure their response. For instance, the key just-war concepts of discrimination and proportionality "are practically meaningless as applied to nuclear warfare." Yet the episcopal conclusions are blunt, clear, and courageous. Third, there is the process itself.[98] Hesburgh applauds the total openness of the procedures culminating in the final draft. "That process was almost as important, for bishops and laity, as the document produced." Finally, there is the modesty of the document, "a quality not true of all Church documents." What it asserts as binding is relatively minimal given the broad sweep of the letter. Furthermore, it is "clearly and expressly a first word," not a final word. Hesburgh has, I believe, put his finger on exactly those dimensions of *The Challenge of Peace* that made its appearance such a fresh and exhilarating experience in the American Church.

[96] *Origins* 13 (1983) 1–32. The official summary is found in *Origins* 13 (1983) 97–101.

[97] Theodore Hesburgh, C.S.C., "Foreword," in *Catholics and Nuclear War*, ed. Philip J. Murnion (New York: Crossroad, 1983) vii. The volume contains commentaries by David Hollenbach, S.J., David J. O'Brien, Peter Steinfels, Charles Curran, William E. Murnion, J. Bryan Hehir, Sandra Schneiders, Joseph A. Komonchak, Gordon Zahn, James Finn, Bruce Russett, George F. Kennan, Lester C. Thurow, John C. Haughey, S.J., Harry A. Fagan, and this author. The book also contains the full text of *The Challenge of Peace*.

[98] For an interesting history of the development of the pastoral, cf. Jim Castelli, *The Bishops and the Bomb* (New York: Image Books, 1983). A good overview of the pastoral is that of Judith A. Dwyer, "The Morality of Using Nuclear Weapons," *New Catholic World* 226 (1983) 244–48.

Other reactions to the document are interesting. Here just a sampling can be cited. The *National Catholic Reporter* editorialized: "It could well be the most important religious statement of our time."[99] McGeorge Bundy refers to the letter as a "landmark in the changing pattern of American concern with nuclear danger." It is an "excellent starting point for what can now be said about deterrence."[100] At the other end of the spectrum was the judgment of philosopher William Mara (Fordham). When asked about the pastoral, Mara responded: "It was overrated. And I think it will have harmful effects." Mara referred to the bishops as "posturing as moral prophets" and wondered "who can take them seriously?"[101]

Charles Krauthammer calls the letter's central position (on deterrence) an "unhappy compromise," a "sorry compromise." Why? The bishops, he says, reject countervalue strategy as indiscriminate and counterforce strategy as violating proportionality. As he puts it, "One runs out of ways of targeting nuclear weapons." Thus, on the one hand, "the logic, and quite transparent objective, of such a position is to reject deterrence *in toto*." On the other hand, this is at odds with Vatican policy (John Paul II). The compromise: "You may keep the weapons but you may not use them."[102] Krauthammer sees this as incoherent and unconvincing. It is incoherent because it requires the bishops to support a policy their entire argument is designed to undermine. It is unconvincing because the deterrent they allow is no deterrent at all. Deterrence requires the will to use.

Krauthammer's analysis, besides assuming that deterrence strategies are efficacious (that is debated), misses the fact that *The Challenge of Peace* did not condemn *any* use of nuclear weapons. It came close, but it

---

[99] *National Catholic Reporter*, May 13, 1983, 1.

[100] *New York Review*, June 16, 1983, 3.

[101] *National Catholic Register*, Nov. 6, 1983, 6. This is also the opinion of Michael Novak, as might be expected ("The Bishops and Soviet Reality," *New Catholic World* 266 [1983] 258–61). According to Novak, the bishops resisted pacifism and did not destroy deterrence. That was to their credit. But they perpetrated a "grave religious as well as political failure" because they underestimated Soviet reality and tied deterrence to progressive disarmament. The *New Yorker* saw the bishops' position as "radical" because it rules out the mainstay of deterrence (the targeting of cities). But the bishops "contradicted themselves" in holding that deterrence can be provisionally tolerated. In trying to steer a course between city-destroying and unilateral disarmament, there had to be a point of ambiguity and that point is the rationale for deterrence. Still, the *New Yorker* judges that the letter has performed "a historic service" (May 23, 1983, 31–32).

[102] Charles Krauthammer, "On Nuclear Morality," *Commentary*, Oct. 1983, 48–52. This was also the criticism of Albert Wohlstetter in "Bishops, Statesmen and Other Strategists on the Bombing of Innocents," *Commentary*, June 1983, 15–35.

did not do so. And it was precisely this tiny opening that allowed its provisional and strictly conditioned tolerance of nuclear deterrence.

Very similar to Krauthammer's is the analysis of François Gorand.[103] The bishops have done both too much and too little. Too much because in opposing the Reagan administration's ideas about a controlled and winnable nuclear war, they have left a kind of *tabula rasa* for nuclear strategy. Too little because their arguments should have led them to question the very notion of deterrence.

Francis Winters responds to Gorand.[104] Gorand's critique had argued that Catholics are confronted with an impossible dilemma: either accept just-war criteria and denounce deterrence, or reject them and preserve the peace by threatening Soviet society. Winters argues that *datur tertium*: strengthening conventional forces while retaining nuclear capacity with no intention to use it. The deterrent effect is in the eye of the beholder, who can never be sure of our intentions as long as weapons exist. This is all that is required for the American bishops to accept deterrence.

Rather than cataloguing reactions, it might be more useful to highlight the issues raised before and after the pastoral. John C. Haughey, S.J., usefully identifies four interrelated concerns, really complaints.[105] First, there is evangelization. The contention is that the bishops' relationship to public life should always express this primary mission of the Church. Specifically, if bishops take a stand on a particular policy issue, they should do so precisely to show that Christ is the norm of their judgment. Merely political argumentation is an inappropriate use of episcopal authority.

Second, there is the question of episcopal competence. If this competence lies in the episcopacy's intimate relationship to the revelation of God in and through Christ, then their policy statements should reveal this linkage. Third, the specificity of recommendations puts the Church in a partisan political posture. Some would argue that this is inappropriate and that the Church should limit itself to general principles. "Otherwise, the contention runs, the Church becomes just another interest group or lobby for this or that position," which can compromise its primary function.

Finally, there is the role of the laity. Some lay people resent what they regard as excessively progressive or liberal positions taken officially. Furthermore, the application of traditional wisdom in the temporal order is the laity's responsibility.

[103] François Gorand, "La dissuasion nucléaire," *Etudes*, Oct. 1983, 377–88.

[104] Francis Winters, "Un regard pascalien," *Etudes*, Oct. 1983, 388–92. Cf. also Francis Winters, "Did the Bishops Ban the Bomb? Yes and No." *America* 149 (1983) 104–8.

[105] *Woodstock Report* no. 2 (April 1983) 1.

Haughey does not attempt to respond to these concerns. But he thinks it important that they are raised because they go to the heart of the significance of faith for public life. Actually, it seems to me that the pastoral has anticipated some of these concerns and responded to them. For instance, with regard to evangelization and competence, *The Challenge of Peace* makes it quite clear why the bishops, precisely as bishops, have a legitimate concern in these matters.[106] As I read the document, it builds this legitimacy in two steps. (1) " The Church is called to be, in a unique way, the instrument of the kingdom of God in history. Since peace is one of the signs of that kingdom present in the world, the Church fulfills part of her essential mission by making the peace of the kingdom more visible in our time" (no. 22). The document speaks of peacemaking as "central in the ministry of the Church." (2) "At the center of the Church's teaching on peace and at the center of all Catholic social teaching are the transcendence of God and the dignity of the human person. The human person is the clearest reflection of God's presence in the world; all of the Church's work in pursuit of both justice and peace is designed to protect and promote the dignity of every person" (no. 15).

Thus it is the centrality of peacemaking in the Church's ministry and the centrality of the person within this ministry that are the bishops' entitlements to address the question. Put negatively, to remain silent on such an issue would be a tacit concession that the *magnalia Dei* have nothing to do with these twin concerns. That is theologically unthinkable.[107]

As for specificity, the pastoral letter is careful to distinguish three types of assertions: universally-binding moral principles, previous magisterial teaching, concrete applications to specific cases. Of this third category the bishops note that "prudential judgments are involved based on specific circumstances" and that "the Church expects a certain diversity of views even though all hold the same moral principles."[108]

As a way of organizing the literature that is only now beginning to appear, we may ask four questions: (1) What is the methodology of the pastoral? (2) What is new about the pastoral's content? (3) How does it

---

[106] Cf. also the Bishops of Haiti, "Les fondements de l'intervention de l'église dans le domaine social et politique," *Documentation catholique* 80 (1983) 641–43. The always perceptive George Higgins takes this up in *America* (forthcoming as I write) in a response to Russell Shaw's "The Synod in Search of a Subject," *America* 149 (1983) 325–28.

[107] Joseph Cardinal Bernardin made this point in a speech at Notre Dame (May 1983): "Today the stakes involved in the nuclear issue make it a moral issue of compelling urgency. The Church must be involved in the process of protecting the world and its people from the specter of nuclear destruction. *Silence in this instance would be a betrayal of its mission* ..." (cited by Hesburgh in *Catholics and Nuclear War* viii).

[108] For an excellent article on authority in the pastoral, cf. Edward Vacek, S.J., "Authority and the Peace Pastoral," *America* 149 (1983) 225–28.

compare with the pastoral letters of other episcopates? (4) What is its major problem?

1) *What is the methodology of the pastoral letter*? Here Charles Curran is very helpful.[109] Curran points out that the *The Challenge of Peace* follows the methodology of *Gaudium et spes* in emphasizing a threefold source of moral deliberation: the signs of the times, Sacred Scripture, human reason. Three signs of the times are mentioned: the need for peace, the curse of the arms race, the unique dangers of the arms race. As for the Scriptures, Curran rightly notes that they do not supply us with detailed answers but "only give a clear, urgent direction when we look at today's concrete problems," a kind of vision.

Curran next turns to and praises the notion of moral theology that structures the pastoral letter. That notion includes: a general vision of reality, an understanding of human history (eschatology) and of human beings in general (anthropology), the virtues and values that must be present in human society, the need for structures to safeguard these values, the importance of the person as agent and as a subject called to continual conversion, the principles and norms that govern conduct, the application of these to specific problems. The admission by the bishops that there can be legitimate disagreement on complex specific applications of principles leads Curran to conclude: "Logically this understanding must also be present in other areas of Christian morality ... [It] is bound to have some repercussions in other areas of moral teaching and Church life."

In another study Curran notes the tensions that constituted the atmosphere of the drafting process.[110] The relationship to Rome and other hierarchies played a notable role. It was well known that some French and German bishops were opposed to condemnation of the first use of nuclear weapons since NATO and the French defense posture rely on the threat of limited nuclear weapons to deter attack even by conventional forces of the enemy. Then there was the Roman meeting chaired by Josef Cardinal Ratzinger during which Ratzinger proposed the rather curious idea that bishops' conferences as such do not have a *mandatum docendi*.[111]

---

[109] Charles Curran, "Metodologia morale della lettera pastorale dei vescovi americani su guerra e pace," *Rivista di teologia morale* 15 (Oct.–Dec. 1983) 487–98. Curran was very badly served by his translator. Curran had spoken of the premoral evil of war. The translator rendered this by saying that sometimes *immoral* acts could be justified by a proportionate reason.

[110] Charles Curran, "Analyse américaine de la lettre pastorale sur la guerre et la paix," *Supplément* no. 147, Nov. 1983, 569–92.

[111] *Origins* 12 (1983) 691–95. For a fine analysis of the teaching authority of episcopal conferences, cf. Avery Dulles, S.J., "The Teaching Authority of Bishops' Conferences," *America* 148 (1983) 453–55.

There was also opposition and conflict within the American Catholic community. A symbol of this was Michael Novak's alternate pastoral letter.[112] One difficulty the bishops faced was consistency with some of their earlier statements. For instance, in their 1976 pastoral letter *To Live in Christ Jesus*, the bishops had stated that it is wrong both to attack civilian populations and to threaten to do so. John Cardinal Krol, in his 1979 testimony, attempted to finesse the implications of this by insisting that deterrence (involving such a threat) cannot be approved but only tolerated.[113] Curran correctly points out that this is a theologically novel use of the notion of toleration, since it involves tolerating one's own immoral (conditional) intent to perform moral evil. However, this worked its way into the second draft of the pastoral. That version was accused of "consequentialism" by certain traditionalists—the moral evil of an immoral intention justified by the good effects of the deterrence. This "consequentialism" was then identified with certain revisionist Catholic thinkers. However, Curran rightly notes that these revisionists would not agree with the Krol testimony and the second draft. One may never intend to do what is morally wrong. Therefore "it is wrong," he writes, "to identify such reasoning with the revisionist theory of proportionalism."

In summary, the final version does accept a strictly conditioned deterrence. It escapes the methodological traps of the Krol testimony and the second draft, but in doing so it offers no satisfactory justification for its position. For this reason Curran's conclusion is right on target: "The thorny question of deterrence and the ethical theory supporting it will continue to be the most important subject for further ethical investigation."

2) *What is new about the pastoral's content?* The American bishops state explicitly in their letter that they "wish to continue and develop" previous teaching on peace and war, and to do this out of the "insights and experience of the Catholic community of the United States." What concretely has this development meant?

In an excellent overview David Hollenbach, S.J., examines three areas: (1) basic perspectives on the morality of war, (2) the moral norms proposed for the use of nuclear weapons, (3) the morality of deterrence.[114] With regard to the first, the pastoral breaks new ground in regarding the just-war ethic and the ethic of nonviolence as interrelated approaches, not as contradictory alternatives. This complementarity had not been

---

[112] Michael Novak, "Moral Clarity in a Nuclear Age: A Letter from Catholic Clergy and Laity," *Catholicism in Crisis* 1 (1983) 3–23.

[113] *Origins* 9 (1979) 195–99.

[114] David Hollenbach, S.J., "*The Challenge of Peace* in the Context of Recent Church Teachings," in *Catholics and Nuclear War* 3–15.

affirmed previously in conciliar or papal teaching. Hollenbach believes the bishops were led to this conclusion by the particular form of the debate in the United States, where an articulate pacifist position has emerged. The strong presumption against war is the link that binds both perspectives together.

As for moral norms on the use of nuclear weapons, *The Challenge of Peace* is more nuanced than any other official statement since World War II. Earlier popes never condemned *any* use of such weapons. The pastoral letter *resoundingly* rejects the use of nuclear weapons against population centers. It *strongly* rejects any first use of nuclear weapons. Finally, on the most debated question of the day (Can any use be discriminate and proportionate?), it expresses *extreme skepticism* that any use can be kept limited.

Finally, there is deterrence. Neither Vatican II nor John Paul II condemned the possession of nuclear weapons for deterrence. Nor did the American bishops. But Hollenbach believes that the American pastoral goes beyond John Paul II "by entering into an analysis of different types of deterrence policies." The conditions set by the Americans for accepting deterrence are considerably more detailed and stringent than are the pope's. They exclude "war-fighting" strategies, the quest for superiority, and all weapons systems that make disarmament more difficult to achieve. Hollenbach concludes that the pastoral involves " a clear development" in tradition and for this reason may be seen as "genuinely prophetic."

In centering attention on the moral legitimacy of deterrence, it is quite possible to overlook this developmental thrust. In a very interesting article, Francis X. Meehan sees the bishops' pastoral as a step in the development of doctrine.[115] How? It is in the relationship of just-war teaching and nonviolence. *The Challenge of Peace* notes that there is a "complementary relationship in the sense that both seek to serve the common good." Furthermore, the pastoral states that the two are "distinct but interdependent methods of evaluating warfare." Finally, the "two perspectives support and complement one another, each preserving the other from distortion."

Meehan sees in these statements a growing resolution of the either-or dilemma (either just war or nonviolence). A new "duality" is emerging that disallows our resting with Christian comfort in either option. Thus "the witness of non-violence makes the use of just-war teaching more moderate and just." Similarly, just-war teaching lends moderation to the nonviolent witness. This complementarity must be seen in the broader

---

[115] Francis Meehan, "Non-Violence and the Bishops' Pastoral: A Case for the Development of Doctrine," forthcoming (1984) in a collection from Paulist Press.

context of the theology of sin and grace. Against such a background, force is "part of the concupiscent world that stems from sin." It ought not to exist. It is a reality to be overcome. Failure to see it in this way leads to an abstract acquiescence in the use of force and an unwitting nourishment of militarism. This means that "we absolve ourselves too easily of a pull which the final kingdom should be exercising on us." Meehan argues that this eschatological pull means "a progressive movement in the Church toward non-violence," Far from being unrealistic, this progression constitutes true Christian realism; for it is a "view of non-violence which is active not passive, historical and public rather than private and interior, assertive rather than surrendering, practical and pragmatic rather than pure other-worldliness."

Meehan is too realistic to think that we will ever overcome the tensions between justice and peace, force and nonviolence. But unless these realities are seen with their deeper rootage in sin and grace, they will remain dichotomous, not complementary. And when they are viewed as complementary, there is a new dynamic at work: toward nonviolence. To brush aside the excellent points in Meehan's analysis would amount to complacency with the *status quo*. At some point that is profoundly unchristian.

John Haughey, S. J., carries this theme forward by noting that in addition to a "norm ethics" we need a "call ethics."[116] The just-war theory has its clear advantages, but it also has shortcomings. For instance, Haughey believes it cannot furnish the power necessary for a "moral-about-face" which the bishops see as necessary. Furthermore, the norm ethics of just-war defense may leave those using it unaware of the violence in their own hearts. True peacemaking must begin by breaking down the walls of hostility in our own hearts. The pastoral is less successful in developing these themes, but Haughey believes it is the direction of the future already foreshadowed in *The Challenge of Peace*.

3) *How does the American pastoral compare with the pastorals of other episcopates?* Before treating the French, German, Irish, and Belgian pastoral letters, let me take note of the Sixth Assembly of the World Council of Churches (Vancouver, July 24–August 10, 1983). The Assembly stated: "We believe that the time has come when the Churches must unequivocally declare that the production and deployment as well as the use of nuclear weapons are a crime against humanity and that such activities must be condemned on ethical and theological grounds."[117]

The Assembly then approached nuclear deterrence. It must be "cate-

---

[116] John Haughey, S.J., "Disarmament of the Heart," in *Catholics and Nuclear War* 217–28.

[117] I work from a manuscript document kindly provided by Alan Geyer.

gorically rejected" as contrary to faith in Jesus Christ. Why? Because "it relies on the credibility of the *intention to use* nuclear weapons." The Assembly insisted that "any intention to use weapons of mass destruction is an utterly inhuman violation of the mind and spirit of Christ."

The Vancouver Assembly then went on to detail further objections to nuclear deterrence. It (1) is the antithesis of an ultimate faith that casts out fear; (2) escalates the arms race; (3) ignores the economic, social, and psychological dimensions of security, thus paralyzing the *status quo*; (4) destroys the reality of self-determination for most nations in matters of their safety and survival; (5) diverts resources from basic human needs; (6) rationalizes the development of new weapons etc.

Several things are notable about this document. First, it goes beyond the moral stance of the American bishops in condemning deterrence. Second, it does this on both ethical and theological grounds. Third, these grounds coalesce in the intention to use nuclear weapons. As I read the declaration, then, it has taken a position on a previously debated point: Does the possession of nuclear weapons as a deterrent necessarily involve the intention (conditioned) to use them? The Assembly's answer is affirmative; otherwise the deterrent is not credible. Thus the World Council links very closely, indeed inseparably, possession and use. This is in sharp contrast with, for example, the pastoral letter of the German episcopate. *The Challenge of Peace* left this dimension of the question untouched.

The German episcopate has issued its pastoral *Righteousness Creates Justice* (April 27, 1983).[118] It is a very long document and in this it resembles *The Challenge of Peace.* The major emphasis in the document is peace—its urgent need, its theological understanding, its human threats, its protection and achievement. Thus, in discussing Church teachings over the past thirty years, it highlights the shift in emphasis from just defense to the mandate of peace. "Although the doctrine of a just defense has not been abandoned, it can no longer serve as a basis for an overall concept of the ecclesiastical ethics of peace."[119] Greater prominence must be given to the "positive precepts of peace and the combating of the causes of war." However, the pastoral refuses to see these emphases as "contrasting." Rather, "these two perspectives supplement each other and we cannot forgo either of them." Still, the doctrine of just defense maintains but a "limited function" within a comprehensive peace ethic.

It is within such a flow of *sic et non* balancing assertions that the German episcopate approaches security policies. There is no longer

---

[118] "La justice construit la paix," *Documentation catholique* 80 (1983) 568–94.
[119] Ibid. 580.

dispute about the goal of preventing war (everyone admits the urgency of the goal). The disputed question concerns the means of prevention, and above all deterrence. After admitting that the efficacy of deterrence is disputed (some say it has prevented war, others say this cannot be substantiated), the Germans cite John Paul II's statement to the Second Special Session of the U.N. General Assembly: "Under present conditions, deterrence . . . can still be judged to be morally acceptable." They then undertake their own analysis.

The Germans accept the papal judgment. They then offer several orienting perspectives for judging a nuclear deterrent. First, there is the *goal* of the deterrent (prevention of war). Politicians and military leaders must "be able to substantiate the fact that war can really be prevented by this strategy and why."[120] Second, there is the question of *means*. The goal must become credible in the choice of means. By this the German document means that weapons must not be judged in isolation but in terms of the overall political objectives.

Such orienting perspectives lead to criteria that judge the moral legitimacy of a deterrent. Three are given. (1) Existing or planned military means must never render war more feasible or more probable. The document notes that this criterion creates almost insuperable obstacles. "After all, weapons only provide an effective deterrent if their use can be threatened in a credible manner."[121] (2) Only those weapons (qualitatively and quantitatively) may be deployed that are required by the deterrent. This excludes any quest for superiority. (3) All military means must be compatible with effective mutual arms limitation, reduction, and disarmament. This reflects the papal assertion that the deterrent must be a "stage on the way to progressive disarmament."

These are the criteria we must apply to live with the dilemma of the horror of mass destruction on the one hand, and totalitarian injustice, oppression, and extortion on the other. In the "interim period," then, the deterrent can be tolerated. "By virtue of this decision we are choosing from among various evils the one which, as far as is humanly possible to tell, appears as the lesser."[122] The document tries to blend rationality (which leads to interim compromise) with an eschatological pull ("which leaves far behind all the currently still necessary compromises").

What are we to make of the German pastoral? The key principle appealed to is that of the choice of the lesser evil when all of the available options include evils. What I find missing in the German document is an awareness that the evils involved may be qualitatively different. Rejecting a nuclear deterrent certainly risks vulnerability to totalitarian blackmail,

[120] Ibid. 586.   [122] Ibid. 588.
[121] Ibid. 587.

expansionism, and takeover. These are clearly enormous evils, but in terms of those experiencing them and trying to prevent them they are nonmoral or ontic in character. By that I mean that if they happened, they would not involve *our* doing moral evil. Tolerating a nuclear deterrent risks its use and this means, to cite the German episcopate, "a horror such as could not be more terrible." Thus the document seems to be balancing two sources of danger, two nonmoral outcomes.

What is obscured in this analysis is that one danger includes (according to some analysts) our own conditioned intention to use nuclear weapons, and that would involve, even on the account of the German bishops, a moral evil. In other words, in adopting as their pivotal principle the choice of the lesser evil (as if the evils were both nonmoral), the German pastoral seems to me to have evaded the very question that led the Vancouver Assembly to condemn nuclear deterrence: the conditioned intention to use nuclear weapons.

One way out of this ethical dilemma is to maintain a limited and morally legitimate use of nuclear weapons. Then the intention to use would not be immoral. What do the Germans say about this? They are deliberately (I believe) ambiguous—much as the American bishops are. They refer to the concerns of "many people" about escalation and ask: "Is not the danger of escalation from their use—however limited—so great that one cannot imagine any situation in which one could accept responsibility after consideration of all factors to use nuclear weapons?"[123] The question is left unanswered, and there is the ambiguity. One senses that the German bishops want to answer this question with a clear "yes." But if they did, the implications for the ethics of deterrence would be clear—especially for those who hold that deterrence is effective only if it involves a credible threat. A similar problem arises in the French, Irish, and Belgian pastorals.

And now to *The Storm That Threatens*, the relatively short July 1983 statement of the bishops of Ireland.[124] The Irish bishops cite both the American and the German pastoral letters. They state: "According to Catholic moral teaching, the possession of nuclear weapons is tolerable only to deter their use by others, as the lesser of two evils and only under certain conditions." The Irish bishops list three conditions. (1) There must be no intention to use the weapons against cities and population centers. (2) The underlying philosophy must be one of deterrence, not superiority or even equality. (3) Possession must be in the context of substantive efforts to bring about disarmament.

---

[123] Ibid. 587.
[124] Catholic Press and Information Office, Dublin.

Several things are interesting about this statement. First, in referring to the tolerability of a nuclear deterrent as the lesser of two evils, the Irish bishops say this is "Catholic teaching." By this I presume they mean two things: (1) The magisterium (Vatican II) has not condemned such a deterrent. (2) John Paul II, in his 1982 U.N. statement, said that deterrence "may still be judged morally acceptable." It seems a bit much to refer to such evidence as "Catholic moral teaching," a phrase that implies more than it can deliver in this instance.

Second, the Irish statement insists that if an *act* is immoral, then the *intention* (even conditioned) to perform that act is also immoral. Thus it insists that there must be no intention to use nuclear weapons against population centers. Yet the letter does two things: (1) It admits that deterrence is based on threat. (2) It tolerates such a threat as the lesser of two evils. The implications are interesting. There are several possibilities. The first is that threats do not necessarily involve the intention to use. The second is that threats do involve such an intention and therefore they must be restricted to morally legitimate use.

The Irish letter does not clearly resolve this problem. I incline to think they had the second alternative in mind, because their only clear and unhesitating condemnation of the use of nuclear weapons is of their indiscriminate use against population centers. They acknowledge the possibility of limited use of nuclear weapons and remain content to cite the German bishops and John Paul II on the unlikely possibility of containing escalation. Thus, though they tie use and intention to use very closely, they do not unambiguously condemn all use, and therefore not every intention to use, and therefore not any possession for deterrent purposes. This leaves a small opening for the tolerance of a nuclear deterrent without that tolerance referring to one's own readiness (intention) to perform immoral actions.

Perhaps this is how the German pastoral should also be read, as noted above. But the opening is very, very small. Indeed, many think it nonexistent. In other words, there is a developing consensus that any use of nuclear weapons is morally unacceptable because of the almost unavoidable danger of escalation. If this is indeed the case, then any appeal to the principle of tolerating the lesser evil is out of place as implying tolerance of *one's own* intention to do immoral things. The principle never meant that.

This impasse has led to two outcomes. First, it has led the World Council of Churches Vancouver Assembly to condemn nuclear deterrence. Second, it has led others (e.g., Francis Winters) to continue to insist that it is possession itself (not any intention to use) that suffices to deter.

And now to the French. In November 1983 they released their *Win the Peace*.[125] The document defends deterrence and denounces unilateral disarmament. Nuclear deterrence is justified because of the "aggressive character of Marxist-Leninist ideology." The central question is the following, according to *Win the Peace*: "In the present geopolitical context, does a country whose life, freedom, and identity is menaced have the right to parry this radical threat with an effective, even nuclear, counterthreat?" The answer: "Until now . . . the Catholic Church has not condemned it."

The absolute condemnation of all war would place peaceful people at the mercy of those inspired by the desire to dominate. The document continues:

> To escape war, these peoples risk succumbing to other forms of violence and injustice: colonization, alienation, removal of their freedom and their identity. In an extreme sense, peace at any price leads a nation to every variety of surrender. Unilateral disarmament can even provoke aggressiveness in neighbors nourishing the temptation to seize a too easy prey.

The French bishops sharply distinguish threats from actual use. They ask themselves: "Is it not wrong to threaten what it is wrong to do?" Their answer: "It is not evident." Threat and use are "moral unequals." What this means is questionable. On the face of it, it would have to mean two things: (1) One may threaten to do what one may never do. (2) Such a threat does not necessarily involve the intention to do, since all admit that one may not even conditionally intend to do what is morally wrong. On this reading the French defense of deterrence is a version of the "bluff theory" or the "mere-possession theory." Many believe that the weakness of that theory is that the deterrent is no longer credible.

The Belgian bishops issued their statement in mid-July 1983.[126] After citing both Paul VI's demand for abolition of atomic weapons and Vatican II's condemnation of indiscriminate destruction, the Belgians turn to deterrence. They recite the positions of those who defend it and those who condemn it. It is no way to a true and stable peace. "At the best it is a 'lesser evil,' a solution of distress strictly provisional in character." They then cite John Paul II's conditioned acceptance of it in his U.N. speech. The brief statement concludes with several suggestions about promoting peace.

How, then, do the pastorals differ? Obviously, there are many points on which they overlap. For instance, the notion of just defense must be seen within the dominant imperative of peace. All accept the legitimacy

---

[125] I work from the manuscript copy kindly provided by Bryan Hehir; cf. also *New York Times*, Nov. 12, 1983.

[126] "Désarmer pour construire la paix," *La libre belgique*, July 20–21, 1983.

of just national self-defense. All are inspired by Vatican II's condemnation of indiscriminate destruction and John Paul II's conditioned acceptance of deterrence.

In an insightful article Stanley Hoffmann has adverted to a major difference between the American and French pastorals.[127] The French present the moral problem as being placed "between war and blackmail." Not so for the American pastoral. The equilibrium of the forces of the nuclear superpowers prevents the exercise of blackmail against the United States.

But the most profound difference between the two pastorals is that *The Challenge of Peace* is fully aware of the recent evolution of strategy and nuclear technology. Deterrence is not what it used to be. The multiplication and sophistication of weapons has made it possible for the superpowers to move from a deterrence involving a threat to cities (apparently still the French concept) to a counterforce threat. This nourishes the idea of a limited, winnable nuclear war. There are two grave consequences to this evolution. First, countercity deterrence demands only a limited number of weapons; counterforce deterrence demands "an astronomic number." Second, the presence of vulnerable nuclear forces may lead one side to a pre-emptive and protective strike. This means a move from a relatively stable deterrent to a destabilizing and disquieting one. The American pastoral realizes this and is composed from this perspective. Not so the French, argues Hoffmann. Thus, the American bishops are much more detailed about arms control, the sale of arms. Further, the Americans condemn first use (thus opposing official N.A.T.O. policy); the French do not.

Second, with Hoffmann I would note that the American bishops are much more reticent about deterrence than the other pastorals. The German, Irish, French, and Belgian letters appeal to the lesser-evil principle; not so the Americans. One can speculate about this, but it is not hard to believe that the Americans had come to see some imposing moral difficulties in such an appeal. However, I can only commend the American bishops for leaving the tensions in their document (e.g., a strictly conditioned acceptance of nuclear deterrence vs. an analysis of nuclear arms that seems to leave no room for it). In tensions there is room for growth.

Finally, the value of nonviolent witness has a prominence in the American document that is not found in the other pastorals.

4) *What is the remaining problem?* Briefly, it is the morality of nuclear deterrence. The American bishops did not condemn *any* use of nuclear weapons. At their May meeting Archbishop John Quinn (San Francisco)

[127] Stanley Hoffman, "Le cri d'alarme de l'église américaine," *Le monde*, Nov. 19, 1983.

had proposed that "profound skepticism" about the morality of any use be replaced by "opposition on moral grounds to any use of nuclear weapons." Originally passed, this amendment was later rescinded because it would appear incompatible with the bishops' acceptance of nuclear deterrence. It was this "centimeter of ambiguity" (Bryan Hehir) upon which the bishops hung their strictly conditioned acceptance of deterrence. But is that analysis persuasive? Several articles highlight this key issue.

Kenneth Himes, O.F.M., reviews the three arguments justifying deterrence and rejects them all.[128] First, there is the position presented by John Cardinal Krol before the Senate Foreign Relations Committee (1979). Krol distinguished between use, threat to use, and mere possession. Mere possession requires no declared intent and hence is tolerable. This is the position still espoused by Francis Winters. Himes rejects this on the grounds that there is an inbuilt intent in the system.

Second, there is the analysis of John Langan and William O'Brien that builds on the idea of a morally legitimate use of nuclear weapons. If some such use is imaginable, then that legitimates the threat of that use. This seems to be the position of *The Challenge of Peace* with its "centimeter of ambiguity." Himes rejects this as being unreal. "The real problem with drawing distinctions advocated by some proponents of this position is that those distinctions would almost surely be among the first casualties in the event of nuclear war." Briefly, this analysis fails to deal realistically with the danger of escalation.

Finally, there is the argument advanced by Michael Novak and David Hollenbach. They distinguish between the intention to use and the intention to deter. Deterrence is built on this latter. Himes rejects this as an immoral bluff. Just as it would be immoral to try to prevent murder by threatening the innocent family members of the convicted murderer (Michael Walzer's example), so too here. The threat itself is morally repugnant.

Himes concludes that there is no convincing rationale for the moral acceptability of nuclear deterrence. He sees this as the "significant flaw" of the American pastoral: it tries to justify deterrence. But that does not mean that Himes calls for unilateral disarmament. Distinguishing moral theological judgments from pastoral judgments, he suggests that it is one thing to judge a policy morally wrong; it is another to ask how we act to reverse it. The answer to this latter question is complicated, is not unilaterally determined, takes time, etc.

Next, there is the study of René Coste.[129] After reviewing the state-

---

[128] Kenneth Himes, O.F.M., "Close but No Cigar," forthcoming in *Cross Currents*.

[129] René Coste, "Le problème éthique de la dissuasion nucléaire," *Esprit et vie* 93 (1983) 513–28.

ments of Vatican II, John Paul II, and two episcopal conferences (American, German), he cites the theological discussion as it has occurred in England and the United States. He mentions the analyses of P. Ruston, Canon Dunstan, Sir Arthur Hockaday, John Langan, David Hollenbach, and this author.

Finally, he concludes by proposing certain guidelines. Some of them are as follows. (1) The fundamental ethical criterion is the promotion of a just peace. (2) The problem of deterrence must be seen concretely, historically, not abstractly. (3) The actual international situation must be said to be gravely evil ethically and sinful from a theological point of view. But it is in such a situation that we must view deterrence. What might not be justifiable in another situation can be "tolerated" in the one we are in. (4) Clarity and a sense of responsibility demand that we take into account the nature of the Soviet regime—as the American and German pastorals do. (5) We must consider it probable that deterrence has prevented a direct military confrontation between the superpowers and that it has protected the freedom of Western Europe. (6) Deterrence can be considered tolerable as a lesser evil as long as it is indispensable for the maintenance of peace. Coste faces the problem of intention by asserting that threat is one thing, one's real intention is another. This latter remains one's secret. This is very close to the Winters position.

Coste's study is careful and his toleration of nuclear deterrence is almost anguished. It is a reflection of what Bruce Russett calls the "ambiguities and contradictions" of nuclear deterrence.[130] Russett lays out very clearly the problems, strategic and moral, with nuclear deterrence. As for the problem of threatening what one may never licitly do or intend, "the bishops avoid it in their letter." He sees their ultimate position as "not so ambiguous as it is frankly conflicted." Russett states: "To avoid totally rejecting nuclear deterrence the bishops had to find some strategy that at least had a chance, in some hypothetical circumstances, of being morally neutral (discriminating, proportionate) rather than intrinsically evil." Did they do so? Russett remains unconvinced. "For myself, I repeat that I see no *good* solution overall."

In a nutshell, that is the moral problem of nuclear deterrence. On the one hand, there is an intuitive sense that it would be irresponsible unilaterally to abandon the deterrent. On the other, there seems to be no satisfactory ethical or theological analysis to support it.

It has been the privilege of this author to compose these "Notes" for nineteen years. In the course of that time I have occupied far more pages than anyone in the history of THEOLOGICAL STUDIES. It is time to turn

---

[130] Bruce M. Russett, "The Doctrine of Deterrence," in *Catholics and Nuclear War* 149–67.

over this task to younger people and different perspectives. But before doing so I should like to express profound thanks to those who have made this task so pleasant: the authors of the articles reviewed and the critics of my writing from whom I have learned so much. To my successors a simple counsel: *in certis firmitas, in dubiis libertas, in omnibus caritas.* And if one is permitted to expand the Augustinian axiom, *in obscuris claritas.*

INDEX

Authoritative teaching, 6, 74, 77
Authority of the Church, 78
Authority of the magisterium, 7, 162
Autonome Moral und christlicher Glaube
  (Auer), 161
Autonomy, 33, 121, 154, 161-162
Balke, Victor (Bishop), 149
Bañez, Dominic, 29
Balthasar, Hans Urs von, 162, 164-165
Barber, Neil, 192, 195-196
Barth, Karl, 162
Bayley, Corrine, 33-34, 36
Becker, Phillip, 27, 32
Bedoyere, Quentin de la, 75
Belfast (Ireland), 86-87, 92
Belgian bishops, 206, 209, 211-212
Belgium, 172
Beneficentia, 112
Benefits, 30-31, 153
Benevolentia, 112
Bennett, John C., 125, 127
Benoit, Pierre, 38
Bernardin, Joseph Cardinal, 132, 202
Best interest criterion, 33, 35-36, 153
Bevilacqua, Anthony (Bishop), 196-197
Bible, 19, 21, 151
Biblical consequentialism, 57
Biblical ethics, 22
Biblical foundations, 38, 162
Biblical morality, 61
Biblical narratives, 21-22
Biblical religion, 151
Bioethics, 23, 156
Biological facticity, 52, 59
Biological knowledge, 183, 186
Biological law, 51
Biological-physiological integrity, 84
Biologism, 58
Birch, Bruce C., 17, 152
Birth control, 41, 186 *See also* Contracep-
  tion
Birth regulation, 37, 186
Birth-room conflicts, 4
Bishops, 43-45, 108, 123, 157, 159
  American, *See* American bishops
  Austrian, 102
  Belgian, 206, 209, 211-212
  Canadian, 41
  Catholic, 25
  Continental, 130
  English, 144
  French, 12, 130, 203, 206, 209-212
  German, 42, 130, 159-160, 203, 206-210,
    212, 214
  Irish, 85-87, 206, 209-212
  peace, 142
  Scottish, 130
  of Texas, 95
  Third World, 81
The Bishops and the Bomb (Castelli), 199
Bishops' Conference of England and Wales,
  Commission for International Jus-
  tice and Peace, 145

Bishops' Joint Committee on Bioethical
  Issues, 174-175
Bishops' Social Welfare Commission, 174
Blackmail, 208, 212
Blank, Josef, 120
Blood transfusions, 8
Böckle, Franz, 2-3, 54, 57, 64, 101, 162,
  171, 183-184
Body, 19, 58-59
Bombing of noncombatants, 62
Bombs, neutron, 95
Bonn, 145
Boyle, Joseph M. 32
Brain damage, 192
Brennen, Keith, 197
Brezhnev, Leonid I., 128
Brinkmanship, 88
Britain, 146
British Government, 86
Brouillard, René, 88
Brown, Louise, 174
Brown, Neil, 165
Brunec, M., 116
Brussels, 145
Bucharest, 111
Bühlmann, Walbert, 44
Butler, B. C. (Bishop), 7, 77, 190
Bundy, McGeorge, 134, 200
Burghardt, Walter J., 180
Bruke, Mary, 197
Burtchaell, James, 32, 75
Caffarro, Carlo, 175
Cahill, Lisa Sowie, 7, 10-12, 71
Caiphas principle, 117
Calculus of values and disvalues, 67, 69,
  166-169
Callaghan, W. S., 87
Callahan, Daniel, 67, 184, 194
Call or calling ethics, 125, 206
"Call to Peacemaking" day, 129
Canadian, bishops, 41
Capitalism, 72-75, 78, 82-83
Capital punishment, 12, 14, 91-92
Carcinoma, metastatic, 153
Cardiac surgery, 155
Carr, Anne, 150-152
Carter, G. Emmett Cardinal, 40
Casaroli, Agostino Cardinal, 72, 132
Casey, Lawrence (Bishop), 31
Castelli, Jim, 199
Casti connubii (Pius XI), 109
Castronovo, Valerio, 72
Casuistry, 17, 162
Catholic Biblical Association, 94
Catholic bishops, 25 *See also* Bishops
Catholic community, 7, 12, 24-25, 128
Catholic ethics, 4
Catholic government officials, 97
Catholic Hospital Association, 71
Catholic hospitals, 71, 83
Catholicism, Liberal, 85
Catholic principles, 33
Catholic revolution, 99

Dogmatic theology, 112
Dominion, J., 39
Donahue, John R., 38
Dotson, Betty Lou, 152
Double effect, principle of, 2-3, 10, 13-14, 60, 90-91, 115-116
Down's Syndrome, 152
Dozier, Carroll T. (Bishop), 129
Draper, Thoedore, 134
Dualism, 19, 58-59
Dubarle, D., 144
Due process, 123, 197
Dulles, Avery, 45-46, 48, 203
Dunstan, Gordon R. (Canon), 214
Duties, 13, 56, 68, 110, 115
Duty, 23, 123
  Christian, 107
  to procreate, 68
Dwyer, Judith A., 199
Dyck, Arthur, 185
Dying, 29, 32-37, 173
Dying incompetents, 34-36, 193
Dying persons, feeding of, 30, 193
Eastern Church, 101, 103
Eastern Orthodox tradition, 19
Ecclesial status of separated brethren, 54
Ecclesiastical politics, 162
Ecclesiastical, positivism, 4-5, 157-158, 164, 186
Economism, 76-74
Ecumenical theology, 183
Edmonds, Patty, 96
Education, moral, 18
Edwards, Carroll, 87-89
Eichner, Philip, 34
Elizari, F. J., 38
Ellis, John Tracy, 161
Embryos, experimental use of, 156, 174, 177
Emperors of China, 186
Empirical science, 11, 15
Ends, 2, 57, 65-66
Ends
  of acts, 14
  good, 7-8, 15, 59
  natural, 53
Engelhardt, Tristram, 32
English bishops, 144
Enterocolitis, necrotizing, 155
Epikeia, 4
Episcopal Conference of Belgium, 172
Ermecke, G., 84, 107, 162
Ernst, Wilhelm, 110, 120
Escalation, 138
Eschatology, 9, 203, 208
Ethical and Religious Directives for Catholic Hospitals (2d rev. ed. Catholic Hospital Association, 1955), 71
Ethical and Religious Directives for Catholic Health Facilities (United States Catholic Conference, Department of Health Affairs, 1971), 71
Ethical deliberation, 121

Ethical duties, 13
Ethical immaturity, 158
Ethical pessimism, 162
Ethical responsibility, 91
Ethics of faith, 162
Ethics, 19-20, 122
  biblical, 22
  call or calling, 125, 206
  Catholic, 4
  Christian, 17, 124-125
  individualistic, 91
  liturgy and, 19
  medical, 186
  norm or normative, 125, 206
  political, 91
  quandary, 165
  sexual, 152
  social, 26
Ethics Advisory Board (DHEW), 71
Études, 88, 185
Eucharist, 26, 38, 40, 47, 55, 100, 159
Eudaimonistic position, 3
Eudaimonistic utilitarianism, 55-56
Eugenics, 175, 179
Euthanasia, 27-29
Evans, Donald, 69
Everett, William, 20-21
Evil, 58, 63, 66-67
  dimensions of, 62
  material, 74
  moral, *See* Moral evil
  nonmoral, *See* Nonmoral evil
  objective, 61, 65-66
  ontic, *See* Ontic evil
  perpetual, 68
  physical, 84
  premoral, *See* Premoral evil
  subjective, 61
Evil actions
  prima-facie, 56
  See also Intrinsically evil actions
Evil means, 7-8, 15, 115
Evils in society, toleration of, 12
Exception-making categories, 10
Exception-making in the Church, 67-68
Exhortation, 5, 22, 58, 114
  sectarian, 23
  See also Parenesis
Existentialism, 40
EXIT, 27
Experience
  of God, 18
  mystical, 18
Experimental use of embryos, 156, 174, 177
Experimentation, human, 16, 175
Extraordinary means of treatment, 28-33, 36
Facility, 5
  biological, 52, 59
Fagan, Harry A., 199
Faith, 19, 44, 77, 121-122, 160-161, 173
  in Christ, 28

221

MacIntyre, Alasdair, 124, 126
McKeever, Paul, 71
McNamara, Robert S., 134, 144
MacSwiney, Terence James, 87-88
Madariaga, José Garcia de, 105-106
Magisteriolatry, 134
Magisterium, 5-8, 38, 42-47, 55, 57-58, 75, 77-78, 105-120, 158, 160, 172, 174, 186-190, 198
  authority of the, 7, 162
  charism of the, 6
  faithfulness to the, 81
  hierarchical, 45-47
  papal, 105-106
  scholarly, 45
  third, 45
Maguire, Daniel C., 52, 64, 67, 121-123, 151-152, 182-184
Maguire, Marjorie R., 185
Mahon, Michael, 134-135
Mahoney, John, 89
Mahony, Roger (Bishop), 129, 134
Mala moralia, 5, 8, See also Moral Evil
Mala natura, 8, See also Physical Evil
Mala physica, 5, 8, See also Physical Evil
Malone, James (Bishop), 187, 189
Mansour, Agnes Mary, 196-198
Manualist teaching, 61, 115
Mara, William, 200
Maritain, Jacques, 27, 119
Marital act, 52-53, 83, 175, 181, 186
Marriage, 49, 52, 164, 174, 177-178
  bond of, 40
  fidelity in, 101
  good of, 66, 84
  indissolubility of, 25, 38, 104
  mixed, 107
  permanent, 9, 12, 16, 100, 104
  sacrament of, 40
Marriage covenant, 179
Marriages
  second, See Second marriages
  sterile, 15
Marriage vows, 53
Married persons, 53, 68
Martin, Malachi, 72
Marty, François, 120
Marxism, 79, 82, 211
Masculinity, 151, 165
Masterson, Patrick 172
Masturbation, 15, 61, 64-66, 69, 109, 118, 159, 166-168, 170, 173, 176
Mater et magistra (John XXIII), 72, 74, 78
Material evil, 74
Material-formal cooperation, 10, 12
Matthiesen, Leroy T. (Bishop), 95-96, 98, 144-145
May, William F., 185
May, William E., 178-179
Mayer, Augustin (Archbishop), 161
Maze Prison (Belfast), 86-87, 92
Meade, Robert (Judge), 34
Means

evil, 7-8, 15, 115
  extraordinary, See Extraordinary
    means, 28-33, 36
  ordinary, 28-33, 36
Medicaid, 198
Medical indications policy, 35-37
Meehan, Francis X. (Bishop), 55, 99, 133-134, 141-142, 144, 205-206
Mercy of God, 8, 100
"Message to Christian Families in the Modern World" (fifth Synod of Bishops), 37
Metaethical suppositions, 128
Metaphors, 22, 125
Method
  in moral decision-making, 1-17
  of proportionality, 2
Methodology in moral theology, 49-71
Metz, Johann B., 103
Micetich, Kenneth, 193
Mieth, Dietmar, 64, 120, 161
Militarism, 93, 99
Miller, Donald E., 18
Miller, Jeremy, 17
Mirari vos (Gregory XVI), 174, 180
Missiles
  cruse, 94
  MX, 93-94
Mixed marriages, 107
Modernism, 85
Moingt, Joseph, 121
Molinski, W., 64, 177
Mollen, Milton, 33
Moral ambiguity, 143
Moral argument, 114
Moral authority of Scripture, 21
Moral decision-making, 46-47
  method in, 1-17
Moral deformity, 169
Moral deliberation, 17, 22
Moral evil, 2, 8-9, 11-12, 15, 61, 64-65, 74, 84, 110, 115-116, 131 See also Mala moralia
Moral finality, 111
Moral formulations, 166
  concrete, 1
Moral good, 8, 10
Moral goodness, 107
Moral heroes, 90
Moral identity, 17
Moral injunctions, 23
Morality, 17-18, 20
  biblical, 61
  Christian, 19
  denial of, 58
  domestic, 74
  familial, 80-81
  formulated-rule, 69
  post-Tridentine, 111
  relational model of, 60-62
  revealed, 22
  sexual, 7, 80-81
  social, 49, 72-83, 141-142

225

Moral judgments, right, 4
Moral justification, 22, 25-26, 119, 125
Moral knowledge, 122
Moral law, 51, 111, 119
  natural, 26-27
Moral life, 3, 19, 22
Moral manuals, 61, 115
Moral norms, 1-2, 15, 17, 105-120, 166, 170
  objective, 9
Moral objects, 112, 114
Moral obligation, 77, 104
Moral orders, 9-10
Moral philosophers, 23
Moral philosophy, 18
Moral purpose of God, 4-5
Moral qualifiers, 114-115
Moral reason, 26
Moral reasoning, 5, 121-128
Moral right, 13, 61
Moral rules, 186
Moral theologians, 3, 159
Moral theology, 4, 17-18, 22
  deviant, 2, 5
  fundamental, 157-173
  methodology in, 49-71
Moral tradition, 17
Moral values, 10-11
Moral virtues, 121
Moral will of God, 5, 110
Moral wrong, 10, 12-13, 61, 64-65, 167
Müller, Heinz J., 1
Multinational corporations, 82, 128
Murder, 14, 115, 118-119, 169, 213, *See also*
  Homicide
Murnion, William E., 199
Murphy, Thomas J. (Bishop), 93
Murray, John Courtney, 174, 180
MX missiles, 93-94
Mysterium ecclesiae (Congregation for the
  Doctrine of the Faith), 181
Nagle, William J., 134
Nascent life, 156
Nasogastric tubes, 192, 194-195
Nassau Hospital, 36
National Catholic Reporter, 75, 95, 200
National Conference of Catholic Bishops of
  the United States (NCCB), 92, 132,
  148, 161
  Committee on Doctrine, 187
National security, 93, 97
NATO, *See* North Atlantic Treaty Organ-
  ization
Natural family planning (NFP), 41, 117, 164
Naturaliter nota, 27
Natural law, 4, 11, 27, 57, 59, 67, 158
Natural Law and Natural Rights (Finnis),
  59
Natural moral law, 26-27
Nature
  human, 176
  sexual, 3
Naud, André, 42-46, 48
NCCB, *See* National Conference of Catholic

  Bishops of the United States
Necrotizing enterocolitis, 155
Neighbors, 68, 82
Nejdl, Robert, 192, 195-196
Nell-Breuning, Oswald von, 73, 76-78, 81
Neo-Scholasticism, 85, 124, 157
Neuhaus, Richard John, 127
Neutron bombs, 95
Neutron warheads, 93, 95
Newborns, 148, 152-155
  terribly defective, 30-32
New Jersey Public Advocate, 192
Newsweek, 161
New Testatment, 165
"New Theology," 85
New York Daily News, 28
New Yorker, 200
NFP, *See* Natural family planning
Noldin, Jerome, 115
Nonmoral evil, 5, 8, 54, 58-60, 74, 112,
  119-120, 209
Nonmoral good, 10, 112
Nonmoral right, 10
Nonmoral values, 10
Nonmoral wrong, 10
Nonviolence, 92, 206
Nonviolent protest, 90
Noonan, John, 186
Normative statements, 16, 163-165
Norms, 9
  concrete, *See* Concrete moral norms
  deontologically understood, *See* Deon-
    tologically understood norms
  human, 4
  moral, *See* Moral norms
  rethinking of, 70
  rigorous, 58
  theological foundation of, 113
North Atlantic Treaty Organization
  (NATO), 203, 212
Northern Ireland, 86-92
Novak, Michael, 72, 134, 140-144, 200, 204,
  213
The Nuclear Delusion (Kennan), 136
Nuclear deterrence, 90, 99, 113, 129-148,
  200-201, 204, 207-212
Nuclear Deterrence Right or Wrong
  (Tuston), 145
Nuclear disarmament, 49, 93-99
Nuclear exchanges, limited, 98
Nuclear freeze, 129, 144
Nuclear proliferation, 93
Nuclear wars, 93, 95, 97-98, 129-148,
  199-201, 212-213
  limited, 134, 138, 147
Nuclear weapons, 93, 96-99, 128-129,
  134-135, 137-138, 146, 203, 205
Nutrition, 193-195
Oberheim, H., 162
Objective conflicts of values, 9
Objective evil, 61, 65-66
Objective moral norms, 9
Objective-subjective distinction, 61

226

Objective wrong, 10
Objectivity, 111
Objects of acts, 14
Obligations, 22, 24, 111, 166
  moral, 77, 104
Obligatory ideals, 52-54, 56
O'Brien, Daniel J., 199
O'Brien, William V., 129, 134, 144, 213
Obsequium religiosum, 188-191
O'Callaghan, Denis, 88-89
O'Connell, Timothy, 64
O'Connor, John J., 129
Octogesima adveniens (Paul VI), 72-74, 79
Oddi, Silvio Cardinal, 161
Oeing-Hanhoff, Ludiger, 77
Odeen, Philip, 133
Office for Civil Rights, 152
O'Fiaich, Thomas Cardinal, 87
Ogletree, Thomas W., 152
O'Hare, Joseph, 140, 142
O'Malley, John W., 105-107
"On Human Work," *See Laborem exercens*
On the Church in the Modern World, *See*
  Guadium et spes
Ontic evil, 5, 58-59, 66, 111-112, 114-115,
  169, 209
Ontic good, 112
Ontic value, 15
Oppression, political, 150
Ordinary means of treatment, 28-33, 36
Orthodox Catholics, 40
Orthodox tradition, *See* Eastern Orthodox
  tradition
Orthodoxy, 86
Ottaviani, Alfredo Cardinal, 160
Our Right to Choose (Harrison), 185
Outka, Gene, 22
Overberg, Kenneth R., 74
Oxygenization, 155
Pacifism, 96, 133, 147, 200
Pain, 8, 153, 193
Palach, Jan, 88-89
Palmer, Dona, 130
Pantex Corporation, 95, 98
Parenesis, 25, 163-165
Parenetic discourse, 5, 58, 112-114
Paris, John J., 33, 192-193, 195
Pascendi (Pius X), 85
Pastoral ministry, 43, 46-48, 124, 160
Pastoral problems, 37, 49, 83-104, 187-199
Patients, 8
  comatose, 31, 193
  families of, 34-35
  friends of, 33
  relatives of, 33-37
  terminal, 30-33
Patriarchal traditions, 151-152
Patrick, Anne E., 150
Patristics, 112
Paul (St.,), 109
  1 Corinthians 7, 109
  Ephesians 5:21-23, 164
  Galatians, 109

Romans, 27
Romans 1, 126
Romans 3:8, 2
  on rules, 70
  on sin, 8
Paul VI, 80, 83
  "Apostolica sollicitudo," 41
  "Crescens matrimonium," 40
  Octogesima adveniens, 72-74, 79
  Populorum progressio, 73, 78, 105
  on sexuality, 52-54, 177
  and the Synod of 1980, 37, 41
  on war, 54, 211
Pax Christi, 93, 96, 129
Peace, 92, 150, 160, 182, 199-214
  theology of, 147
Peace bishops, 142
Penitents, 47, 68
People of God, Church as, 17, 158
Pereira, Aelred, 172
Perico, G., 175-176
Permissiveness, 70-71, 170
Person, 4, 10, 91, 110
Persona humana (Declaration on Certain
  Questions Concerning Sexual
  Ethics) (Sacred Congregation for
  the Doctrine of the Faith), 42, 50,
  118-119, 171, 180
Personal goodness, 107, 158
Personalism, 38, 50, 40-52, 60, 74
Personal well-being, 84
Personhood, 185
Persons, 159
  defective, 31
  human, *See* Human persons
Pesce, G., 175-176
Pessimism, ethical, 162
Petitio principii, 13
Philosophers, moral, 23
Philosophy, 90
  Christian, 80
  moral, 18
Physical evil, 84, See also *mala physica*
Physical force, 90
Physicalism, 60, 168, 186
Physicians, 8, 34, 36-37 *See also* Doctors
Piccoli, Flaminio, 73
Piegsa, Joachim, 172
Pilla, Anthony (Bishop), 93
Pinckaers, Servais, 110-113, 118
Pironio, E., Cardinal, 188
Pius IX
  Quanta cura, 83, 85
  Tuas libenter, 85
  and Vatican II, 54, 174
Pius X *Pascendi*, 85
Pius XI, 80, 83
  Casti connubi, 109
  Quadragesimo anno, 72, 76, 78, 80, 82
Pius XII, 83
  Allocution to Physicians and Anethesio-
    logists, 29
  Humani generis, See Humani generis

227

230

232